Bertie County

An Eastern Carolina History

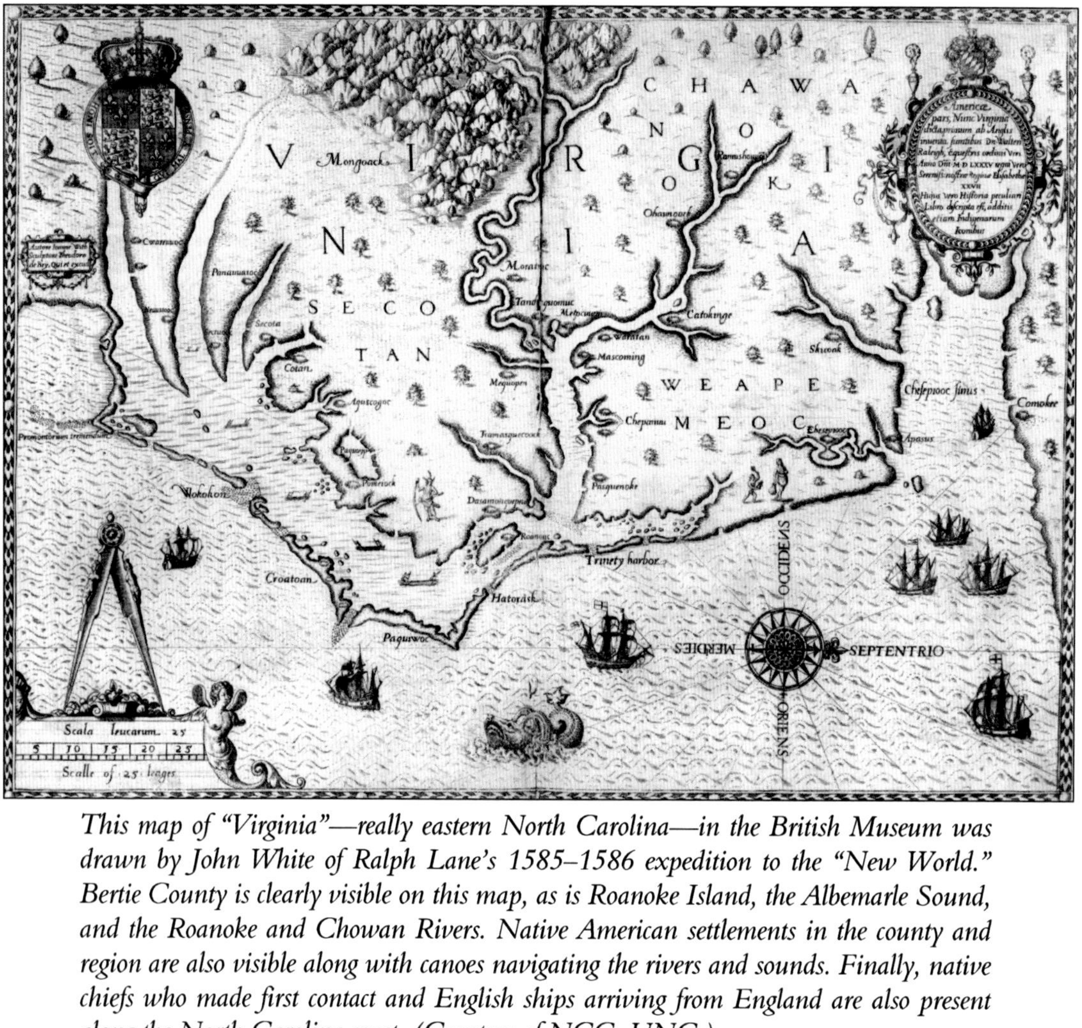

This map of "Virginia"—really eastern North Carolina—in the British Museum was drawn by John White of Ralph Lane's 1585–1586 expedition to the "New World." Bertie County is clearly visible on this map, as is Roanoke Island, the Albemarle Sound, and the Roanoke and Chowan Rivers. Native American settlements in the county and region are also visible along with canoes navigating the rivers and sounds. Finally, native chiefs who made first contact and English ships arriving from England are also present along the North Carolina coast. (Courtesy of NCC, UNC.)

DEDICATED TO MY MOTHER,
LOIS MARIE CHERRY SMALLWOOD.

THE
MAKING OF AMERICA
SERIES

BERTIE COUNTY

AN EASTERN CAROLINA HISTORY

ARWIN D. SMALLWOOD

ARCADIA
PUBLISHING

ISBN 978-0-7385-2395-8

Library of Congress control number: 2002108556

Published by Arcadia Publishing,
Charleston, South Carolina

Printed in the United States of America

For all general information contact Arcadia Publishing at:
Telephone 843-853-2070
Fax 843-853-0044
E-Mail sales@arcadiapublishing.com
For customer service and orders:
Toll-Free 1-888-313-2665

Visit us on the Internet at www.arcadiapublishing.com

FRONT COVER: Pictured here is one of several plantations owned by the Speight family of Windsor, North Carolina, the seat of Bertie County, around the time of the Civil War. This scene was typical of life not only in Bertie County but throughout the South during slavery. (Courtesy of SHC, UNC.)

Contents

Acknowledgments

The great seal of the state of North Carolina, *Esse Quam Videri,* translates from Latin to read "To Be not to Seem," befitting of this state and the people who reside here. It has produced many outstanding individuals of national and international stature, who have been and continue to be both humble and honorable. One may not find any place in North Carolina where the people live up to the state's motto as well as those of the eastern region. Once the wealthiest, and one of the most influential and important areas of the state, today it is one of the poorest and most undervalued. Yet, it still maintains the self-sufficiency and character that has been forged over the past 400 years. Thus, this book is for the tens of thousands of people who have called eastern North Carolina home and, specifically, for those who have called Bertie County home.

This book would not have been possible without the assistance and support of a great many people, especially the following. First, and most importantly, I would like to thank God, my wife and family, particularly my wife's parents, Gerelene and John Mayfield, and the residents of Bertie County, North Carolina. Without God's grace, my wife's and family's patience and support, and the cooperation and assistance of residents of Bertie County, none of this would have been possible. Special thanks are also due Mr. Garfield Jonathan and his family, son of Chief Howard Jonathan, whose Tuscarora ancestors left Bertie County for the Six Nations Reserve on the Grand River in Canada in 1803. In 1997, Mr. Jonathan graciously invited me to stay at his home for a week and discussed his family's roots in Bertie County and the history of those Tuscarora as it had been passed down to his father. He, his son, and members of his family went above and beyond what you might expect and I will forever be in their debt.

I would also like to thank Chief Leo Henry and Kenneth Patterson of the Tuscarora New York Reserve in Lewiston, New York for their hospitality and assistance while visiting and conducting research on their reserve. Also, Chief Leon Lockler, a Tuscarora chief from Maxton, North Carolina in Robeson County, who informed me of the fact that a number of Lumbee Native Americans of the county claim Tuscarora ancestry, including his people, who have roots in Bertie County.

Dr. Onno Browuer, associate director of the Cartography Laboratory at the University of Wisconsin at Madison, and Mr. Eric Rundell, cartographic student assistant, provided excellent work on the maps included in this book. Mr. Rundell took great pains to produce detailed, accurate, and readable maps based on my suggestions to him and I thank him for his patience and the quality of his work. It must also be noted that the support for this and previous projects by the students and staff of the Cartography Lab at the

In this 1890s image, young W.M.R. Capehart rides in a skiff paddled by Robert Robbins, an African American, by the shore of the Albemarle Sound near the Capehart Fishery at Avoco. (Courtesy of NCSAH.)

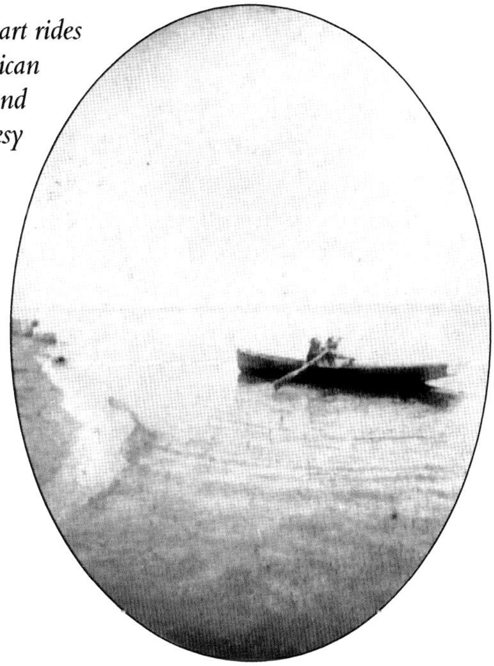

University of Wisconsin at Madison has been exemplary and invaluable. I cannot overstate their importance to the completion of this project and others.

Thanks are also due the staff of the North Carolina Collection Photographic Archives of the Wilson Library, at the University of North Carolina at Chapel Hill, including Jerry Cotton, archivist; Keith Longrotti, assistant archivist; and Bill Richards, photographic lab technician. Thanks also goes to the North Carolina Collection reading room, particularly Mrs. Alice Cotton and Mr. Harry McKown, reference librarians, who assisted me in locating rare books and other sources in the collection. I would also like to thank Dr. H.G. Jones and the North Caroliniana Society, who generously provided me with an Archie K. Davis Fellowship to conduct research on this work in the North Carolina Collection. I would also like to thank the staff of the Southern Historical Collection of the Wilson Library, especially Mr. Timothy Pyatt, former curator of the Southern Historical Collection, now archivist for Duke University; Mr. John White; and Mrs. Rachel Canada.

Mrs. Celia D. Pratt, map librarian for the Map Collection at the University of North Carolina at Chapel Hill, was particularly helpful in assisting me in locating maps of wetlands and swamps in eastern Virginia, North Carolina, and South Carolina. Stephen E. Massengill, head of nontextual material unit for the North Carolina State Archives and History, identified over 100 photographs from Bertie County that were held in the State Archives and I am indebted to him for his assistance. Thanks are also due the staff of the J.Y. Joyner Library's North Carolina Collection, including Mrs. Nancy Shires, Bryna Coonin, and Maury York, and the East Carolina Manuscript Collection, including Mary Boccaccio, Martha Elmore, Susan Midggette, and Jonathan Dembo of East Carolina University.

I am grateful to the staff of the Government Documents and Special Collections of the University of North Carolina at Pembroke, especially Mrs. Lillian Brewington, government documents and special collections librarian, and Mr. Davis Young, both of whom were very helpful in providing me with information on the Lumbee Native Americans and the Tuscarora, who live with them in Robeson County. I would also like to thank members of the staff of the Library of Virginia, including Mrs. Marianne McKee, who worked with me to locate maps showing the relationship between southeastern Virginia and northeastern North Carolina; Mrs. Alexandra Gressitt, head of Archives Research Services for the Library of Virginia; and Mark Fagerburg, manager of photo and digital imaging services for the Library of Virginia. Mrs. Ann Miller of the Virginia Transportation Research Council, Margaret Cook of William and Mary University, and Toni Carter, assistant librarian of the library of the Virginia Historical Society directed me to historic maps of southeastern Virginia.

I would also like to thank the Historic Hope Foundation, particularly John Tyler, director; LuAnn Joyner, administrator; and Timothy Hall, coordinator of education and programs; and the staff and former staff of the *Bertie Ledger-Advance*, particularly J.W. "Russ" Russell Jr., former sports writer for the newspaper and owner of Bunn's Barbecue in Windsor. I would also like to thank Harry L. Thompson, curator of the Port of Plymouth Museum, and Gerald Thomas for the use of photos in this work. I thank individuals who talked with me and, through that conversation, either provided information or led me to individuals who could help—people like William Williams, Bertha Cobb, and Retha Roulhac.

I would also like to thank Dr. Benjamin Speller, dean of the School of Library and Information Sciences at North Carolina Central University in Durham, and Gregory Tyler Peacock. Dean Speller, from Bertie County, has worked tirelessly to document and preserve the history of African Americans from the county and his work on the Ronsenwald schools with Gregory Tyler Peacock, black soldiers during the Civil War, and black Baptist churches, particularly the Indian Woods Baptist Church, is invaluable. I would also like to thank Mrs. Elizabeth Creecy, her colleagues in English, the principal, teachers, and staff at Bertie High School, especially Mr. Styron Bond, my history teacher, and the school's students for their invitation to come and discuss this work in November of 2001.

A special thanks goes to Mrs. Marjorie Manning, a life-long resident of Bertie County, who identified and donated copies of over 20 photos from the 1930s, 1940s, 1950s, 1960s, and 1970s to the Bart F. Smallwood Collection for use in this work. Also, Mrs. Margaret Johnson, the widow of Mr. Frank Roy Johnson, for permission to use several illustrations from her late husband's books on the Tuscarora Native Americans. Mrs. Johnson's husband worked during his life to document and preserve the history and culture of eastern North Carolina. His efforts in researching, writing, and publishing works have left a rich body of literature for anyone who studies the region.

Finally, I would like to thank Mr. Frank Stephenson of Chowan College in Murfreesboro, North Carolina. Mr. Stephenson was the 2000 winner of the Nancy Susan Reynolds Leadership Award from the Z. Smith Reynolds Foundation in Winston-Salem, North Carolina. A native of Northampton County, he has dedicated his life to the preservation of the history and culture of northeastern North Carolina and, as director of Chowan College's Upward Bound Program since 1977, he has assisted hundreds of youths from Northampton, Halifax, Hertford, and Bertie Counties in going to college and becoming teachers, doctors, lawyers, and other types of professionals. He has been a friend and mentor for over 20 years and I know of no one who knows more or cares more about the history and culture of all of the people of eastern North Carolina.

In conclusion, I would like to thank the many decent and honorable people who have called Bertie County and eastern North Carolina home. Over the past 400 years, they have left a lasting legacy of which all past, present, and future generations can be proud.

Arwin D. Smallwood

ABBREVIATIONS USED IN PHOTO CREDITS

NCC, UNC	North Carolina Collection, UNC Library at Chapel Hill
SHC, UNC	Southern Historical Collection, UNC Library at Chapel Hill
LVA	Library of Virginia
NCSAH	North Carolina State Archives and History

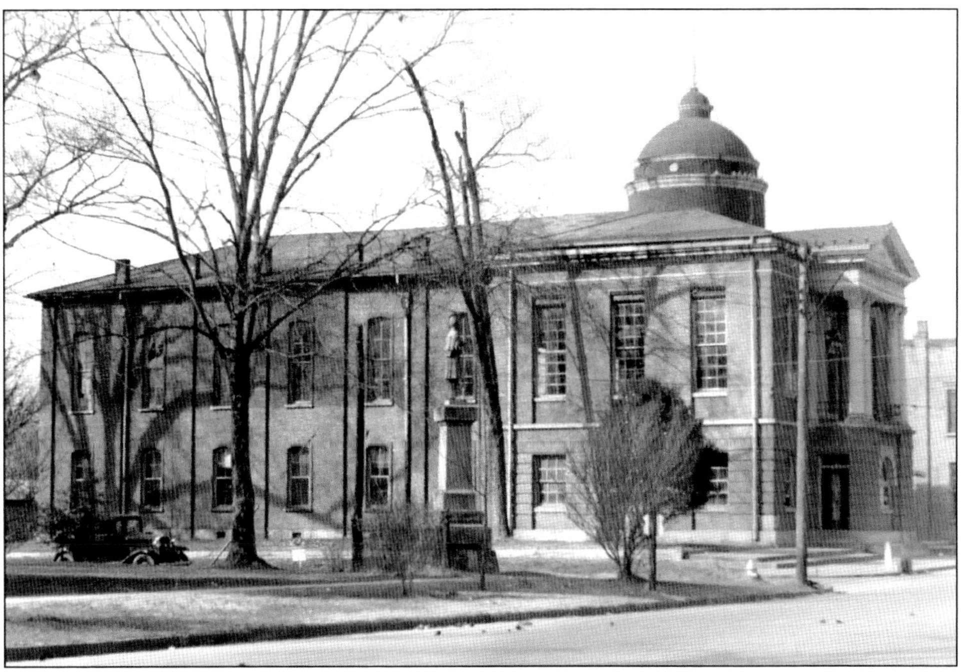

The Bertie County Courthouse is seen from Main Street in the 1920s. (Courtesy of NCC, UNC.)

Preface

This book is based, in part, on my Ph.D. dissertation "A History of Three Cultures, Indian Woods, North Carolina, 1585 to 1995." I chose to publish this work with Arcadia Publishing because of its reputation for being the leader in publishing local and community history. They have mastered the art of publishing visual history, capturing the essence of the communities, towns, cities, institutions, and people their histories are about. In recent years, we have learned to value and respect the contributions that documentaries, photographic histories, and atlases make to scholarship and understanding. This work, I hope, captures what I have dedicated my life to accomplishing: the dissemination of knowledge to the broadest audience possible using the most effective tools available.

Due to the format of this book, the extensive bibliography and endnotes were impossible to include in the book itself, and would offer too much detail for the casual reader. Therefore, arrangements have been made with several archives, libraries, and collections for this material and a copy of the published book to be deposited. This material is being made available to scholars, researchers, and interested individuals, with thanks to the following people, at these locations: Lisa Briley, Historic Hope Foundation, Inc., Windsor, North Carolina; Nancy B. Hughes, Lawrence Memorial Library, Windsor, North Carolina; Dick Lankford and staff, North Carolina State Archives and History, Raleigh; Jonathon Dembo, Special Collections, J.Y. Joyner Library, East Carolina University, Greenville, North Carolina; Kristine Mudrick, Whitaker Library, Chowan College, Murfreesboro, North Carolina; Susan Whitt, Government Documents and Special Collections, University of North Carolina at Pembroke; Tim West, Special Collections, Perkins Library, Duke University, Durham, North Carolina; Floyd Hardy, James E. Shepard Memorial Library, North Carolina Central University, Durham; Roslyn Holdzkom, the Southern Historical Collection, and Robert Anthony, the North Carolina Collection, Wilson Library, University of North Carolina at Chapel Hill; Alexandra Gressitt, the Library of Virginia, Richmond; and Patricia Higgs, Kellock Library, Omohundro Institute of Early American History and Culture, William and Mary University, Williamsburg, Virginia. These materials alone total as many pages as the book and contain both primary and secondary sources, including manuscripts, papers, rare books, diaries from Bertie County residents, articles from the *North Carolina Historical Review*, *The Journal of Southern History*, *The William and Mary Quarterly*, and others on the county, as well as books related to the history of Native Americans, Africans, and Europeans in the region.

I would like to thank Professor John C. Burnham, professor of history at the Ohio State University, a member of my dissertation committee, mentor, and friend, for suggesting that the endnotes and sources for this book be archived for scholars. I would also like to thank the various archives, special collections, and libraries for agreeing to house and make available to the readers of this book this scholarly material. I would also like to thank Sarah M. Williams, editor, and Christine Riley, publisher, of Arcadia's *Making of America* series for their assistance in making the publication of this book possible. They were willing to work with me to find a way to make both this book and its sources available to the academic and general reader.

Arwin D. Smallwood

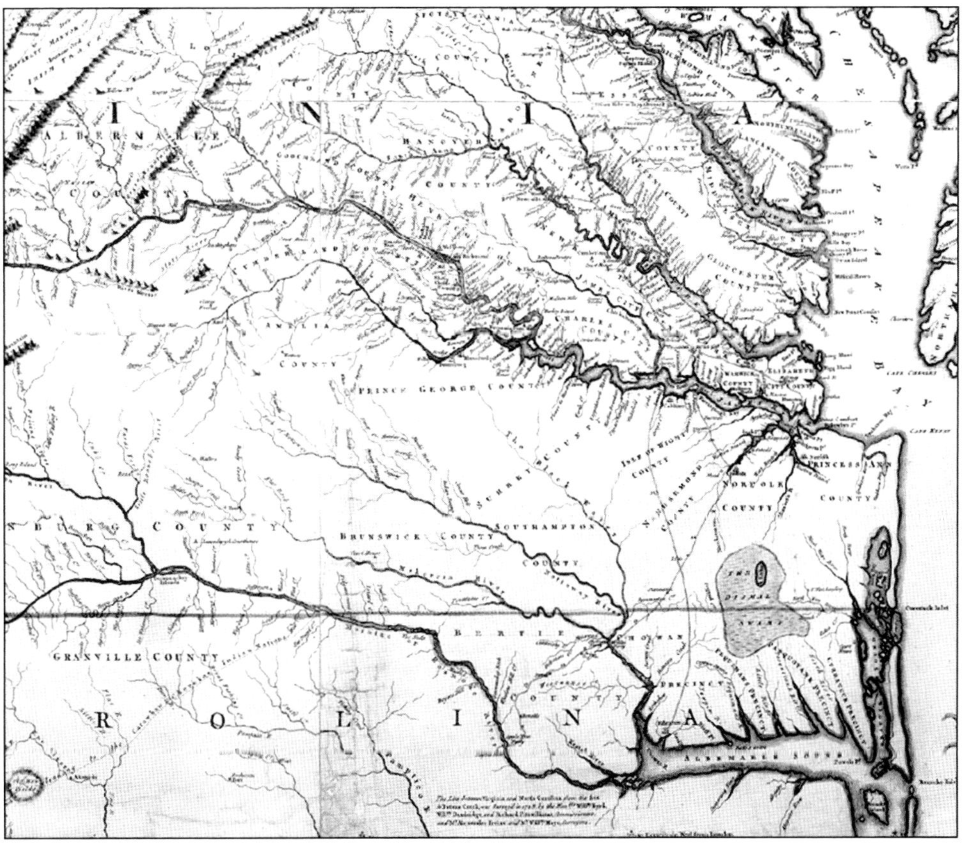

This map, drawn by Peter Jefferson (the father of Thomas Jefferson) and Joshua Fry of Virginia in 1751, shows the relationship between the Chesapeake Bay colonies and northeastern North Carolina, including Bertie County. (Courtesy of LVA.)

Introduction: An Ecological History

We are as much shaped by as we shape our landscape. Depending on whether that landscape is urban, suburban, or rural, who we are and will become are all impacted by our surrounding landscape. Nowhere is that more apparent than in northeastern North Carolina, particularly Bertie County. The lives of the various inhabitants of this county over its 400-year recorded history have not only shaped but been shaped by its landscape. This history has been molded by its natural rivers, creeks, and streams, and the fish and fowl they sustain, as well as the old Native American villages, towns, and forts that were replaced in the 1700s and 1800s by English plantations, such as Avoca, cleared for whites by African and Native American slaves, plantation houses, slave cabins, one-room shacks, and towns, including Windsor, Aulander, Colerain, Roxobel, Lewiston-Woodville, Kelford, Askewville, Midway, and Merry Hill. The landscape and the human relationship to it tells us much about the history, life, and culture of this county and region of North Carolina. Indeed, much can be learned about present-day Bertie County by doing a historical examination of its landscape and studying how that landscape has altered and has been altered by the various people who have lived within and near its boundaries.[1]

Bertie County is located in the western coastal plains of northeastern North Carolina. It is bordered to the east by the tidewater region and to the west by the piedmont region. The tidewater region, which is just east of Bertie County, differs in terrain. The area is generally damp and contains a number of swamps, rivers, creeks, and streams, including the Alligator River and a portion of the Great Dismal Swamp. It also contains a number of natural lakes and savannas, including the largest, Pungo Lake.[2] Together, the tidewater and the coastal plains of North Carolina contain two-fifths of the state's land area and end at the fall lines of the Chowan, Roanoke, Tar-Pamlico, Neuse-Trent, and Cape Fear Rivers, covering a distance inland of 100 to 150 miles.[3]

Along the coast of North Carolina, there is a broken chain of islands known as the Outer Banks, which range in height from a few feet to 100 feet above sea level. Among these islands is historic Roanoke Island, which was the site of the first English settlement in North America. The island is between two great sounds, the Albemarle and Pamlico.[4] North Carolina's five major rivers drain into these large sounds, as well as several smaller sounds, such as the Currituck, Croatan, Roanoke, Boque, and Core. These sounds, along with several inlets, including Currituck, Roanoke, Oregon, Hatteras, Ocracoke, Swash, Beaufort, Boque, and Topsail, are shallow and filled with shifting sands that make the waterways too treacherous for the large-scale commercial shipping the English desired when they arrived in the region in 1584. However, the waterways were ideal for canoeing,

This map shows the location of Bertie County in eastern North Carolina and its proximity to southeastern Virginia, as well as the major rivers, creeks, streams, and swamps of the region.

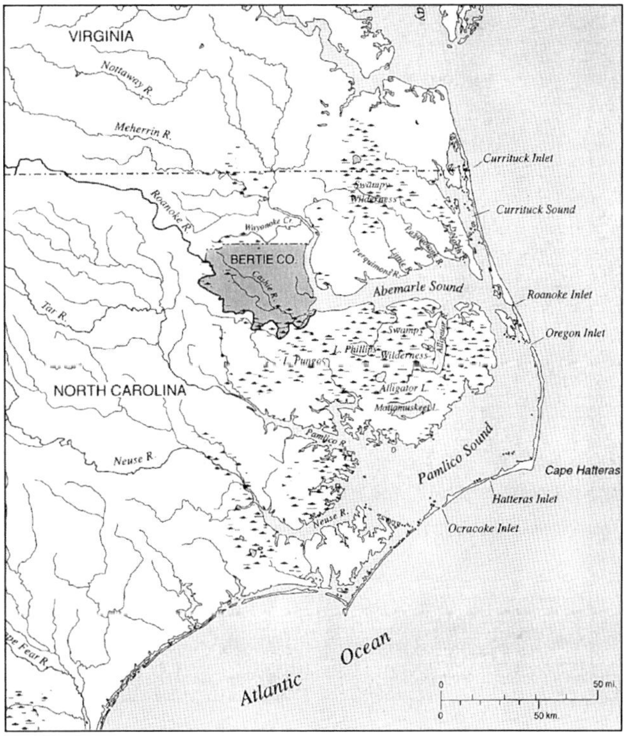

which the coastal and inland Native Americans did in search of fish, crabs, clams, and an assortment of seashells. Trees found on the landscape were used to craft these canoes, make paddles, spears, bows, arrows, and most importantly, to construct and protect their homes and families. They also used trees to make fires that were used to heat their homes, cook their meals, and gather around for religious and social ceremonies.[5]

Today, the county is bordered by five counties that were attached to it at some time in its early history.[6] These counties include Hertford County to the north, Northampton and Halifax Counties to the northwest, and Martin and Washington Counties to the south. Bertie County is also bordered to the east by the Chowan River and the Albemarle Sound, and is divided from its southern and western neighbors by the Roanoke River, which runs from Roanoke, Virginia to the Albemarle Sound, where it drains into the Atlantic Ocean.[7] Bertie County is one of the oldest counties in North Carolina. It was originally a part of Albemarle County, which was established by the English in 1660. It then became a part of Chowan County, which was cut from Albemarle County in 1670. Known as the Bertie Precinct, it was finally given the status of county in 1722 when it was separated from Chowan County.

Bertie County was cut again in 1780 to closely resemble its current shape, with the exception of adjustments that have been made to its northern border with Hertford County. The county would be settled primarily by the English, most of whom migrated down from the Virginia colony and to Virginia from southeastern England, specifically the counties of Essex, Hampshire, Yorkshire, and Norfolk.[8]

All past and present inhabitants of the county have benefited from its easy access to major rivers, streams, creeks, sounds, and, through the inlets of the Outer Banks of North Carolina, the Atlantic Ocean. Since the county is above sea level, it is not adversely affected by the tides or storm surges that can occur during hurricanes, as is the tidewater region to its east. The soil is very fertile and is excellent for growing various types of crops. As a result, all its inhabitants—Native Americans, Europeans, and Africans—have been successful in developing and sustaining a wide variety of agricultural crops, including the "three sisters" (corn, beans, and squash), various peppers, tomatoes, white potatoes, sweet potatoes, and various melons, as well as tobacco.[9]

Once cleared by slaves using slash-and-burn techniques, the county provided excellent land for the large-scale farming that the English would introduce by the late 1600s. The soil was also ideal for growing wheat, tobacco, and cotton in the 1700s and 1800s and, by the late 1800s, peanuts, all of which were produced as cash crops. Most of the agricultural products grown in Bertie County were indigenous to North Carolina, but some new fruits, vegetables, and cash crops, like peanuts and cotton, would be introduced by the English into the landscape.

The county's inhabitants also enjoyed its rivers and their abundance of fish, particularly herring that spawned there in the spring. These fish arrived in such great numbers that several major fisheries were established in the late nineteenth century by white residents of the county. These fisheries exported herring and other fish all over the world. As a result of the fertile soil, abundant fish, fowl, and game, Native Americans—later Europeans and Africans—flourished in the county.[10]

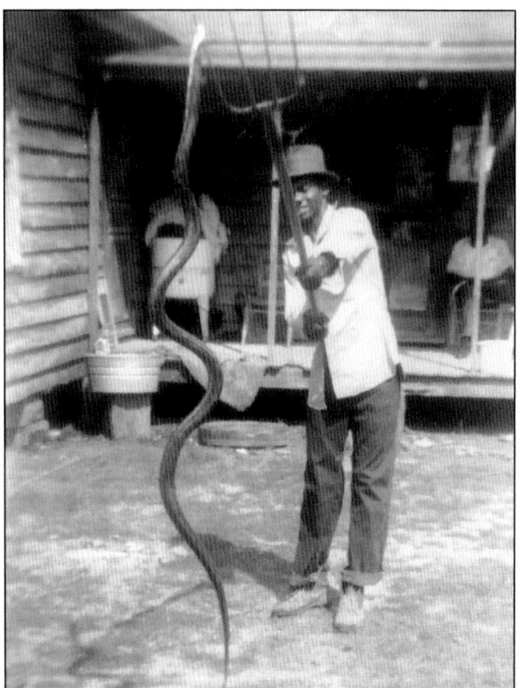

Alfred Bond kills a snake near the home of Ruben Manning as the homeowner watches from the porch. This picture was taken in the 1950s. (Courtesy of Marjorie Manning and SHC, UNC.)

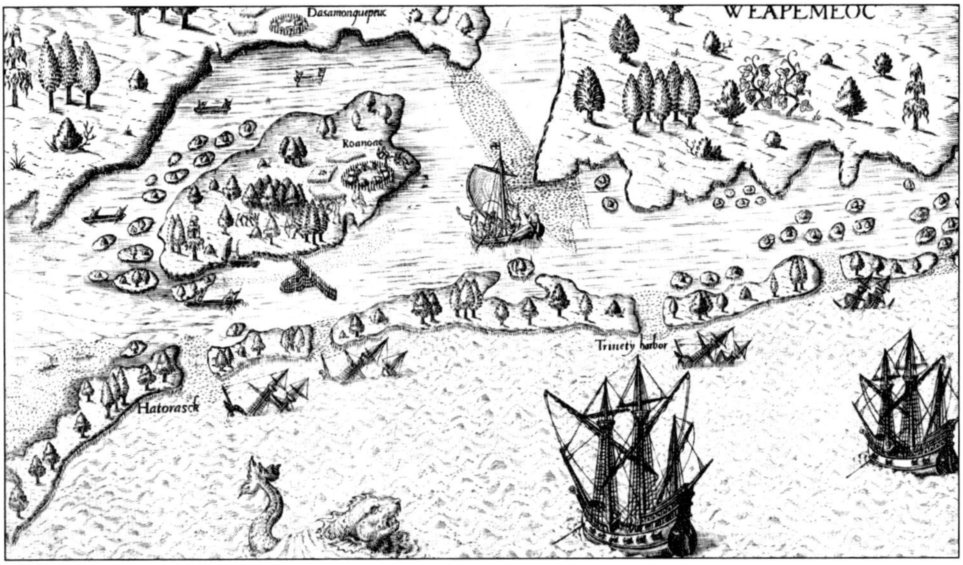

It was clear to the English as early as 1585 when Captains Philip Amadas and Arthur Barlowe lost one of their ships, the Tyger, *off the treacherous North Carolina coast that ships would have great difficulty navigating the area. Ships running aground and sinking therefore remained a major impediment to settling the region throughout the early colonial period. This drawing by John White is in the British Museum. (Courtesy of NCC, UNC.)*

When the coastal region of North Carolina was settled by early colonists, it became clear that heavily loaded ships would have difficulty navigating North Carolina's coast. As a result, the Chesapeake Bay colony of southeastern Virginia drew more settlers than eastern North Carolina. Thus, the North Carolina coast would retard the growth of the region throughout the colonial period. Colonial traders preferred the ports of Virginia, and by 1690, South Carolina, to the treacherous waterways of the coast of North Carolina. In fact, because of its coastline, no attempt was made by the English to settle North Carolina after the failed 1587 colony at Roanoke Island until the 1650s. They instead preferred the Chesapeake area of Virginia for establishing permanent settlements.[11]

Nor were the swamps in Bertie County beneficial to the first English settlers. Two of the largest swamps in Bertie County were the Broadneck, located in the southern part of the county near present-day Indian Woods on the Roanoke River, and the Roquist Pocosin swamp, located in northern Bertie County, south of Piney Woods and near Roquist Creek.[12] These swamps and the many others in eastern North Carolina were full of poisonous snakes, including water moccasins, cotton mouth moccasins, and rattlesnakes. Snakes would remain a problem for residents of the county into the twenty-first century.[13]

Because of the swamps, the county was also infested with mosquitoes, gnats, and a number of biting flies, including deer flies, horse flies, hog flies, blow flies, and common house flies. These pests, especially mosquitoes, which could sometimes carry diseases, proved to be dangerous for early white settlers. Many Africans and Native Americans, on the other hand, tended to be more suited for the environment. This can be gathered by the large numbers of Native Americans and Africans who lived in the swamps of the region to escape slavery and persecution.[14]

There were also large quantities of wild game, including animals that were dangerous. These animals, countless before the arrival of whites, inspired names for the Native Americans and their clans.[15] Even today, there are still surviving members of the Turtle, Beaver, Deer, Wolf, Bear, and Snipe Clans of the Tuscarora, who once lived in the county and the coastal plains of North Carolina.[16]

Because the Native Americans who occupied these lands did not farm the land on the same scale as later white farmers, the landscape was almost entirely covered with trees. However, there were occasional meadows that they cleared and used for gardens and towns. The Native Americans also established a number of early roads that have been referred to as Indian paths. Many of these paths wound their way through thick forests, over creeks and streams, and on the high ground through swamps. These paths connected local Native Americans to their neighbors with whom they traded in eastern North Carolina, southeastern Virginia, and other nations to their north, south, and west.[17] These paths, which became colonial roads and, eventually, modern roads and highways, received a mixture of Native American and English names, and are a lasting reminder of both groups' influence in the development of the county. Many of these early paths and roads made by Native Americans would be improved, widened, and elevated by white settlers and their African slaves, who would eventually be brought into the county.[18]

The landscape of the county and region began to change radically as early as 1700 as better roads were built and new canals dug by Carolina's new colonial government. More whites became interested in settling the county. These settlers, mostly from Virginia, moved into the county as they built plantations and grew tobacco. Many of the early settlers used the county's natural resources to sustain themselves just as Native Americans had for centuries before. The settlers used the Roanoke and Chowan Rivers to catch herring and other fish that spawned there, hunted deer, ducks, quail, and other wild game, and used the soft wood pine forest to develop a turpentine industry, which devastated the forest during the early colonial period and altered the landscape.[19]

There was also an abundance of hard wood trees that supplied timber to make houses, tools, and furniture. Natural materials were readily available to Native Americans, Europeans, and Africans. Animal skins were used to make hats, shoes, gloves, rugs, and bed coverings; animal fat was used to make candles; and timber was utilized to build forts and homes. As more Europeans began to settle the region, the landscape and the inhabitants' relationship to it began to change radically.[20]

Unlike the Native Americans, who lived in harmony with the landscape and took from nature only what they needed to survive, the English over-used and radically altered the county's landscape. They exterminated animals they viewed as pests; they introduced new domesticated animals into the landscape, such as sheep, chickens, cows, horses, mules, and hogs; and they also began to over-hunt and over-fish the rivers, streams, and forests.[21] The most dramatic change, however, was the clear cutting of whole forests to make way for large tobacco plantations.

By the mid-1700s, Bertie County's leading export was naval stores, including tar, pitch, rosin, and turpentine, which were manufactured from the large pine forests of the region that would later be cut to make way for tobacco plantations. Ditches were dug for irrigation purposes. Also, Europeans produced boards, shingles, barrels, and staves.[22] The forest provided the materials for building houses, churches, stores, and other buildings. Timber was also used to build wagons, walking sticks, tables, chairs, desks, stocks for guns, spinning wheels, sloops, and caskets, among other things.[23] Europeans also mined for profit the gold, silver, copper, and iron ore that Native Americans had used in small quantities to adorn themselves and for their sacred objects.[24]

As Europeans radically changed the landscape they also radically changed the way of life for the Native Americans living in the county and region. Surroundings to which Native Americans had grown accustomed for hundreds of years rapidly changed. Their food sources became scarce and some animals disappeared altogether. Their nations were systematically destroyed through war, disease, and alcohol introduced into the region by whites.[25]

The Native Americans taught the whites their methods of fishing, trapping, and dressing skins and furs. They even introduced whites to their methods of clearing land for farming, hill cultivation, and fertilizing. They introduced tobacco to whites and, during the first visit to North Carolina by the English in 1584, they introduced the potato into England and Ireland. The Irish became so dependent upon this vegetable by the 1830s that when the crop failed, millions starved or fled the island for the United States to avoid starvation.

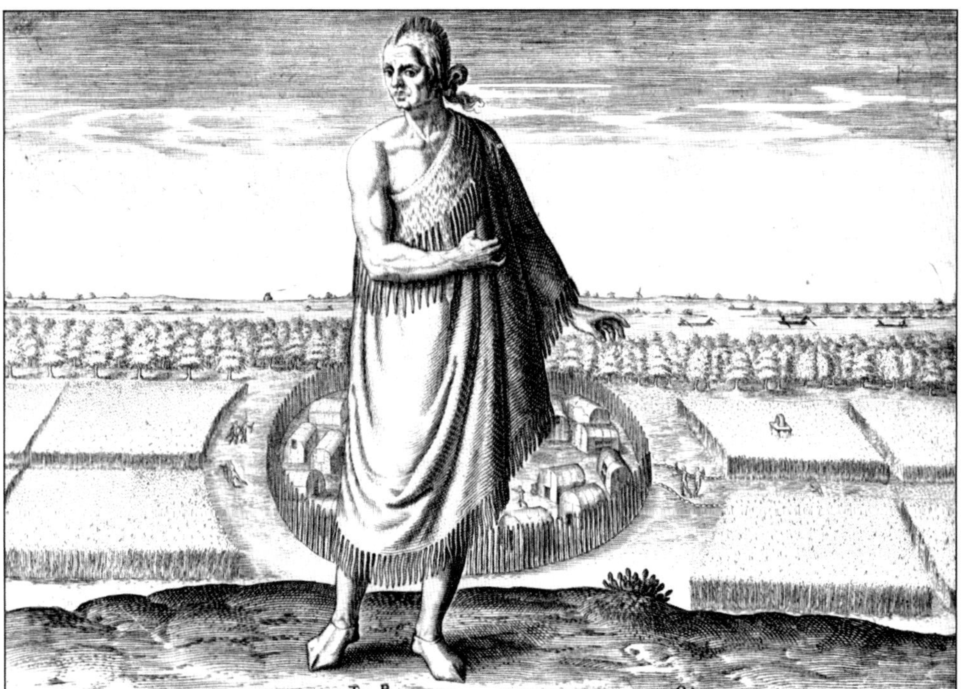

John White's 1585 drawing, in the British Museum, depicts an aged Native American man of "Virginia," (really eastern North Carolina), his settlement, crops, and, in the background, Native Americans canoeing in the Albemarle Sound. (Courtesy of NCC, UNC.)

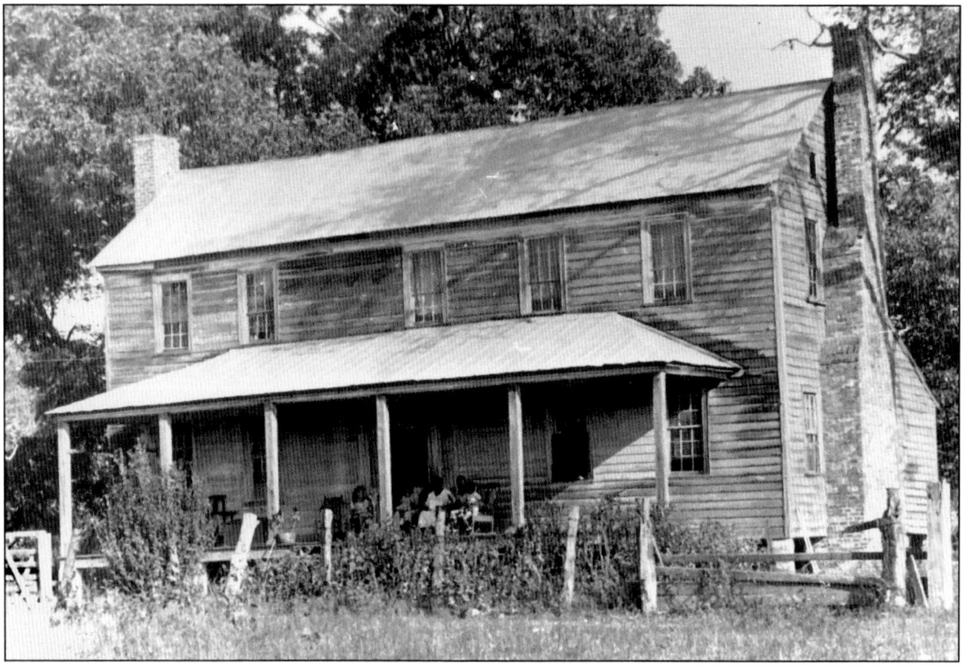

Members of an African-American family living in the Fred Miller house in Oaklawn near Miller's store sit on the porch on a hot summer's day in 1954. (Courtesy of NCSAH.)

Culturally, Native Americans contributed words, political philosophy, myths, legends, traditions, and names for creeks, streams, rivers, swamps, and roads in the county, state, and nation. From 1722 to 1803, Europeans, Native Americans, and African and mixed-blood slaves shared the landscape of Bertie County, trading, hunting, fishing, farming, and passing on to each other parts of their culture—language, religion, music, and art.[26]

In 1803, when the last of the Native Americans left Bertie County, they left behind many artifacts and historic sites that still adorn the landscape. The most significant artifacts were arrowheads, pottery, weapons, and tools. Historic sites include their burial grounds, their punishing ground in Indian Woods, and their trading post, the Gospel Oak. Even today, under a grove of pine trees on Pugh Road, a winding dirt path in Bertie County, one of their burial ground sites is known and respected by the current inhabitants of the area. Their unmarked burial sites, along with unmarked slave cemeteries and marked and unmarked white burial plots on large rural plantations, are today a permanent part of the county's landscape and a reminder of the various people who have shared it.[27]

The labor required to clear forests and run successful tobacco plantations was provided initially by white indentured servants and Native American slaves.[28] By 1730, however, large numbers of African and mixed African–Native American slaves were being utilized in and around the county.[29] Throughout the early 1800s, white farmers continued to clear land to cultivate tobacco and a new cash crop, cotton.[30]

By the start of the 1800s, there were far fewer trees than there had been a century before in Bertie County. Animals that had threatened the crops and the domesticated

English animals, such as wolves, bears, hawks, and snipe, had been hunted to extinction. Many fish were also fished to near extinction for sport and for their commercial value. Large plantation houses, churches, slave cabins, yeoman farmer's houses, and one-room shacks dotted the landscape, along with new bridges over creeks and streams. Ferry boats made crossings over rivers that were too large to have bridges, and fields of corn, wheat, and tobacco grew next to gardens of fresh vegetables, fruits, and nut trees. A number of gristmills would also be constructed by the early settlers to grind their corn into meal and wheat into flour for the plantation owners who moved into the county.[31]

During the Civil War, the landscape of the county was used by plantation owners to grow foodstuffs for the Confederacy. Bertie County was an important part of the fertile Roanoke and Chowan River valleys. To protect the county, the nearby landscape was altered when the state of North Carolina erected "Fort Branch" across the Roanoke River from the county near Indian Woods in Hamilton at Rainbow Bend.[32]

Following the Civil War, the county's landscape changed again. White slave owners would flee the rural areas of the county, leaving their former slaves to sharecrop and tenant farm their land. Many whites would also rent or abandon their homes to African Americans remaining on their old plantations. The few whites that remained, like the Spruill family of Indian Woods, ran businesses and continued to live near them. Spruill operated a general store that provided farm supplies and seed for the plantations that operated in Indian Woods. This store and others like it all over the county would be extremely important to poor white and African-American tenant farmers, sharecroppers, and independent farmers in the county from 1865 to the 1940s. The out-migration of whites from the rural parts of Bertie County changed the landscape for a third time, making what had been black and white communities in the rural areas of the county to most becoming nearly all black and the towns nearly all white.[33]

These communities and towns immediately began to make changes to their landscapes. As early as 1865, African-American churches, serving also as schools and later giving rise to the Rosenwald schools in the early 1900s, were built in rural and urban areas throughout the county. In church cemeteries, residents buried their dead and marked their graves with markers that chronicle their struggles through slavery, Jim Crow, and the Civil Rights Movement. The grave stones also chronicle their involvement in the Civil War, World Wars I and II, the Korean War, and the Vietnam conflict. These newer cemeteries tell the stories of their loved ones that are not told by the many unmarked Indian burial grounds, slave cemeteries, and planters plots that cover the county's rural landscape.[34]

By 1890, a new cash crop, peanuts, took hold in the county. As with tobacco in the seventeenth and eighteenth centuries and cotton in the nineteenth century, peanuts would become the cash crop of the twentieth century.[35] Throughout Bertie County, land that had been cleared in the eighteenth and nineteenth centuries for the growth of tobacco and, eventually, cotton began to be used for the growth of peanuts. By the early 1900s, peanuts had replaced cotton as the leading agricultural crop of Bertie County. Along with peanuts, more farmers also began to grow large quantities of soybeans, which some called "Japan Peas," perhaps because of their resemblance to the shape of Japan.[36]

With the exception of the rise of peanut plantations, the addition of the Rosenwald schools, 20 of which were built in Bertie County, and the grading and paving of the roads, few major changes were made to the landscape in the early 1900s.[37] By the 1930s, electricity was brought into rural communities throughout the United States. It would not make it into rural parts of Bertie County, however, until the 1950s. When it finally arrived, paths were cut through the forest to run power lines and utility poles were run along the roads to connect homes.[38]

By the 1950s, new fertilizers, poisons, and farm machines once again changed the landscape. Added to this was industrialization in nearby towns and counties, which also drastically altered the land and working and living patterns. People began to look for work outside the county in larger numbers, and cars and trucks began to replace horses and wagons. Some new houses were built, and tractors and other forms of farm machinery were common sights on the county's roads during planting and harvesting seasons. As a result, fewer people were needed to work the tobacco, cotton, and peanut plantations of the area.[39] This led to a great out-migration of people from Bertie County to nearby cities, towns, and other urban areas as far away as Virginia, Pennsylvania, and New York.[40]

By the 1980s and 1990s, many of the area's creeks and streams that once were deep enough to canoe in had dried up. The Roanoke and Chowan Rivers, which had sustained huge numbers of herring, perch, and other fish and wildlife, became polluted by industrial and agricultural waste.[41] Many African-American and white residents, who had for generations, first as slaves and masters and then sharecroppers, tenant farmers, and independent farmers, made their living from farming, stopped altogether and were seeking employment outside of the county.[42] Those who continued to farm began to mass-produce chickens for the Perdue Company rather than plant crops. The few remaining forests that had not been cut by the early settlers were cleared and replanted by large timber companies within hours, using machines and less than four men to do work that used to take years and hundreds of men during the colonial and antebellum eras.[43]

In conclusion, Bertie County's past, like that of the rest of eastern North Carolina, has been shaped by and continues to be shaped by the landscape. It, like the rest of eastern North Carolina, was and still is rural and isolated. Because of this, all the inhabitants of the region—Native, European, and African—have used the landscape to house, clothe, and feed their families. They were limited by the landscape initially and, later, they radically altered that landscape to support their needs. However, changes to the landscape have not changed the overall rural nature of the county. The maintaining of the traditions of hunting, fishing, and planting gardens containing the "three sisters," which were taught to the ancestors of the county's current residents, are still practiced without question by many of the county's residents. Thus, the people of Bertie County today and those of the past are as much a part of the landscape as the molders of it. After 400 years, the descendants of the three cultural groups, Native Americans, Europeans, and African Americans that at one time or another lived in the county, still coexist with one another and with the county's landscape.

1. Early History: Roanoke Island and the Chowan and Roanoke River Valleys, 1584–1711

North America was first populated by Native Americans around 10,000 years ago. Archeological digs indicate that the first Native Americans to reach North Carolina and Bertie County arrived between 2,000 and 5,000 years ago.[1] These native cultures changed over time as weaker peoples were conquered and absorbed by stronger ones and North Carolina's first inhabitants developed their civilization. Much of the history of the evolution of Native Americans in North Carolina and the United States consists of legends and folklore. Their histories have been passed down orally for generations and today seem more fiction than fact. Thus, it is unclear when the various native peoples, who were there when Europeans arrived, came to the area, but it is clear from the records we have that Native Americans of Algonquin, Sioux, and Iroquois heritage were in the state in significant numbers by 1584. These early people supported themselves by fishing, farming, and hunting with wood and stone tools. The relatively calm waters of the rivers and sounds assisted Native American fishermen in their attempts to supplement their diet with fresh seafood. The Tuscarora, like many other Native Americans living in the area, used the rivers, creeks, and streams to travel from place to place and to access the sounds.[2]

By 1585, the Native American groups most prevalent in Bertie County were the Meherrin and Tuscarora Nations. Along with the Nottoway, these groups controlled territory from Richmond, Virginia to the Cape Fear River and, as members of the Iroquois family, which included the Delaware, Mohawk, Onondaga, Cayuga, Seneca, and Oneida Nations, created a vast and powerful empire that stretched from the St. Lawrence River in Canada to the Savannah River in Georgia. The Tuscarora Nation, which resided in eastern North Carolina, controlled territory that encompassed all of the major coastal rivers. As a result, the Tuscarora, who held a reputation for being a fearless, warlike, and proud people, shared the bounty of the sounds and Outer Banks with various Algonquin and Sioux peoples that populated the tidewater region of eastern North Carolina and southeastern Virginia.[3] The region's sounds and islands, including Roanoke Island, were areas where different nations of Native Americans fished and searched for seashells without fear of attack. Native Americans valued seashells in much the same manner Europeans valued gold, silver, and precious stones, but for Native Americans, seashells, in addition to having monetary value, also held spiritual value. Seashells were used by the Tuscarora and their Iroquois brothers—the Five Nations of Oneida, Cayuga, Onondaga, Mohawk, and Seneca—to make wampum belts for ceremonies by chiefs and shamans, and to be awarded to certain members of the nations who obtained high levels of achievement.[4]

Since the Iroquois valued seashells that were different from those valued by the Algonquins, and since there was constantly an enormous supply, no conflicts arose between the two groups over them. Likewise, there was no reason for the two groups to develop conflicts over shellfish and salt-water fish, since they too were in abundance.[5] From 1585 to 1715, the Tuscarora were known amongst eastern woodland Native Americans as great traders and travelers, and were recorded by the French, Dutch, Spanish, Swedes, and English to have traded as far north as the St. Lawrence River, south to west Florida, and west throughout the Appalachian Mountains.

The First Europeans to make any contact with North Carolina Native Americans were the Spanish. In 1525, the Spanish explorer Pedro de Quejo sailed along the south Atlantic coast from the Caribbean as far north as Cape Hatteras, North Carolina. The Spanish also introduced into the area the first Africans, brought to North Carolina as soldiers and slaves by the Spanish when they attempted to settle along the Cape Fear River.[6] Most of these Africans died of disease or starvation, or were taken back to the Caribbean after the settlement failed. Quejo was preceded by the explorer Giovanni da Verrazzano, an Italian, who in 1524 also attempted to establish a settlement on the Cape Fear River.[7] Later, between 1566 and 1568, the Spanish conquistador Juan Pardo would

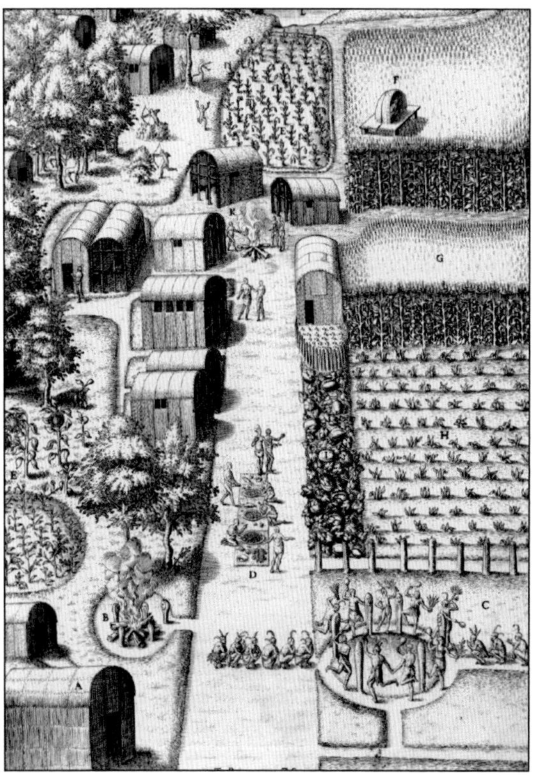

In his drawing of a typical day in a Native American village, John White clearly shows the tasks of hunting and cooking, dwellings, ceremonial grounds, and gardens of tobacco and the "three sisters"—corn, beans and squash. (Courtesy of NCC, UNC.)

This map shows the migration of the Iroquois people (Seneca, Onadaga, Cayuga, Oneida, Tuscarora, and Mohawks) from the Mississippi River valley to the northeast and southeast. Also visible is the Iroquoian wedge in Virginia and North Carolina formed by the Tuscarora, Meherrin, and Nottoway Indians.

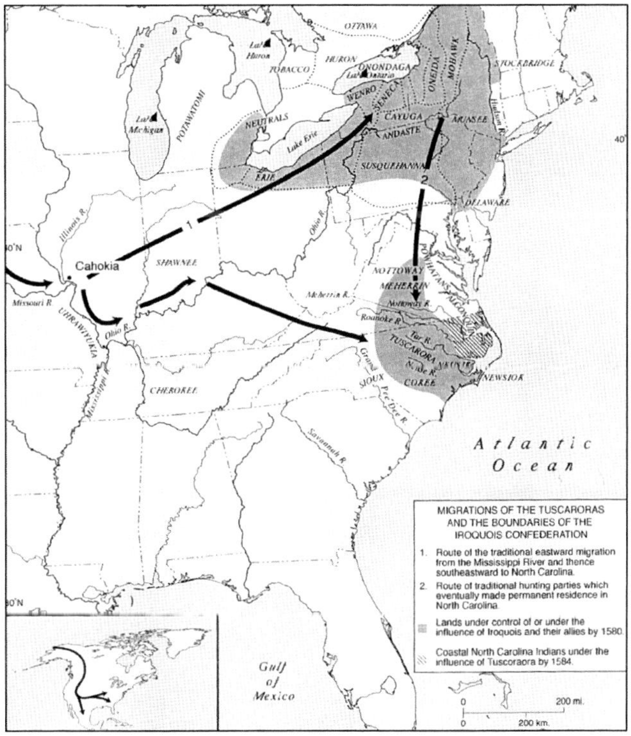

lead a land expedition through western North Carolina up to the Cherokee lands in the Appalachian Mountains.[8]

It is clear from early French, Dutch, and English records that by the time Europeans arrived in large numbers in the late 1600s, the Iroquois people of the Five Nations were the most powerful and prosperous Native American peoples on the Atlantic seaboard. And as a result of the Tuscarora kinship, economic, and military ties to the Five Nations, the Iroquois dominated the Atlantic seaboard from the St. Lawrence River of Canada to the Savannah River of Georgia.[9]

The Tuscarora Nation, which resided in eastern North Carolina, was bordered to the east by the Algonquins, peaceful coastal Native Americans, as well as several other coastal nations. To their immediate south and west, they were bordered by the Sioux, who were war-like hunters and gatherers, and also the Yamasee, Catawba, Creek, and a number of smaller nations aligned with these Native Americans. To their west, beyond the Sioux, were the powerful Cherokee, who anthropologists claim were also Iroquois like the Tuscarora, but neither the Tuscarora nor the other members of the Six Nations (formerly Five Nations) consider the Cherokee part of their group. In fact, all of these North Carolina Native Americans were considered enemy nations, but were held at bay by the Tuscarora's military alliances with the Meherrin, Nottoway, and particularly, the Five Nations.[10]

The Tuscarora, like many of the Northeastern Woodland Indians, were primarily agricultural, but they also were hunter-gatherers. Their nation, like the Iroquois

Confederacy, was made up of large clans that together formed the Tuscarora Nation. The Tuscarora were also separated by region into the Upper Tuscarora and the Lower Tuscarora. The Upper Tuscarora controlled lands from the Tar River north to the Meherrin River and were supported militarily by the Nottoway and Meherrin of Virginia. The Lower Tuscarora were settled south of the Tar River down to the Trent River in eastern North Carolina. The Upper Tuscarora were most likely responsible for destroying the Roanoke settlement in 1587, since Roanoke River and Roanoke Island were within their territory.[11]

Each clan was responsible for making its own laws governing the members of its clan, who were all related by blood, with the blood line traced through the mother. Each clan had a chief that presided over civil and military affairs. In this matriarchal society, these chiefs were elected by the clan mothers. The simplest organized political unit was the *ohwatcira*, which was basically an extended family. The *ohwatcira* included grandparents, parents, children, and daughters and their husbands, who moved in with their wives' families and became part of the clan, which they were expected to defend.[12]

It is not clear how many clans there were before European contact, but by 1700, records indicate that there were at least eight.[13] Clan names were generally descriptive and usually signified the type of game that was plentiful in the territory held by that clan, such as deer, bear, turtle, or wolf. The names also had secondary meanings. For example, turtle also meant "climbing-the-mountain people." Snipe also meant "clean-sand people," which refers to the killdeer and its habit of "running along the clean sand at the water's edge."[14]

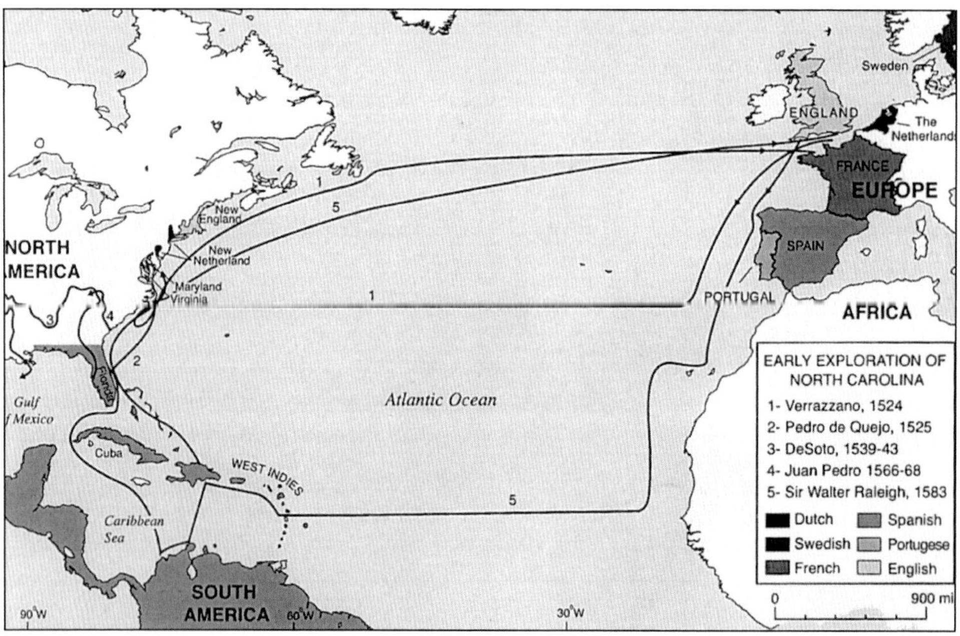

Indicated on this map of America at the beginning of the colonial period are Spanish, English, Dutch, Swedish, and French explorations and settlements in the Caribbean and North and South America from 1524 to 1587.

By the late 1500s, the Tuscarora had established towns on the banks of the Roanoke, Trent, Neuse, and Tar Rivers in eastern North Carolina. These rivers provided the most fertile lands for growing crops. The crops included corn, potatoes, tobacco, beans, peas, and a number of assorted vegetables.[15] The rivers also provided the Tuscarora with an efficient means of travel and large amounts of fish for food. Canoes made from trees were used to navigate these rivers into the Albemarle and Pamlico Sounds, and onto the Outer Banks and coastal islands of North Carolina, including Roanoke, Cape Hatteras, and Manteo, where the Tuscarora acquired seafood and shells. According to the oral accounts of numerous descendants in various states, the Tuscarora were the "Fort Knox" of the Five Nations and traveled frequently to North Carolina's Outer Banks to gather seashells, which were used by all of the Iroquois to make wampum.[16]

In 1578, Queen Elizabeth of England issued the first charter for lands in North Carolina to Sir Humphrey Gilbert, giving him and his heirs lands in North America that were not occupied by European settlers.[17] It would take another six years, until 1584, before the Queen would issue a patent to Sir Walter Raleigh, authorizing him to establish a settlement, which he did three years later in 1587.[18] This settlement and the two expeditions that preceded it brought the first contact between the English and the Native Americans of coastal North Carolina, the Algonquins and those of the interior.[19]

In 1584, Sir Walter Raleigh funded the first of two expeditions to what would become known as the Outer Banks and coastal plains of North Carolina. Utilizing his charter, he sent the first English expedition, led by Captains Philip Amadas and Arthur Barlowe, to explore North Carolina and find a site for a settlement. Amadas and Barlowe sailed from England to the Canary Islands in 1584, then to the West Indies, and from there were carried by the Gulf Stream to the coast of North Carolina.[20] Amadas and Barlowe sailed along the treacherous Outer Banks of coastal North Carolina until they reached the Ocracoke Inlet. From there, they sailed north up the Pamlico Sound until they reached Roanoke Island.[21]

On July 2, 1584, two ships, the *Tyger* and the *Admiral*, commanded respectively by Amadas and Barlowe, landed on Roanoke Island. Three days after the landing, a Native American paddled out to their camp and began trading with the Englishmen, becoming the first North Carolina Native American to make contact with Europeans of English descent.[22] After several days of trading, the friendly Algonquins asked the English for their assistance in defending them against a war-like band to their west along the Neuse River. It is likely that they were referring to the Tuscarora Nation, whose capital city Chattakua was located on the Neuse River near the present-day city of New Bern.[23]

Although the English declined to help the coastal Native Americans in their fight, they did become interested enough in the people, their fighting strength, and their territory to investigate the Pamlico and Albemarle Sounds and the Outer Banks, including the native peoples they found there. After about two months of exploring and mapping the coastal regions around Roanoke Island, Amadas and Barlowe kidnapped two local Native American braves, Wanchese and Manteo, and took them to England to teach them English and show Queen Elizabeth and possible investors what the inhabitants looked like. When they returned to England, they reported their discoveries to Queen Elizabeth. The new lands were named "Virginia" after the virgin queen and plans were made for a second voyage.[24]

The report that Amadas and Barlowe issued, the exposure of Indians Wanchese and Manteo, and a paper written by Richard Hakluyt offered enough information to garner financial support for a second expedition to coastal North Carolina. Thus, in 1585, Raleigh sent a second expedition of 108 men led by Sir Richard Greenville. This expedition also included Ralph Lane, who was to be the lieutenant governor of the colony; Philip Amadas, the admiral of the country; John White, who was assigned to paint the landscape and map the region; Thomas Hariot, who was to record the discoveries and peoples of the area; and Wanchese and Manteo, who were to serve as interpreters.[25]

The second expedition followed a route similar to that of the first, stopping in the West Indies, where the explorers acquired horses, cows, bulls, goats, swine, sheep, bull hides, sugar, ginger, pearls, tobacco, and sugar cane, all of which they took with them to Roanoke Island. After a brief stop at Cape Hatteras, where the Croatan Native Americans were found, and after becoming involved in an altercation with the Secotan of the Native American town of Aquascogoc, the explorers sailed on to Roanoke Island by way of the Pamlico Sound.[26]

After reaching Roanoke Island, where Greenville left the men and sailed back to England, the members of the expedition explored and mapped the coastal areas of North Carolina and erected a fort they named "Fort Raleigh."[27] The coastal Algonquins' relationship with the first white colonists was one of wonderment and brotherhood. They showed no fear or hostility toward the explorers and offered little resistance to their erecting Fort Raleigh at Roanoke Island.[28] They, in fact, traded freely with them for European goods and brought them corn, vegetables, and fish. The Tuscarora, however, proved not to be as trusting.

After ten months of exploring and mapping the Pamlico and Albemarle Sounds and the Chowan and Roanoke Rivers, the Lane expedition, under threat of Native American attack, departed for England. During their expeditions, Lane and his men mapped three towns located in modern-day Bertie County, two along the banks of the Chowan River that were occupied by the Meherrin and one, Moratoc, along the Roanoke River in modern-day Indian Woods, occupied by the Tuscarora.[29]

While camping one night near the Tuscarora town of Moratoc, on the Roanoke River, Lane and his men were attacked by the Tuscarora. Lane believed that Wanchese, one of the kidnapped men who had escaped, had informed the local Native Americans of the Englishmen's presence. The surprise attack forced Lane and his men back to the safety of Fort Raleigh. There, under the threat of another attack by the coastal natives, Lane and his men were forced to flee aboard ships provided by Sir Francis Drake, who had been raiding Spanish settlements in the Caribbean and had stopped to check on and re-supply Lane and his men.[30] When Drake departed, he left over 300 African and Native American maroon soldiers, who had assisted him in his raids, as a reward for their service. These were the first known permanent African residents of the region. What happened to the Africans is not recorded, but some evidence indicates they blended into existing eastern North Carolina's Native American communities, particularly the Tuscarora.[31]

It is clear from the written record that the Tuscarora were neither surprised by Africans when they began to come into contact with large numbers of them, or harbored any hatred for Africans the way they did whites. In fact, *The Colonial Records of North Carolina* notes that the Tuscarora worshiped a black deity along with a red and white one, and that they often covered their skin with bear's oil, which made them appear darker than they were. Whether these practices were the result of unrecorded pre-European African contact is unclear and requires further research.[32]

Shortly after Lane's departure, Greenville, who had brought Lane and his men over from England, returned to the colony to find Fort Raleigh abandoned. Unaware that Lane and his men had departed with Drake for England, or that Drake had left over 300 African, Caribbean, and Central American maroon soldiers on the island, Greenville searched the area and, after finding no one, also sailed back to England, leaving 18 of his men to maintain the fort.[33]

By June of 1586, Governor Lane and his party arrived back in England where they gave a report to Sir Walter Raleigh of their discoveries. Once back in England, however, Lane and some of his men began to speak unfavorably about North Carolina and described the Native Americans living there as hostile. In spite of these negative reports, Raleigh was able to raise enough money and gather enough colonists for an attempt at settling North Carolina. Using funds from a joint-stock company, Raleigh financed the settlement in North Carolina.[34]

John White was selected to govern this planned settlement. White's colony consisted of 93 men, 17 women, and 9 children. They departed in the spring of 1587. John White arrived on Roanoke Island with America's first English settlers in mid-1587 to establish the colony of Roanoke. By the time he arrived, many of the Algonquin Native Americans of the Albemarle and Pamlico Sounds area were weakened or had already died from disease.[35]

When White and his colonists arrived at Roanoke Island, they found Fort Raleigh destroyed and the skeletal remains of one of the men left by Greenville. It was learned

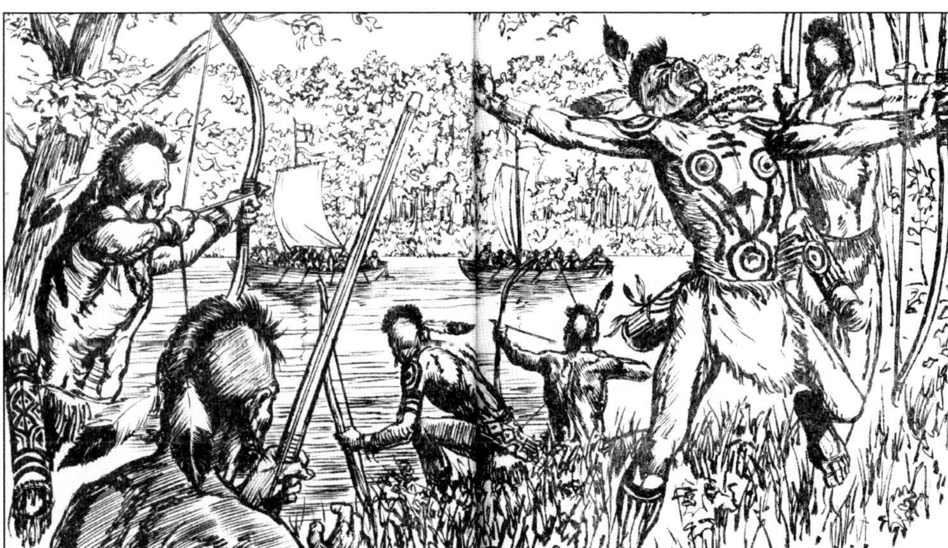

Ralph Lane's expedition was attacked by the Tuscarora Indians on the Roanoke River in 1586. (Courtesy of Margaret Johnson and NCC, UNC.)

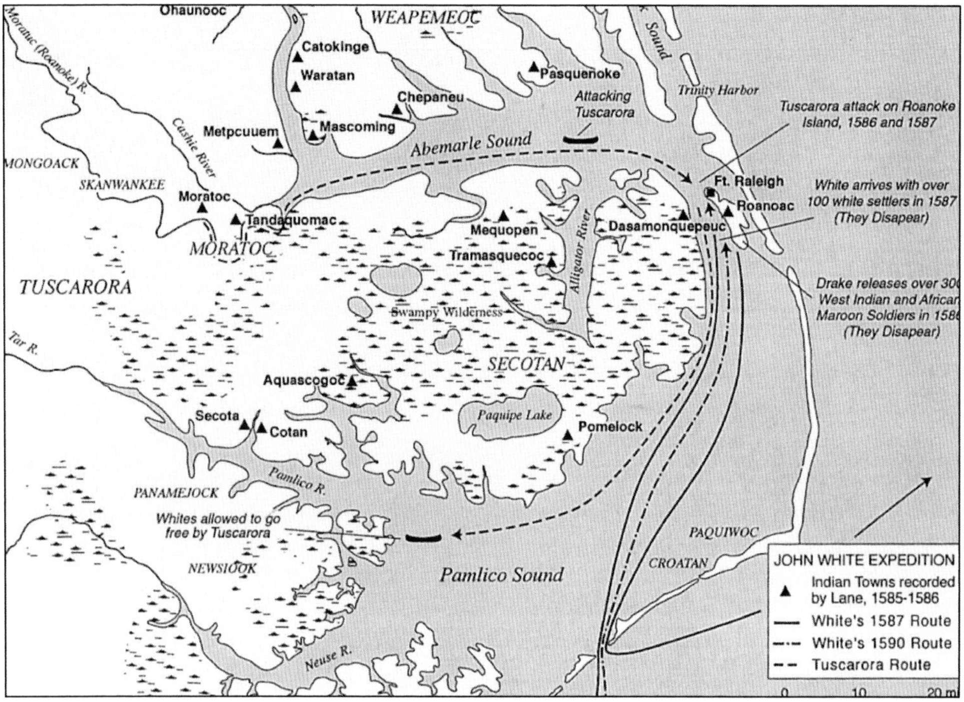

This map shows the Tuscarora attacks on Lane's expedition on the Roanoke River, their attack and capture of 300 African maroons left on Roanoke Island by Sir Francis Drake in 1586, and the attack and capture of the 101 English colonist (known as the "Lost Colony") a year later in 1587.

from friendly Native Americans that the men were killed by natives from the towns of Secotan, Aquascogoc, and Dasamonquepeuc. Even with this information, Simon Fernández, commander of the ships transporting Governor White and his colonists, left them on the island.[36] In fact, White and his colonists were not supposed to be left at Roanoke Island, but rather, taken to Chesapeake Bay after a brief stop at Roanoke to check on the men left at Fort Raleigh. However, Fernández refused to carry them any further. As a result, White had Fort Raleigh rebuilt and settled his colony on Roanoke Island. In the fall of 1587, provisions began to run low and White sailed back to England for additional supplies. While he was in England, war broke out with Spain and later France, trapping him in England until the fall of 1590.[37]

When John White finally returned to Roanoke Island, he found neither his daughter nor granddaughter Virginia Dare, the first English child born in North America. Nor was there anything to indicate where they or the rest of the colonists had gone. He found the houses taken down, bits and pieces of armor, and the word "Croatan" carved into a tree and the word "cro" carved above it. White's failed colony has become known as the Lost Colony. There have been a number of theories about what happened to the Lost Colony, none of which have been conclusive. Tuscarora legend answers with certitude what happened to the colony.[38]

According to legend, the Tuscarora, on one of their foraging missions to Roanoke, took the English women as prisoners and killed most of the men, according to custom. They allowed three men and one woman to go free because they had red and blonde hair, which caused the Tuscarora to be fearful of their spirits, believing them to be children of the sun god.[39] It is believed that these individuals were taken in by the Croatan Native Americans and intermarried with them, creating the Lumbee of North Carolina.[40]

In further support of this legend, colonial records and written statements from French Huguenots note that they saw Tuscarora with blond hair and blue eyes as early as 1696. These Huguenots were settled along the Tar River in 1696 and the Neuse River by 1708, and they were the closest white settlers to the Tuscarora. Since there were no significant European settlements near the Tuscarora until 1660, and any attack by the Tuscarora on Virginia where whites would have been captured would have been recorded by the Virginians at Jamestown, this legend offers a plausible explanation to the perplexing question of "What happened to the Lost Colony?"[41]

The Tuscarora belief in a sun god is also supported by the written record. Baron Christopher de Graffenreid, governor of the New Bern settlement, accounts of a Tuscarora chapel and altar in *The Colonial Records of North Carolina*. De Graffenreid stated the following:

> They had there a kind of altar, cunningly interwoven with small sticks, and vaulted like a dome. In one place was an opening, like a small door or wicket, through which they put their offerings. In the midst of this heathenish chapel was a concavity where they sacrificed beans, corals, and, also wampum. Facing the rising sun, was planted in the ground a wooden post, with a carved head, painted half red and white. In front of it stood a big stick with a small crown, at its end, wrapped up in red and white; on the other side, which looks towards the setting sun, was another image with a horrid face painted black and red. By the first they mean some god and the other the demon, which they know far better.[42]

The taking of the Roanoke women and children would have also been in keeping with the practices of the Tuscarora. De Graffenreid, who was held by the Tuscarora during their raid on the New Bern settlement at the start of the Tuscarora War in 1711, noted that the Tuscarora returned with prisoners:

> I observed that when the Indian soldiers . . . returned with their booty and prisoners, the priest and tallest woman of rank (clan mother) took the poor prisoners and compelled them to dance; when they refused to do it, they took them under the arms, lifted them, and let them down alternatively, as a sign that these Christians had now to dance after their music, and had become their subjects.[43]

After the failure of the Roanoke colony, from 1588 to 1610, several expeditions from England and Jamestown, Virginia were sent to Roanoke Island in search of the Lost Colony. The first two were headed by John White in 1588, being turned back by war with Spain and, again in 1590, arriving safely, but not finding the colonists. Later, in 1602, Captain Samuel Mace arrived in the region from England, but he also was unsuccessful. These explorers searched for the colonists as far inland as the Chowan River valley with no luck. Although these expeditions found no trace of the colonists, they did help to maintain interest in northeastern North Carolina for possible future settlement. However, there were no permanent residents who settled the region until 1655. Fur traders, explorers, and soldiers entered the area from 1622 to 1655.[44] Land grants for territory in North Carolina would be issued from 1629 to 1722 and interest in settling the region remained high. On October 30, 1629, Charles I of England granted Sir Robert Heath land from 31 to 36 degrees north latitude from the Atlantic to the Pacific, including both the current states of North and South Carolina. Heath did not make any attempts to settle his grant and, in 1638, transferred it to Henry Lord Maltravers, who also failed to establish a settlement.[45]

These early grant holders failed to settle Carolina from 1629 to 1660 because of England's internal problems, including the English Civil War that, by 1660, weakened the monarchy and empowered the parliament. While England experienced several decades of turmoil, Virginians from the Jamestown settlement took advantage of the opportunity to gain control of the fertile lands in northeastern North Carolina. From 1622 to 1660, Virginians explored, conquered, and settled the fertile coastal lands that make up the modern counties of Currituck, Camden, Pasquotank, Gates, Perquimans, Chowan, Dare, Tyrrell, Washington, Hertford, Northampton, Halifax, Martin, and Bertie.[46]

In 1607, 20 years after the failure to settle Roanoke, the English began their first successful settlement in Jamestown, Virginia. The Virginia settlement sent several expeditions to Roanoke Island and to the Roanoke-Chowan region in search of the Lost Colony. The first was headed by Captain John Smith in 1608. The second was headed by Captain Samuel Argall in 1610. The final expedition was led by John Pory in 1622, who may have been accompanied by African slaves first introduced into Jamestown by the Dutch in 1619. These African slaves were to work beside white indentured servants and Native American slaves on the tobacco plantations of Virginians. As the size and wealth of the colony of Virginia grew, so did its need for labor and fertile farmland.[47]

By 1622, the Jamestown settlement was a thriving one, with large tobacco plantations and increasing numbers of white indentured servants and African slaves. Because of this growth and the subsequent need for land, John Pory, the speaker of the House of Burgesses in Virginia, headed a 60-mile land expedition into northeastern North Carolina leading south to the Chowan River, which flows along the eastern border of present-day Bertie County. He was pleased with what he saw and encouraged the Virginians to settle the region. Due to the presence of hostile Native Americans, this was not possible until after 1643. In that year, Governor William Berkley of Virginia sent a military expedition by land and sea to the Chowan River valley against the local Native Americans, who were defeated at Weynock Creek, opening northeastern North Carolina to settlement. From 1622 to 1646, settlers from Virginia moved into northeastern North Carolina, clearing land and cultivating tobacco.[48]

From 1650 to 1660, English settlers from Virginia moved closer to Tuscarora lands west and south of the Chowan River. In fact, in 1650, a Virginia merchant named Edward Bland explored the Chowan, Meherrin, and Roanoke River valleys, home to

The sea and land routes depicted here were used by Captain John Smith, Captain Samuel Argall, and John Pory between 1608 and 1622 to search for survivors of the "Lost Colony" and to explore northeastern North Carolina for future settlement.

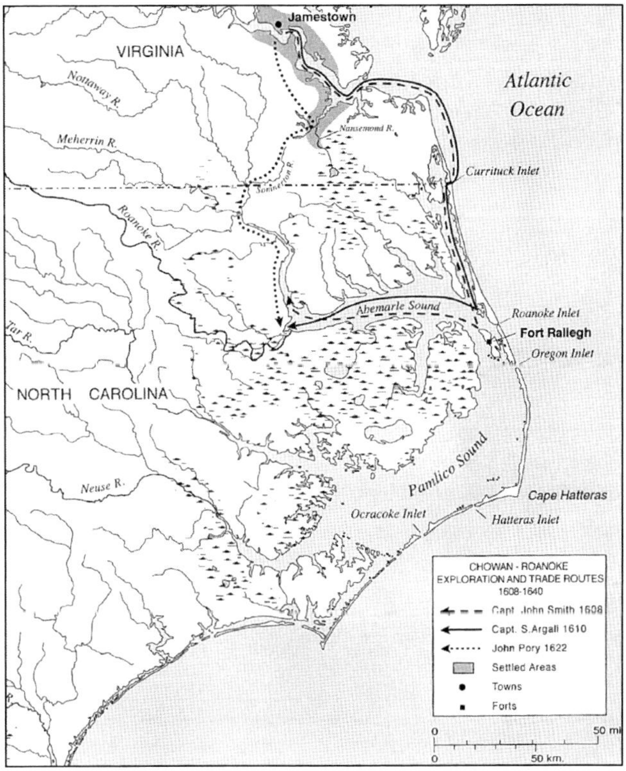

the Meherrin, Nottoway, and Tuscarora people. Upon returning to Virginia, Bland petitioned the colonial legislature for permission to establish a settlement in what is today Bertie County.[49] This request was granted, along with several others between 1650 and 1660, including one to Roger Green, Francis Yeardley, and Nathaniel Batts. Of these men, Nathaniel Batts would become the first white settler in Bertie County in 1655.[50] Tribes residing on Tuscarora lands in and near Bertie complained that their women and children were being stolen and lands belonging to them were being taken by colonists. In fact, the Upper Tuscarora, who had begun trading with white settlers in Jamestown, had been informed of Lower Tuscarora women and children being taken in 1666 by barbarians settled in Clarendon County on the Cape Fear River. They were promptly attacked and driven out as a result. Trade by the Upper Tuscarora with Virginians soon turned to competition which, with the support of their allies the Meherrins and Nottoways, led to a brief war with the Virginians in the late 1660s over white encroachment onto their lands. This war familiarized the Upper Tuscarora with European weapons and made them wary about further hostilities, possibly explaining why Chief Tom Blount was reluctant to go to war with the colony of North Carolina in 1711 and later in 1713.[51]

From 1650 to 1663, most of the charters for land in North Carolina were handed out by the Virginia colony. When Charles II was placed on the throne in 1660, he was indebted to a number of nobles in England who supported him politically and financially. One of the ways Charles II repaid these supporters was by issuing proprietary charters for land in

North America. In 1663, Charles issued such a charter for Carolina. This charter granted proprietors land between 36 and 31 degrees north latitude from the Atlantic to the Pacific Ocean. Charles's charter nullified the earlier charters issued by Queen Elizabeth in 1578 and Charles I in 1629. It included eight proprietors: Edward Hyde, Earl of Clarendon; George Monck, Duke of Albemarle; William Craven, Earl of Craven; John Berkeley; Sir William Berkeley, landowner and governor of Virginia; Sir George Carteret; Lord Anthony Ashley Cooper, Earl of Shaftesbury and landowner in Barbados; and Sir John Colleton, landowner and slave trader in Barbados. In 1663, the new proprietors in England began to assert their control over their lands in North Carolina.[52] In 1665, the boundaries of the charter were revised to the current northern border of North Carolina and the current southern border of South Carolina.[53]

Under the proprietors, three counties were set up: Albemarle County in 1664, which included northeastern North Carolina; Clarendon County in 1665, in the Cape Fear region in southeastern North Carolina; and Craven County in 1670, which would become Charleston, South Carolina. Later, in 1670, John Leder set out from Richmond, Virginia and explored the piedmont and western coastal plains, noting the size and strength of various Native American nations, including the Cherokee and the Tuscarora. This expedition would gather useful information that would prove very helpful in developing alliances to keep the Tuscarora and its allies in check.

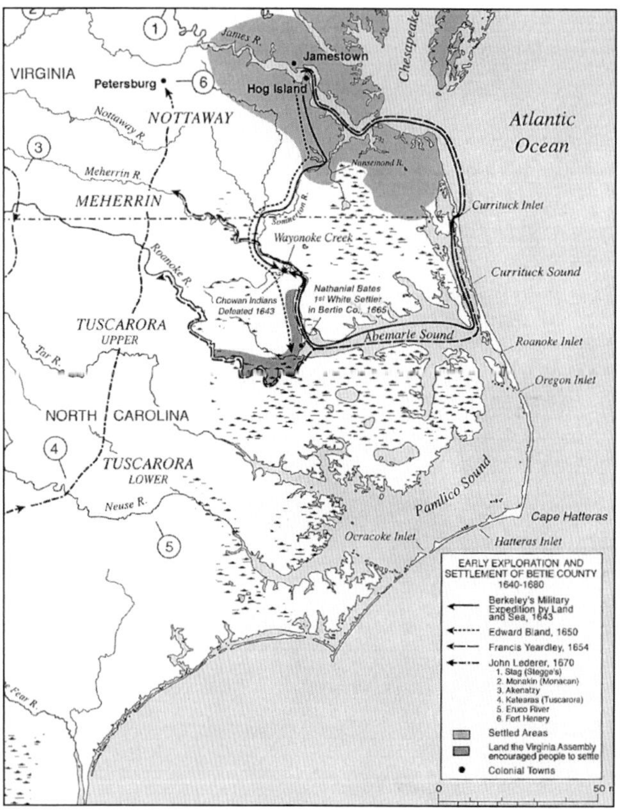

This map shows Native American and English lands in southeastern Virginia and northeastern North Carolina, as well as the routes used by fur traders, explorers, and Virginia government and military officials to trade with, explore, create alliances with, and conquer native peoples in Bertie County and the Albemarle region from 1640 to 1680.

As more and more settlers streamed into the Albemarle region, the need for local government soon became apparent. William Drummond, a Scottish merchant from Virginia, was commissioned as the first governor of Albemarle County in 1664. A year later, Sir John Yeamans became the first governor of Clarendon County in the Cape Fear region.[54] With the appointment of a governor, the Albemarle settlement and trade between it, the Native Americans, and Virginia began to grow.

By 1667, the settlement at Clarendon County failed, and many of its settlers moved to Albemarle County and to Craven County in South Carolina.[55] To promote settlement of Albemarle County so it would not also fail, the proprietors introduced a new constitution on July 21, 1669 known as the "Fundamental Constitution of Carolina" or "Grand Model," which was believed to be written by the English philosopher John Locke.[56] In 1670, Albemarle County was divided into four precincts: Chowan, Pasquotank, Perquimans, and Currituck. Each of these precincts was allowed to have five delegates in the lower House of Burgesses.[57]

In spite of political representation, life for settlers in Albemarle County was very hard. Unlike the Native Americans who lived in the region, the English depended on mercantile trade to grow and prosper, but the county's growth was retarded because of the lack of roads and safe sailing routes to England. Added to this was the fact that Craven County, located in South Carolina, was easier to access by sea and many of the lord proprietors began to steer more money and supplies to settlers in this county, founding Charlestown in 1670.[58]

Many inducements were given to settlers and indentured servants to move to Albemarle County, including land and the right to participate in the governing of the colony. In spite of these inducements, many settlers asked for and received a land grant system similar to that of the colony of Virginia. In 1668, the proprietors of Carolina signed the "Great Deed of Grant," which reshaped Albemarle County's land system to resemble Virginia's. To encourage further settlement, in 1669, the Albemarle legislature passed several laws, the two most significant being tax exemption for one year for newcomers and a five-year stay of suits, debts, and/or other action occurring outside the colony.[59]

These laws and other efforts by the proprietors of Albemarle to attract settlers were met with resistance by both the leaders of the Virginia colony and the many Native Americans occupying the lands being given away. Competition between Virginia and North Carolina for settlers created tension between the two settlements. There was also great fear among many in Albemarle County that Virginia was planning to take over the colony. This fear arose because Virginia insisted that the boundaries of the 1629 charter, under which Albemarle County fell in the boundaries of Virginia, was legal, and the 1663 charter was not. So intense was the competition between North Carolina and Virginia that, in 1679, Virginia closed its ports to tobacco from Albemarle County and many Albemarle settlers believed that Virginians were deliberately inciting the Meherrin and Nottoway, who had towns in what would become Bertie County, to make war on the settlers. As a result of these problems, Virginia and what would become North Carolina had very uneasy relations throughout the early colonial period.[60]

There were also Native American attacks that destroyed crops and homes and frightened away potential settlers. In 1675, there was an uprising by the Chowoncs that was crushed by the colonial government, and not without great loss of life. Albemarle County also suffered three major rebellions from 1677 to 1711. The first of these, the Culpepper Rebellion in 1677, centered around the Navigation Acts of 1673, particularly the Plantation Duty Act. This act required that tobacco and other commodities produced in Albemarle County be traded on English ships rather than on New England ships as had become the custom. The law went unenforced until Thomas Eastchurch was appointed governor of the county and Thomas Miller, president of the council. Miller's attempt to enforce the act was met with fierce opposition and, after detaining a ship bound for New England captained by Zachariah Gilliam, opposition turned to rebellion. Angry colonists led by George Durant and John Culpepper imprisoned Miller and refused to allow Governor Eastchurch to enter the colony from his previous home on Nevis in the Caribbean. The rebels then seized control of the government. Culpepper was eventually caught and tried in England, but was acquitted because of political connections.[61]

In 1683, the last governor of Albemarle County, Seth Sothell, was appointed and he served until 1689. He would be the first of five colonial governors, including Edward Hyde (1710–1712), Colonel Thomas Pollock (1712–1714), Charles Eden (1714–1722), and Gabriel Johnston (1733–1752), and two state governors, David Stone (1808–1810) and Locke Craig (1913–1917), who were either born and raised in Bertie County or moved there, owned and operated plantations, lived, died, and were buried there. The appointment of Seth Sothell as governor did very little to stabilize the colony. Governor Sothel was so corrupt that he was arrested by the citizens of the county, tried, and banished in 1689. Following his banishment, Albemarle County was again rocked by rebellion.

This second rebellion, the Gibbs Rebellion, was led by Captain John Gibbs, who claimed that Sothel had appointed him governor before his exile. After a short-lived armed revolt, Gibbs was deposed and Philip Ludwell was made governor. From 1689 to 1704, the colony was peaceful and continued to grow at a slow pace. As a result of the Vestry Act of 1703, problems between Quakers and Anglicans arose from 1704 until the Cary Rebellion in 1711. The Vestry Act of 1703 sanctioned the first state-supported Anglican churches in North Carolina. The act was originally passed in 1701, but because of opposition from Quakers, Presbyterians, and some Anglicans, who protested the tax increases that the act called for to lay out parishes, organize vestries, erect churches, and a special poll tax on titheables to pay clergymen, it was rejected by the lord proprietors.[62]

Cary's Rebellion, led by Thomas Cary, was basically a struggle between Quakers and Anglicans for control of the colony. In 1710, after years of trouble between the two groups, the proprietors of Albemarle County appointed Edward Hyde as governor. Once he arrived from England, he chose to live at Avoca on Salmon Creek in Bertie where all five colonial governors of the colony lived while governor. This nullified Cary's government, which had been in power since 1708, and led to Cary's Rebellion.[63] With the help of governor Alexander Spotswood of Virginia, the rebellion was quelled and Hyde became the recognized governor of the colony.

By 1711, Native Americans in Virginia, North Carolina, and South Carolina had witnessed first-hand white expansion. They had seen the displacement and destruction of a number of Virginia, Maryland, Delaware, North Carolina, and South Carolina Native Americans. The Tuscarora and various Algonquin tribes left in eastern North Carolina continued to have increasing problems with white settlers who were moving west and south from Albemarle County. As a result of these problems and a desire to avoid war, a conference was called by Robert Daniel, the deputy governor of the colony. At the conference, the Tuscarora chiefs and other leaders from the region negotiated a treaty with the Colony of Virginia that stipulated that no Tuscarora, whom the colonists feared most, would live a day's walk from English settlements and that whites would stop kidnapping and assaulting Native American women and children. Following the conference, in 1709, the Tuscarora sent emissaries north to request permission from the Iroquois Confederacy to relocate their entire nation in their territory. The confederacy immediately granted the request and informed the governor of Pennsylvania of their intentions to have their brothers from North Carolina live among them.[64]

Pennsylvania agreed to allow the relocation in 1710, pending notification by North Carolina of Tuscarora good relations with the colony of North Carolina, a notification that did not come. Nor did the peaceful relations with whites they desired. In spite of the Tuscarora's desire to leave North Carolina and their abiding by their treaty with the colony, whites continued the practice of assaulting them, settling their land without permission, murdering those that resisted them, and kidnapping and selling into slavery their women and children. All these things led to one of the bloodiest wars in colonial American history and the dispersion of a proud, expansive Indian nation, the Tuscarora.[65]

When the war started in 1711, there were approximately 5,000 Tuscarora living within the present boundaries of the state of North Carolina and perhaps as many as 2,000 in southern Virginia. There were around 15 towns and forts with the most important ones, including their capital, being located on either the Roanoke, Tar, or Neuse Rivers

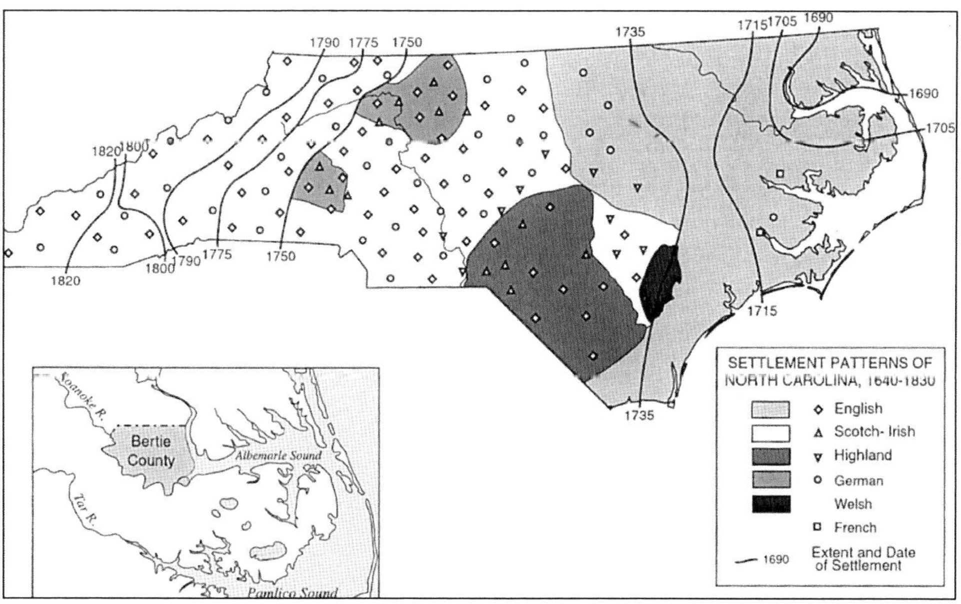

This North Carolina map shows the settlement patterns of whites. Once Native Americans were defeated in war, they were either killed, enslaved, or removed to reservations.

and on Contentnea Creek.[66] The forts were Fort Torhunta, Fort Conneghta, and Fort Nooherooka, or "Nohoroco," on Contentnea Creek. The towns included Chief Hancock's, a leading war chief during the second Tuscarora War, further downstream on Contentnea Creek. About 30 miles east of Chief Hancock's town on the banks of the Tar River was Ucohnerunt, Chief Tom Blount's town near modern-day Tarboro. As an ally of North Carolina in the second war, Blount captured Chief Hancock, ending the war in 1713. About 40 miles northeast of Ucohnerunt on the banks of the Roanoke River were the towns of Oaneroy, Refootketh, and Moratuck, in what is today Bertie County and the town of Cheeweo across the river in present-day Martin County. These towns had been functioning Native American settlements since 1586 when the Lane expedition mapped and visited them.[67]

These towns, the women and children they sheltered, the fertile lands that they occupied, and the lucrative trade they carried on with whites and other Native Americans became the prize in the growing conflict between them and their white neighbors by 1711. The very people who had been taught how to live and prosper in North Carolina and Virginia were now destroying the ones who were responsible for the education. Cultures that just a century before had coexisted and accepted each other with reservations now loathed each other and could only see conflict in their futures. The resulting conflict would forever change both groups and eastern North Carolina, for which they would fight bitterly for control.

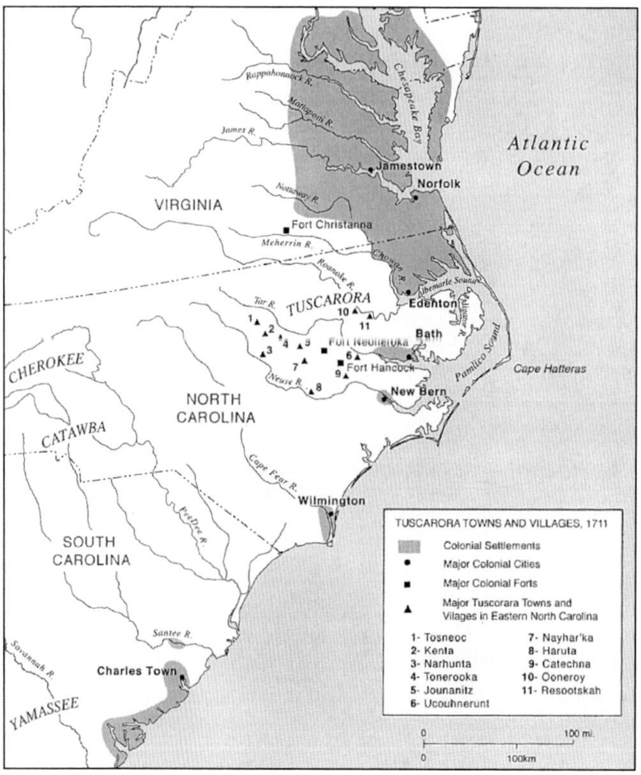

Depicted here are the Tuscarora and other southeastern Indian and English settlements in eastern Virginia, North Carolina, and South Carolina by 1711.

2. CULTURES IN CONFLICT: THE TUSCARORA WAR AND FORCED MIGRATION, 1711–1722

During the late 1600s, the Tuscarora Nation and its allies the Meherrin and Nottoway controlled lands that stretched from the present-day Cape Fear River in North Carolina to the James River in Virginia. As a result of their military alliance with the Meherrin, Nottoway, the Five Nations (or Iroquois Confederacy), and other smaller nations scattered from North Carolina to Pennsylvania, they dominated Native American trade and trading routes to the southeast and southwest as far north as New York and south as Georgia. By 1711, all this had begun to change. Although they still maintained control of vast territories and influenced many nations of Indians, the Tuscarora Nation and its allies were losing influence and ceding power to whites and their enemies, particularly the Cherokee, Yamasee, Creek, and Catawba.[1]

John Lawson, surveyor-general for the colony of North Carolina, noted that the Tuscarora were quite prosperous and lived in houses constructed of poles and covered by the bark of cypress, red or white cedar, and sometimes pine. They had plenty of corn but little meat because of their large settlements, which frightened animals away. Lawson also noted that both men and women smoked tobacco, which stained their teeth yellow and described their skin as being tawny or darkened by the habit of placing bear's oil, which contains a pigment resembling burnt cork, on their bodies for adornment.[2] He recorded that they had many dances, one for every occasion, and would hold public feasts prepared by the clan mothers where the dances were performed. Lawson also noted that the Tuscarora would come to these feast from towns as far away as 50 or 60 miles and would trade goods during these feasts.[3]

At these gatherings, many of the Tuscarora enjoyed gaming. So passionate were they about gaming that they sometimes lost all their property and even bet on themselves, after which they would serve as slaves for the winner until their debts were paid. Two of their most popular games were the bowl and plum-seed game, and the other, the name of which was unrecorded, involved a bundle of split reeds about 7 inches in length. This bundle was thrown ten times and the opponent had to guess how many reeds were in the bundle each time it was thrown.[4]

As the first European settlers migrated to what was known as the Bertie Precinct, Native Americans befriended and traded with them as the coastal tribes had done. John Leder in 1670 and John Lawson in 1700 did extensive trading with the Tuscarora, recording that they were known as great traders by both the white settlers and other Native American

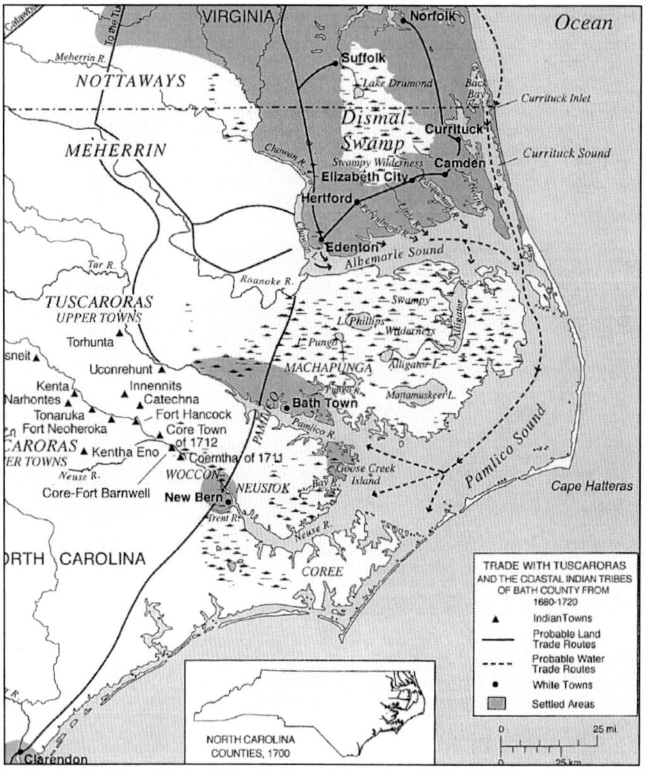

These are the major trading routes between the whites of Virginia and eastern North Carolina, including Albemarle County, Clarendon County, New Bern, and Bath, and the Nottoway, Meherrin, and Tuscarora Indians between 1680 and 1715.

nations. They were reported to have traded wooden bowls and ladles for rawhides with the Shakori and Occaneechi and, by 1708, traded rum rundlets, which they secured from the white settlers, in exchange for furs and rawhides to Native Americans over 100 miles west of their territory and towns.[5]

Although trading with the Tuscarora was profitable for white settlers, it was not long before the settlers began to desire and take the Tuscarora's fertile lands on the banks of the Chowan, Roanoke, Tar, Trent, and Neuse Rivers, and deny them access to the Outer Banks of North Carolina where they gathered their most prized trading commodity, seashells for the Five Nations.[6] The settlement of whites along the mouths of these rivers and throughout the rest of coastal North Carolina, and their refusal to allow the Tuscarora to travel freely to what had been for years neutral lands, began the hostilities between the two groups. The Tuscarora also saw many of their people kidnapped and sold into slavery as far away as Pennsylvania and the Caribbean.[7] In fact, Pennsylvania received so many Native American slaves from North Carolina that in 1705, the legislature passed a law forbidding the importation of any more, under the threat of war with the Five Nations if the trade was not stopped.[8] Although banned by the Pennsylvania colony, the North Carolina slave trade continued to operate as evidenced by the petition sent by the Tuscarora to the governor of Pennsylvania in 1710.[9] The Tuscarora petition called for Pennsylvania to intervene and stop, in their words, the kidnapping and enslavement of Tuscarora women and children.

Tuscarora women who were enslaved by North Carolinians and Virginians were often bred with African males or with the white slave owner himself to produce as many slaves as possible. These slaves found themselves working side by side on Virginia and North Carolina plantations with their full-blooded Native American and African parents and under the watchful eye of their sometimes-white fathers. Encouraged by a headright system that awarded slave owners 20 acres of land for every male African or slave brought to the region, and 10 acres of land for every female African or slave brought into the colony, whites and their slaves settled along the Chowan and Roanoke Rivers from 1650 to 1711 in what would become known as Bertie County.[10] By 1710, there were 900 Africans living in the North Carolina colony.[11] Most of these early African slaves who ended up in Bertie County were moved down from Virginia and arrived after having lived in or being seasoned in Virginia and the British Caribbean.[12] Many of these Virginia slaves were shipped from Guinea on the west coast of Africa to the British Caribbean, or directly to Virginia and then sent over land or by water to Bertie County and the Albemarle region.[13]

As more Tuscarora became caught up in the slave trade, their anger and resentment toward whites grew. The more aware they became of how African, Native American,

This map shows the trade routes of the Native American slave trade, which operated in Virginia, North Carolina, and South Carolina. This trade exported Indian slaves throughout the British colonies as far south as the British Caribbean and as far north as Massachusetts where the Iroquois Confederacy, who opposed the trade, threatened to go to war with the colonist if it was not ended. It must be noted that the reason for this threat was due to the enslavement of Tuscarora men, women, and children in North Carolina. The Tuscarora were members of the Iroquois Confederation although they resided in eastern Virginia and North Carolina.

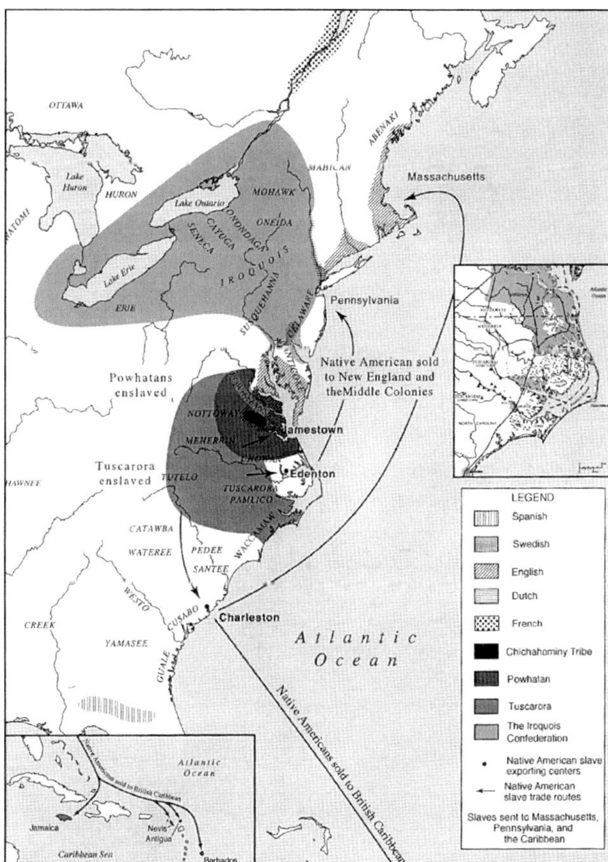

and mixed-blood slaves were being treated, the more they disliked the institution and the white settlers who practiced it. Although the Tuscarora made no references to the African slave trade that was occurring at the same time as the Native American slave trade, it is clear that they did not approve of the trade and that it was one of the most significant of the many grievances that the Tuscarora had against the colony of North Carolina before declaring war in 1711.

In 1711, after twice negotiating with the colonies of Virginia and North Carolina to stop the assault, abduction, and enslavement of Tuscarora women and children and the encroachment upon their land, the Tuscarora decided to go to war with the latest settlers on their land along the Neuse River. The conflict was actually made up of two wars, one that lasted from 1711 to 1712 and involved all the Tuscarora and their allies, and a second that lasted from 1712 to 1713 and involved only the Lower Tuscarora. The Tuscarora War began following the Cary Rebellion of 1711, which was a major colonial rebellion, and took the colonists by surprise.[14] The colonists believed that the Tuscarora were aware of this rebellion and took advantage of the confusion to attack white settlements from the Roanoke River south to the New Bern settlement on the Neuse River. Although there is no evidence to support this theory, it turned out to be an opportune time for their attack.[15]

There were three major causes of the Tuscarora War. The first was a tribal war near New Bern caused by the illegal selling of Tuscarora land by the surveyor-general of the North Carolina colony, John Lawson. The second cause was anger over deaths among the Tuscarora from European diseases, particularly an epidemic of yellow fever that broke out in the colony early in 1711, which Tuscarora shaman interpreted as evil magic. Third was the aforementioned kidnapping of Tuscarora women and children.

The war began most directly over the Palatine settlement on Tuscarora land along the Neuse River at New Bern.[16] In fact, the New Bern settlement had been established on 10,000 acres of land supposedly sold by the Tuscarora to Baron de Graffenreid in 1709.[17] They were particularly angry over the growth of the Palatine settlements near their capital city Chattakua (New Bern) on the Neuse River. When the Palatines first arrived at New Bern, the Tuscarora, who were already living at Chattakua, treated them very well, trading with them and allowing them to settle land that had not been sold to de Graffenreid. They even assisted the settlers in hunting wild game and fish.[18] However, by the fall of 1711, hundreds of Tuscarora began to fall ill and die from European diseases that led to increasingly negative perceptions among the Tuscarora of the settlers moving onto Tuscarora lands without permission.[19] This land served as the Tuscarora capital and was stolen by whites, according to the Tuscarora. This and the tribal war that resulted led to a council of chiefs and the decision in favor of war.

On the day of the attack, September 22, 1711, the Tuscarora captured and held the leader of the Palatine settlement, Baron Christopher de Graffenreid, as well as John Lawson. While exploring the Neuse River and surveying the lands for future white settlements, Baron de Graffenreid and Surveyor-General Lawson, along with two friendly Native Americans and two slaves, were seized for trespassing on Tuscarora lands without permission. They were held for several days while a Tuscarora council of chiefs decided their fate.[20] De Graffenreid and Lawson were tried on charges of kidnapping women and children and taking Tuscarora land. De Graffenreid explained in his diary that during his capture in 1711, it was asserted by the chiefs present that Surveyor-General Lawson had, by illegally selling Native American lands, caused a tribal war near New Bern. This cost many lives and caused much hatred for the surveyor-general.[21]

After much discussion and debate, it was agreed that all would be allowed to go free. Lawson, however, reopened hostilities when he quarreled with one of the chiefs, Core Tom.[22] It appears that during the quarrel, Lawson threatened revenge against the Tuscarora and insulted the council of chiefs. After this, the two whites were condemned to death. During the deliberation on how they should die, Chief Tom Blount spoke against killing de Graffenreid, thus saving his life, after he agreed to a treaty that basically purchased his life and freedom.[23]

In an effort to save Lawson's life, de Graffenreid attempted to blame the two African slaves that accompanied them for Lawson's behavior, saying they had angered him the night before.[24] This, however, did not save Lawson. In fact, the slaves were immediately released with no complaints made against them by any chiefs present. According to de Graffenreid, once released, one slave ran away and was never seen again.[25] The other slave remained with de Graffenreid and verified his story of Lawson's death. It is clear from de Graffenreid's account that the Native Americans did not harbor any ill feelings against African slaves and, in fact, probably had more compassion for them because of the enslavement of their people by Europeans.

However, the Tuscarora and their allies had become angry with whites over the continued abuse inflicted upon their people by the colonists. Thus, tribes of the lower section of the Tuscarora Nation and their allies the Core, Pamlico, Motamuskeet, Bear, and Machapungo joined forces with the upper section of the Tuscarora Nation and their allies the Meherrins and Nottoways to create an alliance, led by Chief Hancock from the south, who held the strongest forces.[26]

The compact planned to cut off the colonists from each other and drive them from Native American territory. The compact conducted coordinated raids on the Roanoke, Tar, Neuse, Trent, and Pamlico River settlements on September 22, 1711. The coordinated attacks between the Upper and Lower Tuscarora and their allies that followed killed hundreds of white settlers along the Roanoke, Tar, Trent, and Neuse Rivers[27]; 130 colonists were killed on the Roanoke River alone.[28] The Palatines, who were attacked at the same time at New Bern, had established thriving settlements along the Trent, Neuse, and Pamlico Rivers, with homes, schools, churches, and large farms that they cleared themselves. Their settlements contained blacksmiths, tanners, shoemakers, millers, wheelwrights, carpenters, and teachers.[29]

During their attack, the Tuscarora burned houses, the school, the courthouse, and other buildings of the Craven and Bertie Precincts. It was initially difficult for the colonists to fight back. Colonists from the Albemarle region feared going to their aid because of the possibility of another attack on their own homes while they were away. In his diary, de Graffenreid described the Tuscarora preparation for the war, John Lawson's execution, and their victory over the white settlers on their land, particularly the Palatines:

> In the open space or public square mentioned there was a large fire, near which was the shaman or high priest, a grizzled sorcerer, who made two rings

> on the ground, whether flour or white sand was not stated. In front of the two victims was placed a wolf skin, and a short distance farther there stood an Indian in a terrifying posture, holding in one hand a knife and the other a tomahawk. He did not move from the spot. On the farther side of the fire were assembled young men, women, and children, who danced with weird and frightful contortions and attitudes. In the center of the circle of dancers were seated two singers who intoned a dismal song, rather fit to provoke tears and anger than joy. Within the circle of dancers the shaman stood unterrified uttering his threatening and adjurations and performing his exorcisms against the foes of his people and their orenda or medicine, when there would come a pause in the dancing. Finally, with shouts and howls the dancers ran into the neighboring forest. In a short time they returned with their faces painted black, white, and red, in bands, and with their hair loose and flying, oiled and sprinkled with fine down or cotton from the cattail flag and with small white feathers, and some returned arrayed in all kinds of furs. After they returned the dance was renewed.[30]

De Graffenreid continued, noting that when the braves returned from their attacks on the river settlements, they held a feast and built several bonfires that night. The largest one was in the execution area where they made offerings and danced.[31]

When the news of the attack reached Governor Hyde, he appealed to Virginia for help, but Virginia attempted to take advantage of the attacks by demanding land cessions in the Albemarle region in exchange for their assistance.[32] Governor Hyde finally approached

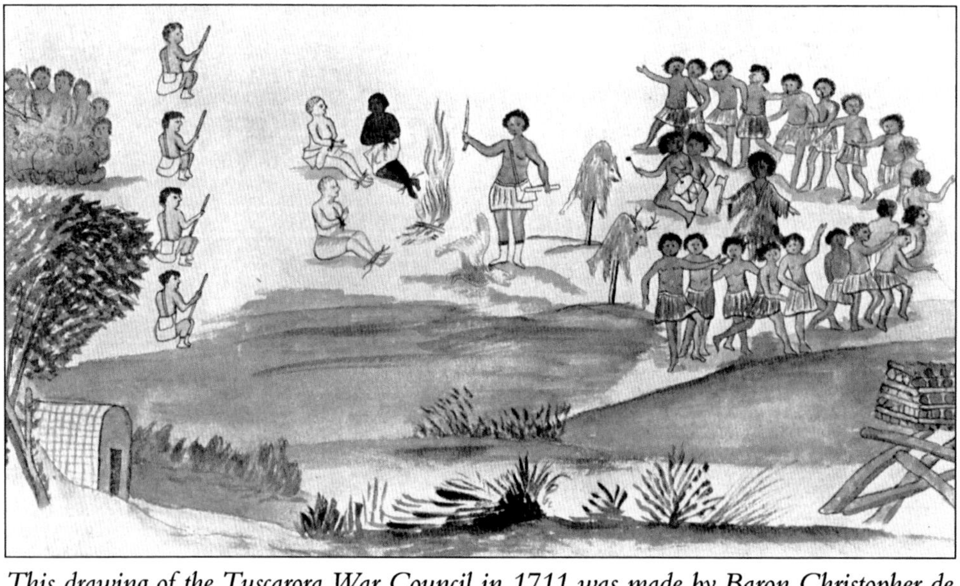

This drawing of the Tuscarora War Council in 1711 was made by Baron Christopher de Graffenreid who, along with John Lawson and two slaves, was held by the Tuscarora at the start of the war in 1711. (Courtesy of NCC, UNC.)

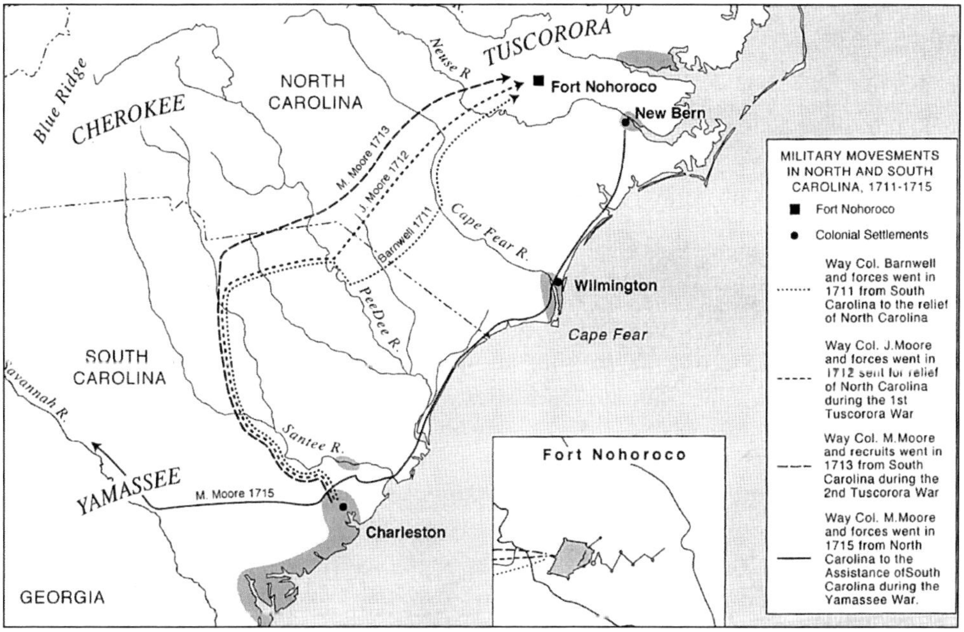

These routes were used by South Carolinians and their Indian allies to aid North Carolina during the Tuscarora Wars in 1711, 1712, and 1713 and by North Carolinians and their Tuscarora allies to aid South Carolina during the Yamasee War in 1715.

South Carolina with a request for military aid. South Carolina responded by sending 40 white men and 800 Creek, Cherokee, Catawba, and Yamasee, who were enemies of the Tuscarora.[33] With the aid of these South Carolinians and their Native American allies, armed with guns and colonial artillery, the colonists were able to end the first Tuscarora War and secure the release of a number of white women and children whom the Tuscarora had taken prisoner during their raids.[34] The South Carolina troops were commanded by Colonel John Barnwell, who marched his men through eastern North Carolina, while Governor Hyde, who was working with Virginia's governor, attempted to secure the release of de Graffenreid and John Lawson.[35]

In his statements to the governor following his release, de Graffenreid acknowledged that the Tuscarora did not start the war without provocation. De Graffenreid insisted, however, that he and his colonists had nothing directly to do with starting or encouraging the war, and he emphasized three points in his report to Governor Hyde of North Carolina: the Native Americans spared his life as a sign of their respect for his dealings with them; he, in purchasing the land called Chattaqua, paid for it three times, once to L.L. Props, once to the surveyor-general, and the third time to the Native American king called Taylor; and during his capture and the convening of the Great Assembly of the Tuscaroras (where the wrongs committed against the Tuscaroras were discussed), not one chief lodged a complaint against him.[36]

On January 30, 1712, Colonel Barnwell and his men finally reached the Tuscarora stronghold, Narhantes. Narhantes was filled with Tuscarora fleeing attacks on fortified villages that were being indiscriminately assaulted by Colonel Moore, his forces, and other colonists. Barnwell, once rested, mounted an attack on Narhantes and, in the ensuing battle, killed 62 Tuscarora, 52 men and 10 women, and captured 30 prisoners. Barnwell's losses included 13 killed (7 whites and 6 Native Americans) and 60 wounded (32 whites and 28 Native Americans). Barnwell continued to march on to Chief Hancock's village, destroying the Tuscarora village of Core, about 30 miles outside of New Bern, along the way. Chief Tom Core and his forces fled and took refuge in Chief Hancock's town, where they halted Barnwell on January 28, 1712.[37] A treaty was negotiated at Fort Barnwell on March 12, 1712, but just as quickly broken by Barnwell, who was disappointed because he was not paid by North Carolina. Thus, he seized the Tuscaroras and made them slaves. When Barnwell returned to Charlestown, he took over 100 Tuscarora men, women, and children with him, many of whom ended up in St. Helena several miles south of Charlestown.[38] This destroyed all Tuscarora confidence in the word of the white colonists and initiated the second Tuscarora War.

In retaliation for breaking the peace and the further kidnapping and enslavement of Tuscarora by Barnwell, the Tuscarora renewed their attacks on white settlements in North Carolina. At the start of the second Tuscarora War in November of 1712, Colonel Thomas Pollock, the governor of the North Carolina colony and the colonial council, held a conference with the peaceful chiefs of the Tuscarora Nation, who did not want to see further loss of life. At this conference, Pollock coerced six chiefs, with the threat of violence against their villages and towns, into signing a treaty of alliance with North Carolina. The treaty read that if there were further hostilities between the colonists and warring Tuscarora chiefs, the six friendly chiefs, who became known as the "Chief-Men-for-Peace," would remain neutral.[39] During the second Tuscarora War, 11 chiefs aligned themselves against the colony of North Carolina. Chief Hancock, whose fort "Nohoroco" was the site of the final battle, joined the warring chiefs at the end of the war, after breaking the treaty he signed with Chief Blount, the other peaceful chiefs, and the colony of North Carolina, remaining neutral only in the early days of the second war.[40]

Again, North Carolina asked South Carolina for assistance. This time, South Carolina sent Colonel James Moore with a force of about 900 Native Americans, including Creek, Catawba, Yamasee, and about 400 Cherokee. This conflict ended when the warring Tuscarora were defeated at Fort Nohoroco, their strongest fort, near the present-day site of Edwards' Bridge in Lenoir County, in 1713.[42] A letter dated March 27, 1713 to Governor Colonel Thomas Pollock of Salmon Creek in Bertie, who became the third governor from Bertie County after taking over for Edward Hyde after his death from yellow fever on September 8, 1712, described the final battle. The altercation left 392 prisoners taken and 192 scalps taken. A total of 950 losses to the Tuscarora Nation included 200 killed and burned in Chief Hancock's village, as well as 166 killed and removed from the village.[43] Colonel Moore and Baron de Graffenreid, who accompanied Moore on the campaign, reported the following in spite of these losses:

> the savages showed themselves unspeakably brave, so much so that when our soldiers had become master of the fort and wanted to take out the women and children who were under the ground where they were hidden along

> with provisions, the wounded savages who were groaning on the ground still continued to fight . . . there were wounded savages, crawling on the earth who tried to hurt the victors . . .[44]

The loss of this fort, along with the capture of Chief Hancock by the northern Tuscarora under Chief Blount, forced the warring Tuscarora to surrender in 1713.[45] After their surrender, arrangements were made by the Tuscarora to relinquish most of their lands in North Carolina, including their capital Chattakua, modern-day New Bern.[46]

After the Tuscarora War and the loss of nearly one-quarter of their people to enslavement and death, Tuscarora survivors recalled a threat made against them by white colonists in 1587 after they absorbed the Roanoke settlement. This threat was passed on orally among the Tuscarora for over a century. In the threat, as Geroux, a descendant of the Tuscarora who emigrated to New York, noted after the war, the Tuscarora were told by the whites in 1587 that if they (the whites) were harmed, the mother boat would return and would "make thunder and spit fire at them," a reference to the ships' cannons that could have been used to defend the settlement. Whether this threat was remembered by the Tuscarora during the war with North Carolina is not clear, but the Tuscarora were reportedly terrified of colonial artillery, which "spit fire and made thunder."[47] After the war, the Tuscarora began to repeat the threat and blamed the mixed-blood descendants of those responsible for the Roanoke colony's destruction for their misfortune. Thus, many Tuscarora in 1713 believed they were being punished by their ancestors and the Great Spirit as a result of the abduction of the colonists in 1587.[48]

Dr. Hamilton of East Orange, New Jersey, who was part-white, part-African American, and part-Tuscarora, confirmed Geroux's story with one of his own before he died in the 1930s. He noted that not only did the Tuscarora believe they were being punished for what they had done at Roanoke, but certain members of their tribe were cursed with the "Tuscarora Eye" or "Evil Eye," which ran in his family.[49] These Tuscarora, who may have been descendants of the white women taken from Roanoke Island, were born with blue, green, or gray eyes. As time passed, the eye became more prevalent throughout the tribe, along with problems with white settlers. In fact, in 1707, French Huguenots, who settled near the Tuscarora along the Tar River, reported that the Tuscarora had many members with blue, green, and gray eyes.[50]

Aunt Tamar, a former slave who died at 127 or 129 years of age in the mid-1920s in Salisbury, Maryland, was also part-Tuscarora and stated that her great-grandmother was a Tuscarora and said they were cursed. She recited a story similar to that of Hamilton and Geroux, in which her Nation had offended their ancestors and was being punished as a result. Part of this punishment included their being forced to go to the north where it was cold. Tamar stated that her great-grandmother did not want to live in a cold climate and chose to stay in Maryland on the eastern shore of the Chesapeake Bay, which was similar to her home in North Carolina, and marry Tamar's great-grandfather, an African slave.[51] It is not clear if Tamar or her family had the "Tuscarora Eye," but Hamilton did state that marrying African Americans eliminated it for a while in his family before it began to reappear in his generation.

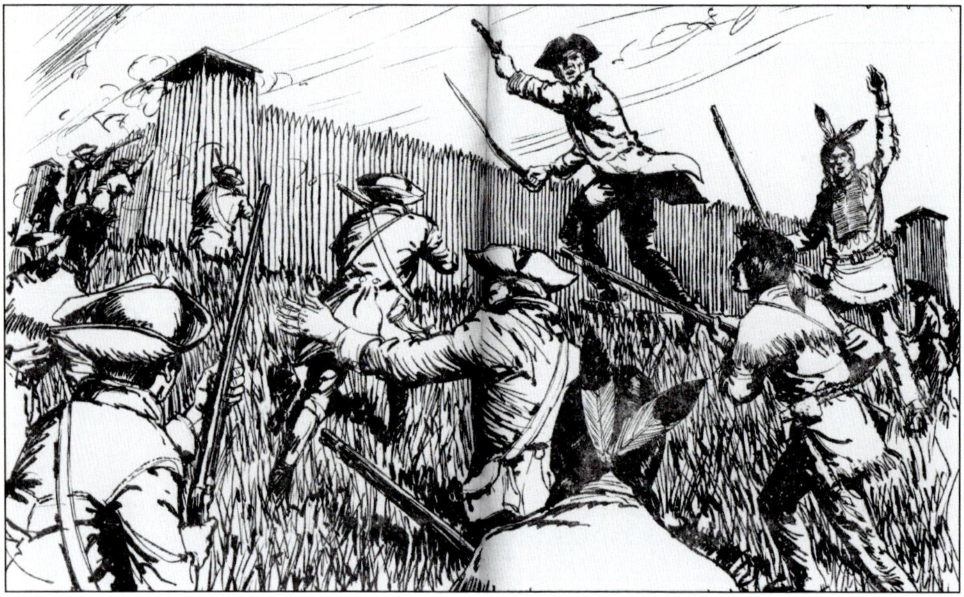

In the final assault on the Tuscarora stronghold Fort Nohoroco in 1713, 36 whites and more than 900 Cherokee, Catawba, Yamasee, and Creek Indians succeeded in driving the Tuscarora out of North Carolina. (Courtesy of Margaret Johnson and NCC, UNC.)

Even today in Bertie County, particularly in the Indian Woods township, large numbers of African Americans who are obviously mixed with Native Americans still carry this trait. There are several families in Indian Woods who still possess the Tuscarora Eye, including the Freemans, Smallwoods, Bonds, Outlaws, and Rascoes. Many of the current residents' customs, gardening, and farming practices appear to be a combination of Tuscarora, English, and African practices.[52] Based on research, including their traceable ancestry back to antebellum slavery and even farther back than this orally, most families lived on farms and land that was farmed by their families since the end of the Civil War. Based on the fact that Indian Woods in Bertie County was the last home of the Tuscarora, and that those who settled there refused to leave even under the threat of enslavement, and from research visits to the Tuscarora reserves in New York and Canada, it is clear that these people are of Tuscarora, African, and obviously European descent. Hamilton also noted that as the Tuscarora suffered more and more misfortune, those with the Tuscarora Eye were ostracized, and many found it better to leave the Nation and their clans.[53]

The Tuscarora War brought about the destruction of the Tuscarora as a powerful nation and was the beginning of what can be called the "Tuscarora Diaspora." The war accelerated what the Native American slave trade had begun, the dispersion of the Tuscarora people and their allies to over nine states, two countries, and the British Caribbean. Isolated Tuscarora communities would also stretch from Virginia through the Catskill, Kittochtinny, and Ramapos Mountains of Pennsylvania, New York, and New Jersey.[54]

In North Carolina, small, isolated Tuscarora communities remained scattered in their old territories throughout eastern parts of the state, but without their traditional political organization. From Maxton in southeastern North Carolina to Murfreesboro in northeastern North Carolina, communities like Enfield, Ahoskie, Goldsboro, and Indian Woods remained on their ancestral lands. Many of the people in these isolated communities were enslaved and eventually mixed with Africans or whites who moved into eastern North Carolina.[55]

When the Tuscarora War ended, over 1,000 Tuscarora were dead and hundreds were wounded and enslaved. Those who remained free were forced to give up their lands in eastern North Carolina and denied access to the Outer Banks. Because of the destruction of their capital, major forts, and towns, small villages became politically and culturally isolated from each other. Worst of all, these Tuscaroras were forced to work through the courts of white colonists to resolve complaints they held against their white neighbors.[56]

From 1713 to 1715, the Tuscarora honored an uneasy peace with their white neighbors in North Carolina. Even the Chief-Men-for-Peace, who had agreed to remain neutral during the second war, were appalled at the loss of life and destruction of their brothers' property. The entire nation despised their historic enemies, the Cherokee, Creek, Catawba, and Yamasee, who aided the colonists in both wars and the Tuscarora Nation's destruction and enslavement. As a result of this hatred, several clans numbering several

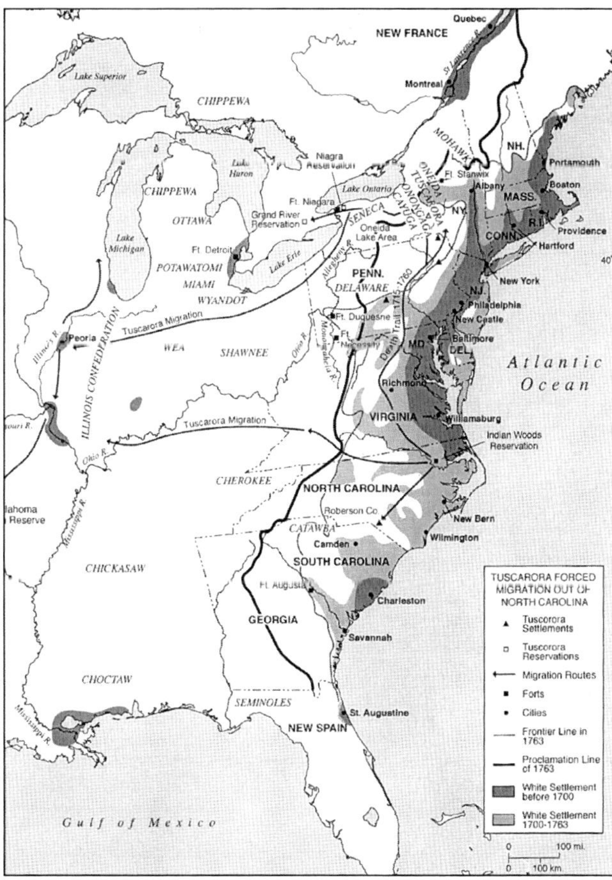

After their defeat in the Tuscarora War in 1713, the Tuscarora and their allies were scatted from Charleston, South Carolina to Canada on the Atlantic seaboard and as far west as Kentucky, Illinois, and Oklahoma.

hundred, which had migrated to Port Royal, South Carolina, joined Colonel Moore of South Carolina in the destruction of the Yamasee Nation in the Yamasee War of 1715.[57] The Five Nations, referred to as the Six Nations after 1722, also attacked and raided Cherokee, Creek, Catawba, and Yamasee villages and towns from 1713 to 1812. Even as allies of the British during the Revolutionary War, the Iroquois fought pitched battles with the Cherokee, Creek, and other southeastern Native Americans who had participated in the Tuscarora War. As late as the Civil War, Creek and Cherokee Confederate soldiers killed Iroquois Union soldiers at battles like Petersburg, Virginia, still remembering the Tuscarora War.[58]

Clans that abided by the peace in North Carolina found that they were no longer allowed to protect themselves from thieving and murdering whites. Often, their complaints about abuses by whites went unanswered by the courts. In fact, when the Tuscarora of Core Town were accused of wounding white colonist Robert Schrieve in a disagreement, it was declared that the Native Americans of Core Town were in revolt, and the North Carolina Colonial Assembly, governed by Charles Eden, the fourth colonial governor from Bertie, ordered "the entire destruction of ye said nation of Indians as if there had never been a peace made with them." The indiscriminate slaughter and enslavement of the Tuscarora that resulted from this order led to the forced migration of the Tuscarora from North Carolina to Virginia, Maryland, Pennsylvania, New Jersey, and New York.[59] On what became known as the "Tuscarora Trail" or "Death Trail," thousands fled North Carolina for the protection of the Five Nations in New York. Those who made it were taken in by the Oneida Nation during a special tribal council and settled at Oneida Lake in New York. As the Tuscarora left North Carolina, the once proud and strong people were fractured, battered, and demoralized. Division over whether or not to fight the second war had split the nation into the followers of Chief Tom Blount and those of Chief Hancock. Clearly, Blount and his supporters were not loved since they were responsible for capturing Chief Hancock, which led to the defeat of the Tuscarora in 1713.[60]

However, Chief Blount was considered by the General Assembly of North Carolina to be the leader of the remaining Tuscarora clans. Of the many Tuscarora who fled North Carolina following the General Assembly's order and the destruction of Core Town, the exception was Chief Blount and his followers. Authorized by Governor Eden, Chief Blount was allowed to retain his town, Ucohnerunt, and a small area in modern-day Edgecombe County along the Tar River.[61]

There were still bands of hostile Tuscarora and their allies, however, who raided white settlements and the villages of Blount's people. They included the Core, Pamlico, and Machapungo tribes. These bands avoided capture by staying on the move and hiding in the swamps. As early as April of 1713, about 50 of these Native Americans attacked and captured settlers along the Alligator River.[62] Raids like these were conducted well into 1718, causing as much, and in some cases more, damage than the war itself. As late as October 1718, the General Court was disrupted by threats of Native American attacks.[63]

As a result of attacks by the defeated Tuscarora and their allies, and the threat of attack by the Yamasee, Creek, Catawba, and Cherokee, Chief Tom Blount's followers were moved from their original town, Ucohnerunt on the Tar River, to Moratoc on the Roanoke River in 1717. Since Chief Blount had aided Governor Pollock during the war,

Governor Eden and other members of the colonial assembly believed he and his people should be protected from Native American attacks and unprovoked attacks by whites, who believed that all Tuscarora should be exterminated.[64] The fertile lands along the Roanoke River, known as Indian Woods in Bertie County, had always been a part of Chief Blount's territory. The original boundaries of this reservation extended well beyond the present boundaries of the Indian Woods township. The land in the Bertie Precinct was given to Chief Blount on June 7, 1717 and called Indian Woods. The Meherrin were also given a reservation in what is Colerain today. At the time, Governor Charles Eden thought that the reservation only contained 10,000 acres. Surveyor Colonel Edward Moseley later discovered that the reservation contained over 40,000 acres.[65]

Although many clans blamed Chief Blount and those of their nation that carried the "Tuscarora" or "Evil Eye" for their defeat, clearly all of the Iroquois (Mohawks, Oneida, Layuga, Onondaga, Seneca, and Tuscarora) must share the blame for what happened. They all in one way or another violated or ignored the teachings of their ancestors. First, they ignored the words of Da-ka-nah-wi-da, who warned the Iroquois "never to seriously disagree among yourselves. If you do you might cause the loss of any rights of your grandchildren, or reduce them to poverty and shame." The Tuscarora chiefs chose to disagree seriously over whether to go to war a second time or not, splitting the nation which, had it been united, may have lost fewer people. Also, had the Five Nations not allowed the governors of Pennsylvania and North Carolina to cause them to hesitate on becoming involved in the war, North Carolina may not have been able to raise a force strong enough to destroy the Tuscarora.[66]

Second, they further ignored "Never, never disgrace yourself by becoming angry." Chief Tom Crow became angry with John Lawson, who threatened Crow's imminent destruction upon Lawson's freedom from captivity. This brought about Lawson's death and a call for war that had not been asked for in the first council. Third, no heed was paid to "Your skin must be seven hands thick to stand for what you know is right in your heart." Were Chief Blount and the Chief-Men-for-Peace right in their stance against the war?[67]

Finally, following the war, the Nation violated another important teaching by Great Hawk when they turned on each other. Great Hawk had warned that "no matter how good people are, some things happen that are not preventable, but being good and obeying the law of brotherhood makes one strong in spirit and able to withstand misfortunes."[68] After the war, the Tuscarora began to blame those among them who carried the Tuscarora Eye for their downfall, further fragmenting their already weakened nation. This only accelerated the break up of the nation and caused many Tuscarora to isolate themselves in various parts of eastern North Carolina from the larger nation. Today, there are known descendants of the Tuscarora in North Carolina, South Carolina, Virginia, Maryland, Pennsylvania, Delaware, New Jersey, New York, Connecticut, Oklahoma, Canada, and possibly the British Caribbean as a result of the Native American slave trade before, during, and after the war. Also, based on Tuscarora legends describing their migration routes to North Carolina from the Mississippi Valley through eastern Kentucky and western Virginia, what have been referred to as Melungeons in eastern Kentucky, western Virginia, and West Virginia may be related to their diaspora.[69]

Many of the 3,000 or so Tuscarora and their allies who departed on the Tuscarora or Death Trail never made it. Some stopped in Virginia and Maryland and settled along the Chesapeake Bay because they preferred the warmer climate of the south, even though it meant enslavement.[70] Others settled in valleys of the rural isolated Catskill, Kittochtinny, and Ramapos Mountains of Pennsylvania, New Jersey, and New York, which they had passed on their many trips along the Tuscarora Trail to New York to trade seashells with the Five Nations.[71]

Some young lovers were separated due to family or clan obligations. Many who had the Tuscarora Eye found themselves ostracized by others in the nation who blamed them for their misfortune. The women who carried this trait often chose to marry outside the Nation because they found that neither black nor white men were bothered by the trait. As a result, many of these women never made it to New York, but found husbands along the way and remained with them.[72] Many clans encountered hostile Algonquin Native Americans who harbored ill will because of previous trading trips made by different Tuscarora clans, who had not respected their territory and were abusive, destructive, or were caught stealing food and wildlife.[73]

Some Tuscarora clans were even annihilated by enemy tribes on the way, as was the case in Carroll County, Maryland around 1715.[74] Most of the Tuscarora who made the trek were either very old, very young, female, or wounded and thus died on the trail. One group that was filled with very old Tuscarora and could travel no further camped at Slide

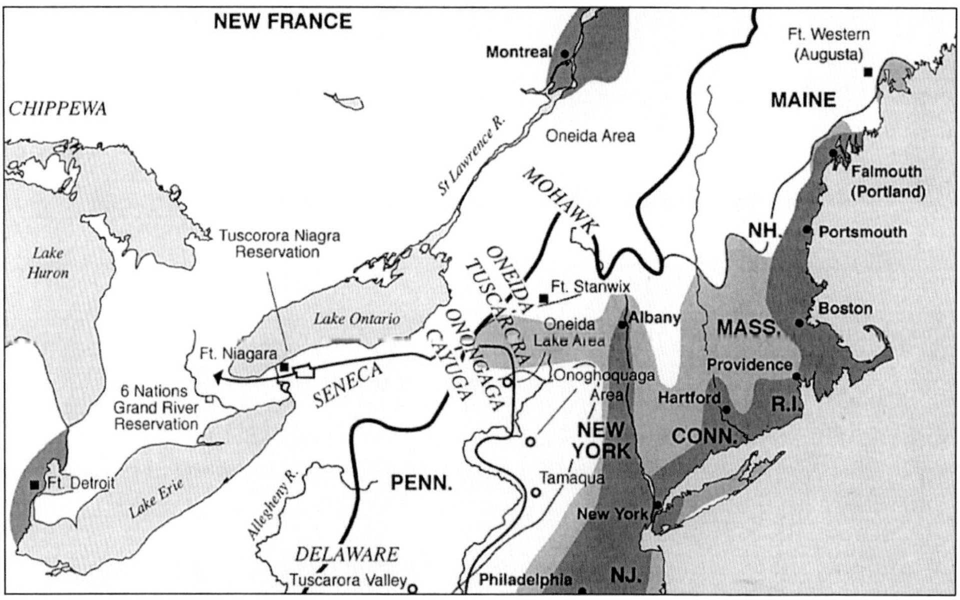

The majority of the Tuscarora settled in lands held by the Iroquois Confederacy in New York, New Jersey, Pennsylvania, and Canada after 1715. In 1722 the British government officially recognized the Tuscarora as the Sixth Iroquois Nation. Most of these recognized Indians settled either on the Tuscarora Reserve in Lewiston, New York in 1803 or on the Six Nations Reserve in Oshweken, Canada after the Revolutionary War.

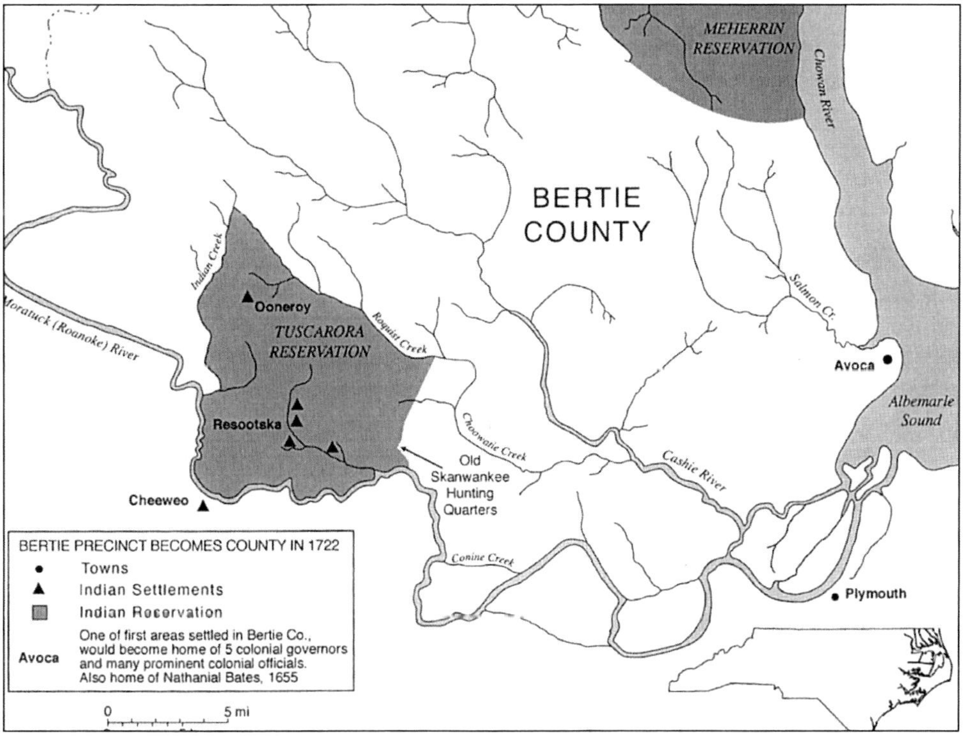

This county map shows the Tuscarora and Meherrin reservations established in Bertie County at the close of the Tuscarora War for those Tuscarora and Meherrin Indians who had remained neutral during the second Tuscarora War in 1713.

Mountain, New York. They were there for about three days when a band of Mohawks arrived and carried them away. This gained the attention of local whites because they knew of the fierceness of the Mohawks and had begun to arm themselves, becoming surprised when the Mohawks left carrying the elderly Tuscarora, taking them to the Mohawk settlement in the Five Nations.[75]

Not long after the first migration to New York and New Jersey, the Tuscarora who had broken with their brothers over the war with North Carolina and remained in Bertie County began to experience the same types of problems that their brothers had before the war. Whites sold the braves' liquor, raped their women, and established plantations on their land without permission.[76]

Reservation life proved to be harder than Chief Blount and his followers expected. As early as 1721, whites began to encroach upon the Tuscarora land, claiming that the boundaries were uncertain.[77] Because this land belonged to the Tuscarora Nation before the war and was considered frontier territory, there had been few attempts by whites to settle it for fear of attacks. Nevertheless, by 1722, with the Native American threat largely removed, great numbers of white settlers began to migrate to Bertie County and claim land around and on Chief Blount's reservation.[78] So numerous and aggressive were the white settlers that the Tuscarora petitioned the Colonial Assembly in Edenton for protection in 1722. They stated that the whites did not respect the boundaries of the reservation set by the colony.[79]

As a result of the complaints by the Tuscarora, the boundaries of the reservation were redrawn in 1722 by General William Maule, effectively reducing the size of the original reservation. The feuds over land, and the inability of Blount's people to adjust to the confinement of the reservation, caused many of the Tuscarora to leave and join others already in New York. By 1731, only about 600 of the original 800 Tuscarora remained in Bertie County.[80] Today, many residents of Bertie, black and white, readily admit they have Native American ancestry, but have mistakenly called it Cherokee. This is understandable in light of the order issued by the General Assembly following the war, calling for the complete annihilation of the Tuscarora in the colony at the time. Those who were not killed or enslaved would have possibly referred to themselves as Cherokees, who were great heroes of the colony for their major role in the defeat and destruction of the Tuscarora during the war. Although it is remotely possible that some of these residents could be of Cherokee origin, knowing the history of white settlement of eastern North Carolina and the Cherokee territories that began in the piedmont and moved west into the Appalachian Mountains, the evidence supports their being Tuscarora. Today, the descendents of the Tuscarora in Bertie County and surrounding counties, nearly all of whom are mixed with either African Americans or whites, still carry on their oral traditions, hold pow-wows, and tell their story about the history of the establishment of the county and the state.[81]

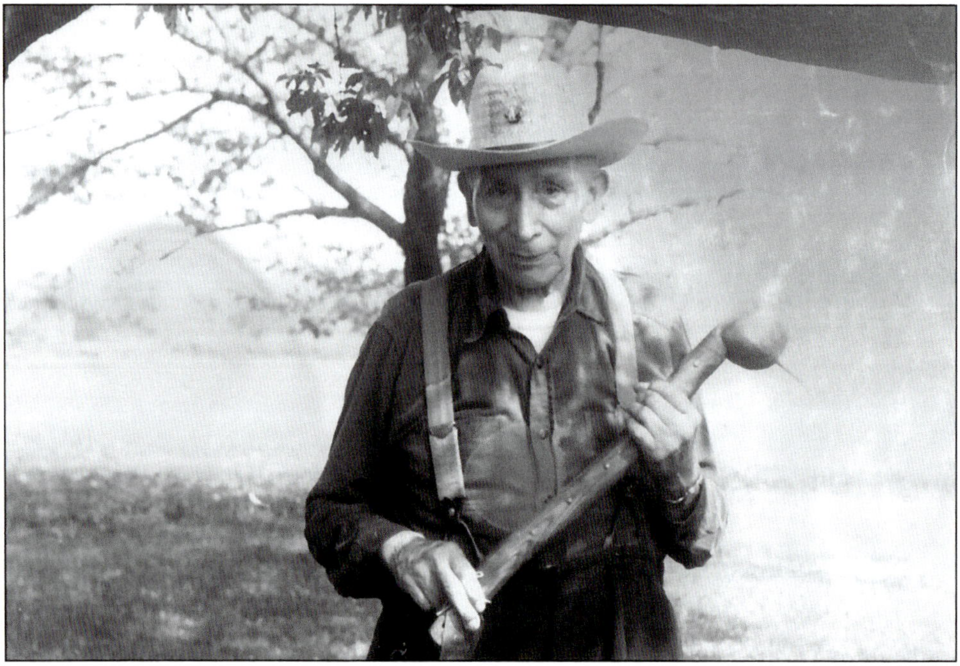

A part-white Tuscarora of Indian Woods, Bertie County, holds a Tuscarora War club. This picture was taken sometime in the 1960s.

3. Life during the Colonial Era, 1722–1774

After the Tuscarora War, the Tuscaroras' removal from North Carolina, and the end of their raids from 1715 to 1718, more and more white settlers and their African and Native American slaves migrated to what would become Bertie County. The area had, from 1664 to 1670, been part of Albemarle County, the first North Carolina county. It then became a part of the Chowan Precinct which, along with Perquimans, Pasquotank, and Currituck, were the first four precincts created in North Carolina.[1] It remained a part of the Chowan Precinct and, later, a part of Chowan County as the Bertie Precinct until it was separated from Chowan County and given the status of county in 1722.[2]

Before 1722, Bertie County was sparsely populated, with most of its settlers living along the banks of the Chowan River, the Albemarle Sound, or at the mouth of the Roanoke River. However, once the Tuscarora threat was removed, Bertie County's population began to swell. As the population grew, the need for better laws and effective government became apparent and residents began to demand their own local government. The residents of the area petitioned the Colonial Assembly in 1720 for a central and convenient meeting place to govern themselves. Answering their petition in 1722, the Colonial Assembly, which convened in Edenton, North Carolina, established the County of Bertie, which would later become present-day Bertie County. Named for James and Henry Bertie, it would from that time until 1759 produce all or part of four additional counties. From its southeastern territory, Tyrrell County would be formed in 1729, eventually becoming present-day Tyrrell and Washington Counties.[3] From its southwestern territory would be formed Edgecombe County in 1741, which would become present-day Halifax, Martin, and Edgecombe Counties. From the northern part of the county would come Northampton County, also in 1741, and Hertford County in 1759, giving Bertie County, with minor adjustments, its current political boundaries.[4]

After giving Bertie County status, the assembly decided that there should be a regular place for holding court in Bertie. Because the county at that time contained Hertford and Northampton Counties, it was decided that the courthouse would be built at St. John's near the Cashie River, which was located midway between the Chowan and Roanoke Rivers. This was considered an ideal location because the rivers were main arteries of transportation and most of the major plantations were built along their banks.[5] These plantations grew in number and size from 1715 to 1730. As their plantations grew, so did the need for labor. As a result, the number of slaves entering the county and colony grew during this period to a total of 6,000 for North Carolina by 1730.[6]

During the early colonial period, because of the lack of good roads, churches, and schools, most white residents of Bertie lived isolated rural existences with their slaves. This brought on boredom and a desire for a meeting place for social gatherings. Rather than churches, which were almost nonexistent at the time in Bertie or anywhere else in eastern North Carolina (most settlers had very little interest in religion except for the wealthy), the gathering place became the county courthouse. This would not change until religion finally did come to the county and region during the Southern revival movements of the late 1790s and early 1800s.[7]

As a result, the Bertie County courthouse remained the central meeting place as late as 1760, when Bertie County was reduced to its current size and the courthouse was moved to Windsor. For many whites, holding court was an opportunity to end a year-long seclusion on their isolated rural plantations. On most plantations, even the large ones, the only other whites there were the planter's wife, children, and overseers.[8]

As a result, the whites of Bertie County desired the company of other white settlers, particularly those of their class. In spite of the fact that many of the rural areas had poor roads, white residents religiously made the trips to the courthouse. Meetings at the courthouse, held only four times per year, were desirable times for social gatherings. As the white residents' need for more activities and interaction increased, they became more creative in their pursuit of things to do. Thus, they participated in religious meetings, horse races, cockfights, and military musters. While the court was in session, residents traded horses and bought, exchanged, or sold their home-grown commodities.[9]

African and Native American slaves were often at these gatherings, too. Slaves often accompanied their masters to help bring home a heavy load or were there to be sold. But most slaves who lived in Bertie County on rural plantations never got farther than the fields owned by their master.[10] Native Americans that remained in Bertie on the Meherrin and Tuscarora reservations rarely ventured beyond the boundaries of their reservation, primarily due to fear of being kidnapped and sold into slavery. If they left the reservation, they were often beaten, arrested, or sometimes even killed; thus, most trading was done well within the boundaries of the reservation. In Indian Woods, trading was conducted near the area most residents today refer to as Grabtown by what slaves would later name the "Gospel Oak." This was where Indian Woods Road began and forked north to Windsor and south to Williamston, which was across the Roanoke River.[11]

At courthouse meetings, colonists bought and sold slaves, gamed, drank large quantities of rum, and often fought one another. Newspaper accounts demonstrate that it was not uncommon for the gatherings to have fights, which were described as generally being started by bullies who had consumed too much strong drink. One article described such an incident:

> A stout man in liquor wanted to fight with another man not so disposed. The intoxicated man lay down on the tavern floor upon his back with his legs and arms extended. He called, "Now strike me, hit me, kick me, stomp me!"; yet the man would not be provoked to start a fight for which he would shoulder the blame.[12]

This was typical day-to-day life in rural Bertie County. So unrestricted and relaxed were the behaviors of the average eastern North Carolinians that it drew comment from the citizens of neighboring Virginia. Most notable among those citizens was William Byrd II, the Virginia commissioner, who in 1728 helped to clarify the dividing line between the southern boundary of Virginia and the northern boundary of North Carolina.[13] Byrd observed that Carolinians did what they pleased and lacked the rules of sportsmanship. He noted that Bertie residents had a reputation for looseness and overindulgence in sex. Women were known to become with child before marriage. This can be gleaned from reviewing the bastardly bonds from the county courthouse. As early as 1739, they show a number of women with children out of wedlock throughout the 1700s and into the early 1800s. In these bonds, the fathers of the illegitimate children, as named by their mothers, were forced by the courts to either care for their children through marriage or face imprisonment.[14]

Byrd went on to say that there were also instances during fights where people gouged each other's eyes out, slit each other's noses, cut out each other's tongues, and bit fingers and ears off, and that some fights could be described only as gnarling coon-and-dog scraps. Byrd further stated that this behavior was not limited to the poor and lower classes, but that a furious quarrel was recorded between Governor Burrington and Chief Justice Gale. This was a conflict in which, after a heated exchange of words, the judge swore that if he saw Burrington again, he would slit his nose and crop his ears.[15]

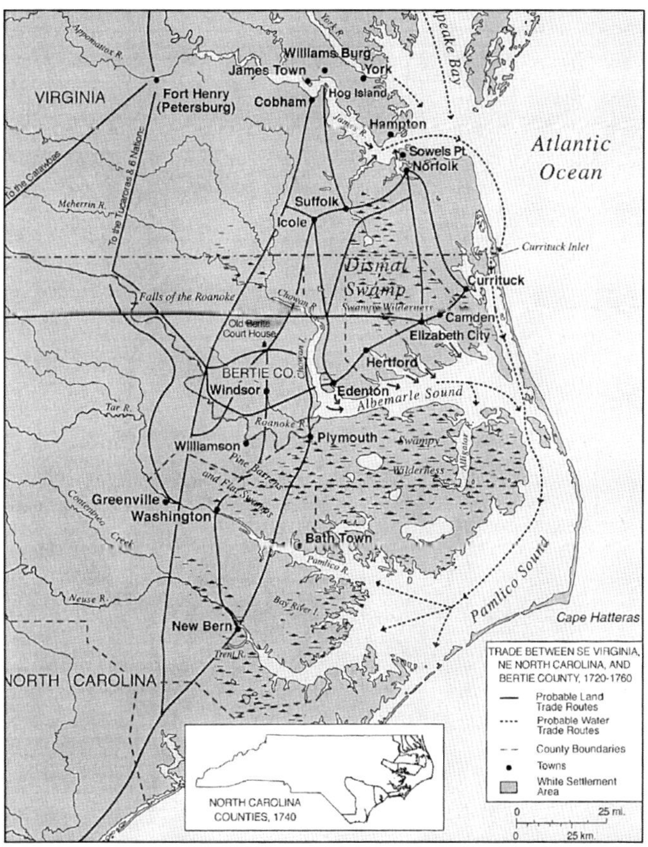

These major colonial roads through Bertie County and eastern North Carolina connected North Carolina towns with southeastern Virginia towns and ports where goods, including tobacco and African slaves, were traded from 1720 to 1760.

The people of Bertie County had even less respect for colonial authority. In one instance, a magistrate of the Currituck Precinct took it upon himself to order a rabble-rouser to the stockade for being disorderly and drunk. So ill-tempered were the citizens of Bertie concerning this act that the magistrate was forced to take flight, and he narrowly escaped without being whipped. Even Governor Gabriel Johnston, who lived in Bertie at Salmon Creek, noted in 1738 that the people of Bertie were of rebellious spirit.[16] He reported in a letter to the London Board of Trade that in the precinct of Bertie, 500 men, after hearing of a man being accosted about not paying his taxes, or "quit-rents" as they were called, threatened the tax collector with violence, made rebellious speeches, and cursed the king's name. They disbanded only after hearing that the man and the tax collector had come to an agreement.[17]

In spite of the fact that Governor Johnston and the Speaker of the House for the Colonial Assembly William Downing both lived in Bertie, the majority of the people that settled Bertie were of questionable character. One of their primary reasons for moving to Bertie was to escape the taxes and laws of the Virginia colony. There were men of wealth and reputation who served in the colonial assembly at Edenton, but these men were few and hated by the majority of poor white settlers. These settlers, however, were just as hated by the wealthy legislators and planters in Edenton and Virginia, a fact made clear by William Byrd II when he surveyed the boundary between Virginia and North Carolina.

After the settling of the boundary between North Carolina and Virginia in 1728, North Carolina would remain in the hands of its proprietors until 1729, when all colonial charters were ceded to King George II of England, making them and North Carolina a

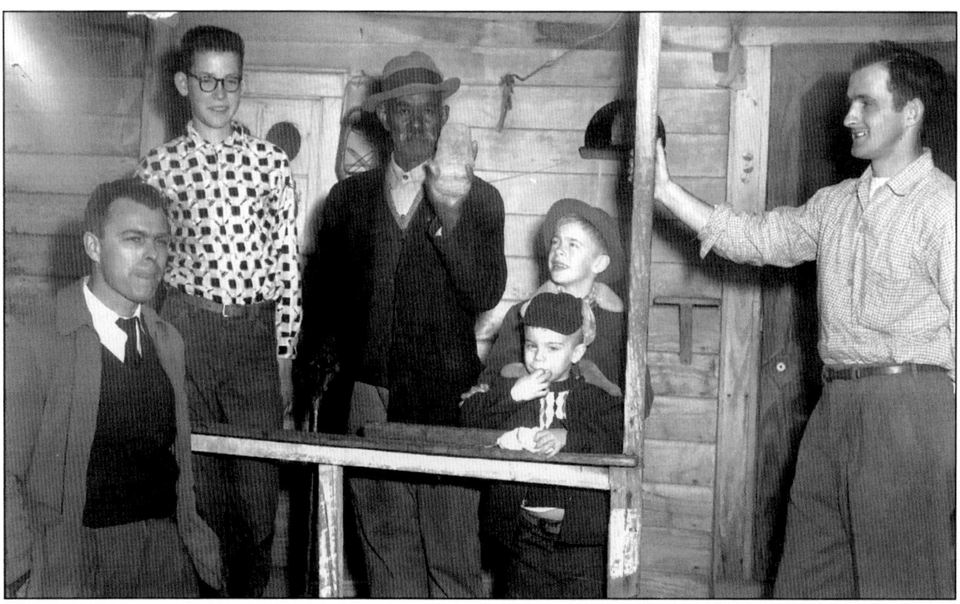

In this 1960s image, a part African-American Tuscarora from Indian Woods holds up an authentic Tuscarora stone tablet carved and passed down to him by his ancestors. (Courtesy of Frank Stephenson, Chowan College.)

royal colony.[18] Because the King of England purchased the colony, the government of the colony became more efficient. As a result, the colony experienced steady and rapid growth in its population from 1729 to 1775, particularly in the Cape Fear and Piedmont regions. Also evident was a rise in the colony's standard of living, including better homes, furnishings, clothes, food, tools, schools, libraries, churches, and the printing of its first books, newspapers, and pamphlets. Royal rule and the growth of the naval stores industry in the coastal plains of North Carolina, of which Bertie County was a major part, helped to bring this about.[19]

Although during these years Bertie County residents witnessed the arrival of German Moravians, Scottish Highlanders, and Scotch-Irish settlers to North Carolina, these groups tended to settle the Cape Fear region to the south or the Piedmont region to the west. Thus, Bertie County remained mostly English, African, and Tuscarora. As early as 1663, a well-defined class structure existed in the colony, and from 1729 to 1775, it became more pronounced. There were four basic classes: gentry or planter aristocracy; farmers; white indentured servants; and Native Americans, Native American-white mix, white-African mix, Native American-African mix, and full-blood African. Gradually, the white indentured servant class disappeared and was replaced by the poor, or whites who worked as skilled and unskilled laborers, such as millers, blacksmiths, overseers, and farm and port laborers for the wealthier classes.[20]

By 1735, lands that had been given to the Tuscarora and Meherrin in Bertie County were again being seized by the neighboring white farmers to expand their tobacco plantations.[21] When the soil was ruined from only growing tobacco year after year, the farmers cleared new lands and expanded their plantations or moved away from their old farms. Because the Tuscarora in Indian Woods and the Meherrin in Colerain held fertile lands bordering their plantations, it seemed logical to the colonists that those lands should belong to them as well.[22] Indian Woods contained thousands of acres of very fertile land and was greatly desired by local whites. In spite of new boundaries being drawn in 1722 to protect Tuscarora lands, conflicts still arose between the Tuscarora and local whites. In 1735, the Tuscarora living in Bertie again complained to North Carolina authorities about abuses by local whites and their taking of reservation land to expand plantations. This time, complaints by the Tuscarora brought Governor Gabriel Johnston, the fifth colonial governor to reside in Bertie County, to Indian Woods to investigate personally.[23] The governor was told that whites sold the Native Americans rum, which prevented braves from performing their duties, particularly hunting, and that white traders and keepers of the ferries were not fair with them and overcharged them for fur goods and for transporting them across the Roanoke River, sometimes refusing to transport them at all.[24]

These hardships caused more Tuscarora to leave Indian Woods and rejoin the larger Nation in New York with their kin in the Iroquois Confederacy, which still held considerable power and influence in the north. Chief Blount and those loyal to him, however, continued to remain on their reservation in Bertie in spite of their problems with local whites. When Blount died in Bertie in 1739, he was known throughout North Carolina as the greatest Tuscarora chieftain ever.[25] The Tuscarora who remained in Indian Woods were loyal to the colony of North Carolina in spite of their hardships.

Many of the concerns of the Tuscarora might have been better addressed if the colony had not been distracted by internal strife. In what might be seen as a prelude to the Representation and Regulation conflicts of 1755 and 1771, Governor Johnston, who led the colony from 1733 until his death in 1752, became involved in a similar conflict between the Albemarle region of the northeast and the Cape Fear region of the southeast. Starting as a debate over whether or not to move the colonial capital from Edenton to New Bern, the conflict soon escalated to a near-war over control of the colony's government. Bertie, along with the rest of the Albemarle region, had been settled by Virginians who were English. They had struggled for autonomy from Virginia and after finally securing it by 1700, they had developed a successful and prosperous colony based on agriculture and mercantile trade. By 1730, with the growing importance, size, and success of the Cape Fear settlement, their power and dominance was slowly being undermined. Quit-rents were supposed to end up in the colonial treasury, but usually ended up being paid to private proprietors living in the Granville District of which Albemarle was a part. The residents of the southern counties, by 1744, demanded not only relief from quit-rents, but also equal representation in the colonial assembly. Both these things were nonnegotiable from the point of view of the residents of the Albemarle region, including Bertie County.[26]

Many in Bertie County and the Albemarle region were particularly upset at even the suggestion of giving up or sharing control of the Colonial Assembly with people they viewed as inferior. The Cape Fear region was populated, as the back country would be by 1771, by mostly Scotch settlers for whom the English of Bertie and the Albemarle region cared very little. It must be noted that before the unification of England, there were ethnic and religious wars on the island, which resulted in the English and the Anglican church becoming the dominant ruling group. Their hatred for non-English ethnic groups and their dislike of other Europeans of different ethnic backgrounds during this period, particularly the Spanish, Irish, French, and Germans to name just a few, is well known to students of English history.[27]

Salvation from what could have been another rebellion came in the form of Governor Johnston himself. Johnston, a Scot, supported the southeastern settlers whom he had encouraged to come to North Carolina. As governor, he agreed with the Cape Fear region that they should be given equal representation in the Colonial Assembly and that the colonial capital should be moved from Edenton to New Bern. To drive home this point, he convened several assemblies in Wilmington, outraging members from Bertie and the Albemarle region who promptly refused to participate in the government. As governor of North Carolina and with the full backing of the King, Johnston held the power to force changes in the location of the capital, taxes, and representation, but instead he sought compromise and, by 1744, was successful in reaching one that eased tensions in the colony.[28]

After resolving the conflict between the northern and southern parts of the colony, the governor married the step-daughter of former governor Charles Eden, Penelope Galland, who was a wealthy widow from Bertie. Once married, he moved into her home "Eden House" near Salmon Creek in Bertie County and lived there until his death in 1752. It is highly likely that his decision to do both these things, in spite of his owning property in the Cape Fear region and supporting the settlers there during the crisis, did much to heal the colony and promote unity among them, regardless of whether they were Scotch or English.

War between England and Spain in 1740, which forced the raising of two companies of militia from both regions to protect the colony from attack, and between England and France in 1744, which led to the building of Fort Johnston at the mouth of the Cape Fear River, surely also helped bring an end to the sectional crisis.[29]

Between 1733 and 1757, under Johnston's rule, North Carolina's population tripled, with Bertie County growing faster than any other county or precinct in the colony. This was due in large part to the expansion of trade and the growth of the slave population. From 1733 to 1757, the slave population of North Carolina and the county increased as a result of a growing inter-colonial domestic slave trade and whites forcing sex on their female African and Native American slaves, in most cases to produce more slave laborers for their plantations and farms and, in other cases, to sell the offspring. The slave population of the whole colony alone grew from 6,000 in 1739 to 40,000 by 1767.[30] By the end of the Seven Years' War in 1763, Bertie County was one of the most populous slave counties in North Carolina, with about 3,000 slaves.[31] Due to the increase in tobacco production in northeastern North Carolina and its relationship with southeastern Virginia, the slave population grew at a much faster rate than it did in other parts of the colony.

The cultivation of tobacco also continued to lead to intense feuds over land between the Tuscaroras and white residents of Bertie County. These feuds prompted the colonial legislature to pass legislation in 1748 that defined the boundaries of the Tuscarora Reservation in Bertie yet a third time. Those boundaries, as later reported in Article 1 of the legislation between the North Carolina colony and the Tuscarora Nation, included the following:

> Allotted to time by the Legislature of said state, situated in the county of Bertie, beginning at the mouth of Quitsnoy Swamp, running up the said swamp four hundred and thirty poles, to a scrubby oak, near the head of said swamp, by a great spring. Then north ten degrees, east eight hundred and fifty poles, to a persimmon tree in Roquist Swamp and along the swamp and pocosin, main course north fifty-seven degrees west, two thousand, six hundred and forty poles to hickory on the east side of the Falling Run or Deep Creek, and down the various courses of the said run, to Moratoc or Roanoke Rivers; then down the river to the first station.[32]

Even this measure, however, was not enough to keep the discontented Tuscarora on the reservation or the land-hungry whites from taking reservation land to develop new tobacco plantations.

By 1750, there were a number of residents in Bertie County who were either African-Tuscarora mix, English-Tuscarora mix, or African-Tuscarora-English mix. Many Tuscarora women after the Tuscarora War had even married whites, runaway slaves, or African slaves they were enslaved with on plantations. Most Tuscarora women, however, preferred to marry African men to eliminate their European characteristics, particularly the Tuscarora Eye in their children. These marriages succeeded in eliminating the Tuscarora Eye, with the exception that every other generation children would often

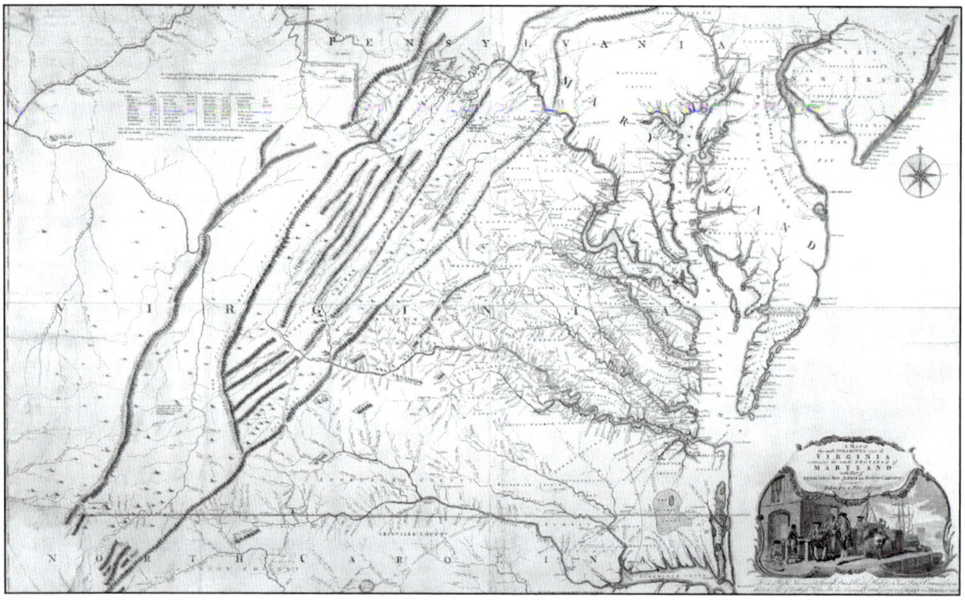

This map, showing Bertie County and its relationship to Virginia, was drawn by Peter Jefferson, the father of future president and author of the Declaration of Independence Thomas Jefferson, and Joshua Fry in 1751. (Courtesy of LVA.)

be born with green, blue, or gray eyes.[33] Because of these marriages and the continued enslavement of Tuscarora women and children by neighboring white plantation owners, all the Tuscarora and their Iroquois brothers, the Six Nations, began to develop a great dislike for the institution of slavery and the condition of African, Native American, and mixed-blood slaves. As a result, the Tuscarora of Bertie County developed friendships with the Quakers, Moravians, and leading abolitionists of the day. In 1752, the Moravian bishop August Gottlieb Spansenberg from Pennsylvania passed through Bertie County and visited with the Tuscarora on his way to western North Carolina to settle the land that the Moravians had purchased in what would become Winston-Salem, North Carolina.[34]

In New York around the same period, the Tuscarora, along with the other members of the Six Nations, met with the Quaker leader Anthony Benezet.[35] It was most likely no coincidence that two of the leading anti-slavery groups were meeting with and talking to the Tuscarora and other sympathetic nations in Pennsylvania, New York, New Jersey, and North Carolina. Nor is it a coincidence that the route of what today is referred to as the Underground Railroad runs through Tuscarora and other reservations and communities in Tuscarora Valley, Pennsylvania and the Catskill, Kittochtinny, and Ramapos Mountains of New York and New Jersey. Many slaves ended up in Buffalo, New York and in the Grand River area of Canada. The Tuscarora and Meherrin of Bertie were also accused of giving aid to and harboring runaway slaves.[36]

In fact, the Tuscarora, Meherrin, and other reservations and isolated communities were an important part of the Underground Railroad. The Underground Railroad included a network of Iroquois and other friendly reservations and communities in North Carolina,

Virginia, Pennsylvania, New York, New Jersey, and Canada, as well as the homes of Quakers in cities like Philadelphia, New York City, Albany, Buffalo, and Niagara Falls. The Tuscarora smuggled slaves out of Bertie County, gave slaves directions to other reservations and communities where they could find help, and even served as guides for slaves since they were familiar with the "Tuscarora Trail" throughout the colonial period. They also took slaves with them to New York during their various migrations from North Carolina between 1715 and 1803.[37]

When, in 1754, the colony of North Carolina conducted a survey to determine the population, it recorded only 301 Tuscarora remaining in the Indian Woods portion of Bertie County: 100 men and 201 women and children.[38] As the white and slave population grew in Bertie County, so did the pressure on the Tuscarora to give up the small remainder of land on which they lived. Whites complained that the Native Americans were not utilizing the land properly and that they were harboring runaway slaves, an allegation that whites did not have to prove to relieve the Tuscarora of their land.[39]

Because of a growing mistrust of local whites from around 1754 to 1803, the Tuscarora of Indian Woods became increasingly involved with harboring and assisting runaway slaves in their flight to freedom. They continued to give them directions to other Tuscarora and friendly reservations and communities where they could find refuge on their way north to freedom. Many hid runaway slaves from slave catchers on their reservations, since whites would be confronted by a large number of hostile Native Americans if they attempted to enter.[40]

In Bertie County, conditions continued to worsen for the few Native Americans who remained. Because many of the large plantation owners wanted the fertile lands located in Indian Woods, through a series of leases, the county land office and these individuals conspired to confiscate as much land as possible from the Tuscarora. There were trials held in Bertie County in which Tuscarora were charged with a host of crimes, particularly helping slaves escape. The charge alone was often enough to successfully relieve many Tuscarora of their lands. Nevertheless, the Tuscarora of Indian Woods continued to remain loyal to the colony of North Carolina and the British government.[41]

When the French and Indian War broke out in 1754, warriors from Indian Woods, under the leadership of Chief Blount's son, went to Virginia to join the fighting. In 1756, a company of these warriors fought with George Washington at Fort Duquesne on the western frontier. As a reward for their bravery and loyalty, they were given 105 pounds.[42] This incident is significant for a number of reasons. Not only did it demonstrate the bravery of the Bertie County Tuscarora in volunteering and fighting, but it also shows that the Tuscarora had no aversion to traveling great distances as they had done on their treks to New York to trade with the Five Nations before the arrival of the English in 1587. Their participation also demonstrated their unquestionable loyalty to the colony of North Carolina.[43]

During the French and Indian War, or Seven Years War, the Tuscarora of Indian Woods found themselves fighting alongside other Tuscarora braves and their Iroquois brothers of the Six Nations.[44] It is unclear if members of the two Tuscarora Nations actually fought together on the battlefield during the war, but they both demonstrated loyalty to their common allies, the British.[45]

In spite of their bravery and service to the colonies, the Tuscarora of Bertie County still found themselves the targets of abuse, enslavement, and deceit. As a result, in 1766 when a Tuscarora chieftain arrived in Bertie from New York, as many as 160 of the youngest warriors left Indian Woods for the Six Nations. Among them was Chief Blount's son. Arrangements were made with Governor William Tryon for the removal of as many remaining Tuscarora as would leave. In the resulting agreement between the chieftain and North Carolina, the colony agreed to lease 8,000 acres for 150 years from the Tuscarora. This was only about one-half of the land allotted to the Tuscarora in 1748. They were given $1,500 in exchange for the 150-year lease. The land was leased to three prominent white plantation owners, Robin Jones, Thomas Pugh, and William Williams. The deal was ratified in New Bern, North Carolina with the help of Alexander McCulloch, who was promised 100 acres of land on the reserve.[46] When the chieftain finally left, fewer than 100 Native Americans remained on the rest of the land. These Tuscarora asked for protection of their remaining land and themselves from the increasing number of whites moving onto their reservation. Thus, the governor did act to salvage the remaining Tuscarora lands.[47]

On their way to New York, the Tuscarora braves stopped to visit with the Moravians in Friedenshuetten, Pennsylvania. After several weeks with the Moravians, they continued their march to the Six Nations in New York. The group was robbed by whites of horses and property worth $300 at Paxtang, Pennsylvania before they arrived in lands held by the Six Nations. They finally arrived at Mt. Johnson, New York on December 16, 1766. The few Tuscarora left in Bertie County were the very old who refused to leave their ancestral home. Many were looked after by their children, who refused to leave them.[48]

By 1774, white settlers were in firm control of Bertie County. Wealthy white plantation owners routinely planted and cultivated tobacco, bought and sold slaves, and lived prosperous lives with luxurious homes and fine linens, china, furniture, libraries, and huge estates. They and their male children could also look forward to voting, holding office in the Colonial Assembly, and visiting Europe to vacation or study if they desired. They could train for military service as an officer and compete for government appointments, with the exception of being governor of the state, which was always filled by an Englishman appointed by the King. It was also still the custom of the wealthy in the county to will their entire estates to their eldest son. In fact, in cases where there was no will, it was mandated by the courts. This proved precarious for sisters and younger brothers who fell out of favor with their older brothers and helped to drive them to seek ways to acquire their own fortunes.[49]

With the exception of inheritances, life for the planter class and their children was without restriction in Bertie. This was not the case for the other groups that shared the county with them. Yeoman farmers, poor whites, and slaves had a much harsher realty. With the exception of the rare individual, they could not afford an education nor the luxuries of the planter class. By the time of the American Revolution, many of these people in Bertie disliked what they viewed as the excesses of the privileged class. They also disliked the growing number of laws enacted by the Colonial Assembly and resented the social legislation enacted during this period, including the regulation of marriage, taverns, and religion. As stated earlier, most of the poor practiced no religion, whereas, for elites, attending church was expected and practiced unequivocally.

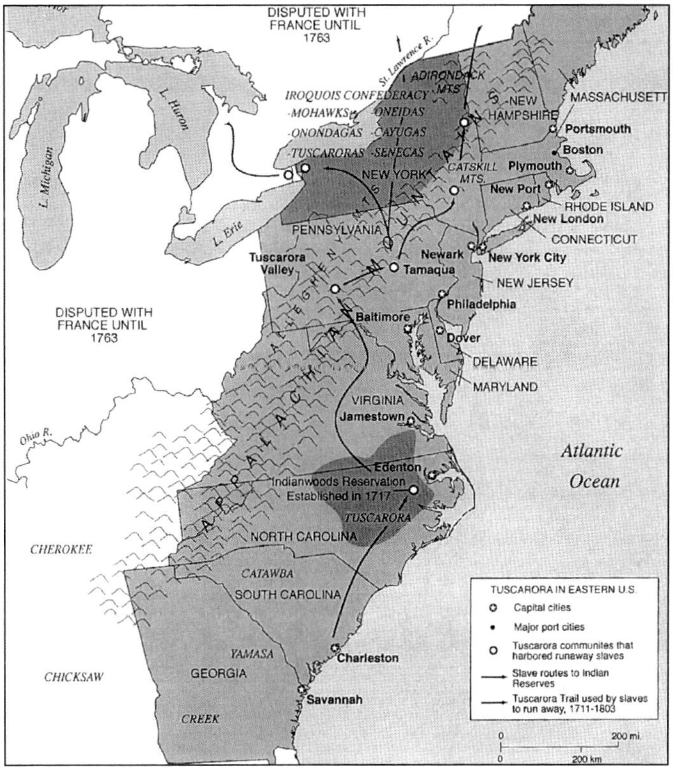

The Tuscarora Trail, or Death Trail, used by the Tuscarora to trade and, later, to flee North Carolina became one of the first routes of the Underground Railroad. Indians sometimes took with them runaway African, Indian, and mixed-blood slaves. The trail would be used later by Moravians, Quakers, and other anti-slavery groups to smuggle slaves out of North Carolina, South Carolina, Georgia, Virginia, and Maryland.

Thus, when one act required each person to apply themselves on Sunday to the duties of religion and another forbade, under penalty of 14 shillings, all work and amusement on Sunday, many were outraged. Governor Johnston and the Colonial Assembly also set out to end the unacceptable sexual behavior that drew criticism from William Byrd in 1728 by passing an act that jailed unmarried mothers until they disclosed the paternity of their children. This law did not apply to African or Native American women, slave or free, thus it was not as a rule applied to plantation owners who tended to abuse their slave women. And since English law was interpreted as not covering Africans or Native Americans, the law was not enforced when it came to those women of color who were considered free. The enacting and enforcing of these laws on the white population of Bertie County, however, had a profound impact on not just whites, but the entire population of the county. With the arrival of the "Great Awakening" and the Southern revival movement of the 1790s and early 1800s, religion and respect for religion would root itself deeply in Bertie County and eastern North Carolina. So deep that even as late as the twenty-first century, religion and its components—sermons, music, and the church as the source of information and guidance in political matters—are still revered in a way unseen and unknown anywhere else in North Carolina with the exception of Charlotte.[50]

With the enacting of social legislation and the ending of tensions between the northern and southern sections of the colony, Bertie County and the rest of eastern North Carolina began to take on a shared identity. After all, the Scotch in the South were as dependent on slaves and the institution of slavery as in the northeast. Because of this and their shared economic interest in international and intercolonial trade, the two groups, following Governor Johnston's lead, made peace. Prominent families from the northeast or their children migrated to the southeast, purchasing land and bringing their slaves.[51]

Thus, from 1722 to 1740, the settlement of Bertie County and eastern North Carolina followed three basic patterns. First, it was for the most part a north-to-south movement with the county and region being primarily settled by Virginians moving south from the Jamestown settlement. These people initially settled the Albemarle and Chowan regions, which would become Bertie County. From there, they moved further south into the Pamlico and Cape Fear regions where they intermarried with the Scotch and developed their economic interests.[52] Second, the settlers who came to Bertie and the rest of eastern North Carolina were mostly English and the elites, members of the Anglican church, forging a common identity as eastern North Carolinians. The Anglican church, through social legislation from 1741 to 1757, was forced on all the colony's people regardless of class or ethnic background. Third, they brought with them their African and Native American slaves on whom, like the Virginia colony, they became dependent. During the years from 1722 to 1740, Bertie County and eastern North Carolina fashioned a society that was modeled after colonial Virginia. Not only was it modeled after the tobacco culture of Virginia, but it was begun by prominent and not so prominent Virginians. The colony contained the best and the worst of Virginia society, including the ever-growing system of slavery with the trans-Atlantic slave trade.[53] As a result, Bertie County and the rest of eastern North Carolina became prosperous and gave rise to a number of well educated men who, by their travels and trade in the Americas, Caribbean, and Europe, gained power and influence in the colony, while working to maintain and expand for themselves and their children.[54]

With the defeat and removal of North Carolina's various western Native Americans by 1740, an increasing number of settlers began to move into the western part of the colony. Unlike the earlier settlement of the east in which settlers came by water, these settlers traveled over land to start their farms and towns on the hilly and rocky soil of the piedmont and mountains. Due to these factors, there tended to be poorer and more subsistence farmers in the west than there were in the east. These settlers were joined by displaced poor whites from the east who, because of slavery, looked to the west for better livelihoods. These were not the only differences between the easterners and westerners. These westerners were also more ethnically and religiously diverse than those who had settled the southeast.[55]

The back country, as it became known, was settled by Highlanders, Scotch-Irish, Welsh, Germans, and poor Englishmen from eastern North Carolina, all of whom the colonial aristocracy of the east and southeast, which governed the colony, saw as persons who could not be trusted with political power. Some of these settlers brought their native religions, but most had none. Nor did they share the east's dependence on slavery, preferring to do their own farming. As the population of the west continued to grow and eventually outnumber the white population of the east, tensions began to grow over governing the colony. From 1740 to 1755, the east, which dominated the Colonial Assembly, refused to allow for the creation of more counties in the more populous west in an effort to maintain control of the colonial government.[56] This and their stated differences fostered mistrust between the two regions, which rapidly evolved into tension that peaked in 1755 in what became known as the "Representation Controversy." This controversy revolved around the west's complaint that they lacked equal representation in the Colonial Assembly based on their free white populations, which were significantly larger than that of the east. When the Colonial Assembly refused to alter its makeup to give the more populous west more representatives and an equal vote in colonial affairs, the west's leaders became bitter. This bitterness would eventually give rise to the regulators and armed combat between the east and the west in 1771.[57]

When William Tryon became the seventh royal governor of the North Carolina colony in 1765, he took over a government and colony that was divided. This was a division he was unable or unwilling to make whole. Instead of trust and confidence being fostered under his reign, tensions between the east and west erupted into violence. Trouble began with the building of the governor's new palace at New Bern, the new colonial capital, in 1767. Westerners began to complain that the governor's administration was corrupt, extravagant, and unwilling to hear their old complaints over taxation, the lack of equal representation, and their inability to regulate their own affairs.

Tryon's palace, which was to be built at New Bern and brought higher taxes throughout the colony, was viewed by westerners as an unnecessary waste of money. Most easterners, including many from Bertie, supported the building of the palace and noted that when completed it would be considered "the finest government house in English America."[58] The dispute over the taxes required to build this palace and the lack of representation in the Colonial Assembly from the west brought loud protest against Tryon's government. These protests from 1765 to 1771 were not without merit. Not only did the east dominate the colonial legislature, but it had complete control of all branches of government: all councilors, judges, the treasurer, and the speaker of the house lived in the east.[59] In fact, most western local governmental officials were appointed by this government and many of

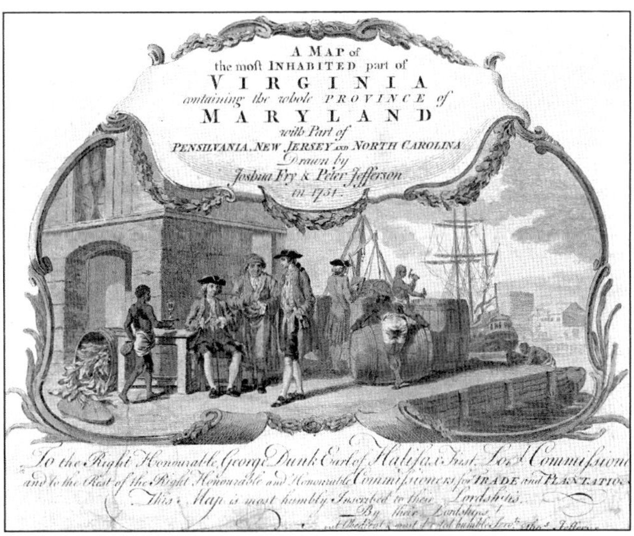

This picture, inset on the Jefferson and Frye map, depicts African slaves loading and unloading ships and prominent colonist conducting business at a southern port in Virginia in 1751. (Courtesy of LVA.)

them were corrupt. The west had no vote or input into deciding who these officials would be; many were unable to even vote or hold office due to the high poll taxes they had to pay, taxes that excluded not only poor whites in the west from voting, but many yeoman farmers as well, who could not afford to pay the tax in spite of being landowners.[60]

After years of complaints, resolutions, and petitions, the westerners rebelled against the east. On May 14, 1771, an army of 2,000 westerners, or Regulators as they became known, met a state militia force of 1,452 men led by Governor Tryon at Great Alamance Creek. In the battle that followed, Governor Tryon defeated the Regulators and captured 12 of their leaders, who were promptly tried and convicted. Six were hanged, six were pardoned, and the men who had participated in the uprising against the east were given clemency after disbanding and laying down their arms.[61]

Although it would take until 1835 for the western part of the state to gain equal representation, this conflict did lead to an acknowledgement by eastern planters, including those from Bertie serving in the Colonial Assembly, that the west had been treated unfairly and that some government reform was called for. It also led to one of the first mass exoduses from North Carolina. Former Regulators, who saw no change in the government and feared reprisals, fled the state in droves for Tennessee and other sparsely settled areas.[62] The collapse of the Regulation Movement in 1771 and the exodus that followed ended the east-west conflict. With the start of the American Revolution, east-west differences gave way to conflicts between loyalists, North Carolinians loyal to England, and Patriots, those who were supporters of the revolution.

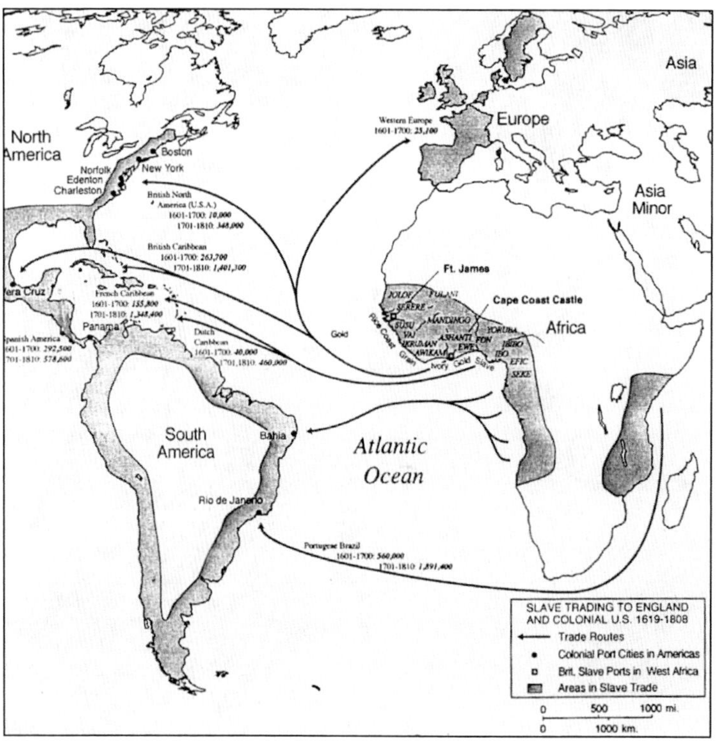

The trans-Atlantic slave trade, which lasted from 1502 until 1888, brought between 9 and 12 million African slaves to the Western Hemisphere and over 2 million to the British colonies in the Caribbean and North America. Thousands of these slaves ended up in Bertie County.

4. The American Revolution and the Early Years of the New Republic, 1774–1803

By the start of the American Revolution, Bertie County had undergone nearly two centuries of change. It had evolved from the tranquil home of the Meherrin and Tuscarora to a thriving English colony with large prosperous tobacco plantations worked by thousands of African, Native Americans, and mixed-blood slaves. It had developed lucrative trading ties with its neighbors Virginia and South Carolina, as well as intercolonial and international trade with New England, Britain, and the British Caribbean. By 1774, Bertie County was one of the most prosperous counties in North Carolina. It had benefited greatly from being adjacent to Edenton, the colonial capital, and from serving as home for five colonial governors who guided the colony through difficult times.

From its beginning as an English colony, it also had been a hotbed of anti-government feelings. From the start, the county had been settled by explorers, former soldiers, traders, trappers, Native American slave catchers, criminals, and others who lacked respect for the colonial government or the established church.[1] The Virginians who settled the county wanted to rid themselves of colonial authority and the social constraints of Virginia society. The county and many of its early settlers allowed pirates and piracy to operate from its shores as noted by Virginia officials during the "Golden Age of Piracy," 1689 to 1718. The most well-known pirate was Edward Teach or "Black Beard" as he was commonly known. Black Beard was fond of saying that there was not a home in the Albemarle region, of which Bertie was a part, that he was not welcome.[2]

This contempt for colonial authority and outright lawlessness brought strict legislation from 1722 to 1752 with the establishment of Edenton in 1722, across the Albemarle Sound, as the colonial capital. With the establishment of what today is called Avoca, a 10,000-acre plantation on Salmon Creek purchased and first lived on by Seth Sothell in 1685, as well as a number of prominent families, including four colonial governors and a number of men who served in the colonial assembly, the importance and status of the county began to change. As the image and reality of the county changed, more plantation owners arrived with their slaves, bringing with them the social and governmental structure of Virginia. These planters enforced the laws of the county and enacted new ones, bringing order and stability to the county. As a result, anti-government protests and actions declined from 1760 to 1774.[3]

By the start of hostilities between Britain and the New England colonies in 1770 with the Boston Massacre, residents of the Bertie County were still concerned about the Regulators in the western part of the colony. With the defeat of the Regulators in 1771, residents began to follow events in other parts of the colonies, but due to the lack of a daily newspaper in the county, news of the trouble in New England was little and far between. When the Coercive Acts were enacted in 1774, many of the planter class in Bertie found themselves torn. On the one hand, they looked to England for validation and identity because they were, after all, of the same blood, religion, culture, and class; yet, they believed that the taxes and restrictions imposed on Boston by the parliament were excessive and unjust and required redress. Eventually, the majority chose to take action against or protest England's unjust actions.[4]

This was no small decision considering that many residents of the county had friends and relatives in England. In spite of this, many residents chose to voice their opposition to British policy. One of the most famous acts of defiance in North Carolina history was the Edenton Tea Party in 1774 in which 51 prominent women from Edenton protested the Tea Act of 1774 by issuing a written statement condemning the act and committing to stop buying British manufactured goods and tea until the act was repealed.[5] Beginning with the Edenton Tea Party on October 25, 1774, residents of the Chowan and Roanoke region began to show their dissatisfaction with British rule by protesting. During this period, many poor whites in Bertie County found themselves aligned with a number of vocal individuals from the planter class, including John Campbell and William Gray, who represented the county in both the Hillsboro Convention in 1775 and the Halifax Convention in 1776, where the state's constitution was written. Others included William Johnston Dawson, member of the Hillsborough Convention of 1788 to ratify the United States Constitution, and William Blount, member of the Continental Congress and signer of the Constitution.[6]

Along with disagreeing with English policy toward the colonies, these men saw the potential for unrestricted trade if the revolution was successful. Bertie County was built during the colonial period on mercantile trade initially with the Native Americans for furs and animal hides from 1640 to 1722, and then on tobacco and slaves from 1722 to 1774. By 1774, the county contained a number of large merchant and plantation owners who were dependent on what had become known as triangular trade.[7]

These planters exported their tobacco and other agricultural goods to England that once the ships were unloaded in English ports, set sail for Africa with guns, rum, and English manufactured goods. Once in Africa, these same ships were unloaded and reloaded with African slaves bound for the British Caribbean where they were exchanged for seasoned slaves, slaves who had been in the British Islands for three to four years and knew English customs and the language, and sugar, molasses, and rum, which were traded to the Native Americans on the frontier for furs. Some ships returned directly from England with English manufactured goods, including guns, munitions, and a number of luxury items, including, books, furniture, china, crystal, fashionable clothes, and tea.[8]

Thus, Bertie planters were dependent on trade and, since British law required that all this trade be done on British ships and that tariffs be paid whenever ships were unloaded and reloaded, the planter class of Bertie was not inclined to support more or higher taxes. This taxation was even present during intercolonial trading, which North Carolina had been conducting with New England since 1686.[9] Yet in spite of the discontent over taxes,

Bertie, like the rest of eastern North Carolina, held a strong religious and cultural tie to England. Most of the planter class and their children in Bertie had been educated in England and were proud of their English blood line, which they believed to be superior to other races and ethnic groups around the world and in Europe.[10]

Many had been involved in governing themselves by voting and serving in the North Carolina Colonial Assembly, and enjoyed freedom and happiness that neither slaves nor poor whites of the county could. It must be noted that when Parliament enacted the Coercive Acts in 1774 to punish Massachusetts, North Carolina was not targeted and that the same men in the county and the colony, who took up arms and crushed the Regulators and their movement in western North Carolina, now convened in continental congresses in North Carolina and Philadelphia to decide how best to respond to the escalating tension between New England and England over the very same issues.[11]

To select the delegates to the Continental Congress, North Carolina held its first provincial congress in August of 1774. It was decided that safety committees would be organized in towns and counties around the state for protection. As tensions continued to increase, North Carolina held two more congresses to state clearly the colony's position on the coming conflict. The third congress raised minutemen, of which two companies were required from Bertie County. The resulting companies were commanded by Colonel Thomas Whitmell and Lieutenant Colonel Thomas Pugh.[12] Although there was support for the revolution across all classes and races in the county, including the Tuscarora and Meherrin, free African Americans and most slaves hoped the freedoms and equality of which these revolutionaries spoke so passionately would extend to them

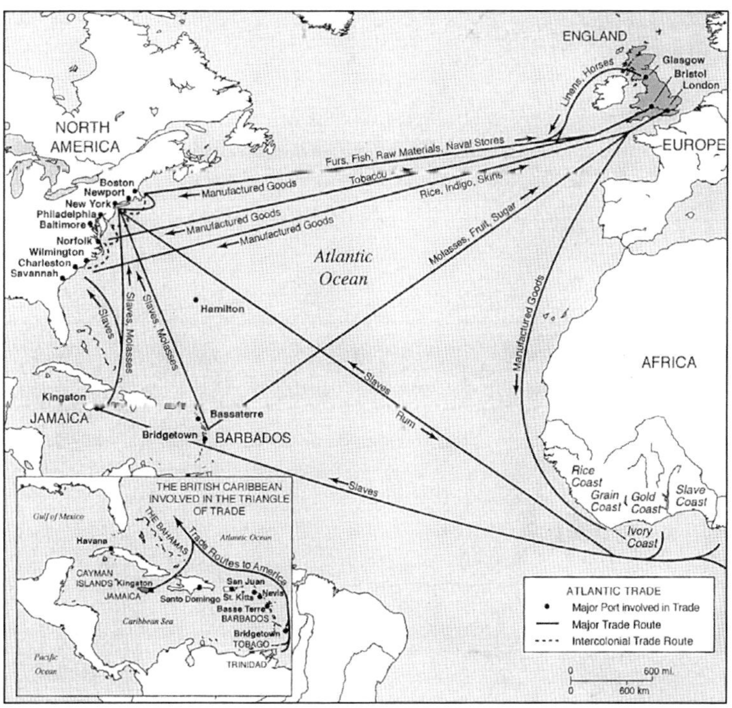

In this triangle of trade, British colonies could only trade with other British colonies and Great Britain. They were also allowed only to use British ships and had to pay a tax to the crown every time a ship was loaded and unloaded.

as well. There was also a sizable number of wealthy whites, free blacks (after the royal governor of Virginia Lord Dunmore's proclamation giving any slave who fought for the British their freedom), and slaves. These supporters of the crown became known as Tories or Loyalists. The white Loyalists tended to be large land and slaveholders, people who held royal appointments, or at least planned to one day hold such appointments, and free blacks and slaves answering Lord Dunmore's call to arms. For these last two groups, the choice was simple—they understood that the promise of freedom from the British was preferable to perpetual slavery under the Patriots in the county.[13]

Thus, when hostilities broke out in 1775 in Lexington and Concord, Massachusetts, the county was torn over whom to support. When the last royal governor of North Carolina, Josiah Martin, dissolved the colonial legislature in 1775, a legislature in which Bertie County and the rest of eastern North Carolina were well represented, residents begin to support the revolution in greater numbers.[14] This was tempered, however, when Lord Dunmore issued his proclamation extending freedom to any slave that would join the British in the war. Bertie County slaveholders and many others in the colony and in the South found the proclamation outrageous. And with the proclamation coming from Williamsburg, the colonial capital of Virginia only a few miles north of the county, it created fear and a sense of immediacy not felt in other parts of North Carolina.[15] This, along with the fact that slaves constituted roughly half of the county's population and in some parts of the county were well more than half, gave white residents legitimate cause for concern.

During the provincial congresses that convened at Halifax on the Roanoke River just northwest of Bertie following Governor Martin's actions in 1775, Bertie elected and sent representatives to decide what course of action should be taken. Bertie was represented at all five of the provincial congresses held during the revolutionary period and those residents and their children who served would emerge from the American Revolution as state and national leaders.[16] In response to Governor Martin's dissolving of the colonial legislature, the provincial congress issued the Mecklenburg Declaration of Independence and adopted the "Mecklenburg Resolves." These documents, rebellious acts, and threats to Governor Martin's safety forced him to flee the colonial capital at New Bern.[17]

Exiled but not defeated, he sent an army of North Carolina Loyalists to subdue the rebels in the state, but in the first battle of the revolution fought in North Carolina by Whigs from the old colonial assembly, the Loyalists were defeated at the Battle of Moore's Creek Bridge on February 27, 1776. By April, the provincial congress had authorized its delegates in the Continental Congress to sign the Declaration of Independence and, by December of 1776, the provincial congress had drafted the state's constitution and formalized North Carolina's new independent government by 1777.[18]

All did not go well, however, in Bertie County during the war. As Alan Watson notes in his book *A Brief History of Bertie*, the county was the center of an extensive Loyalist plot known as the Llewelyn Conspiracy. John Llewelyn, a prominent Martin County planter with roots in Bertie and other northeastern counties, organized it. The conspirators included people who were devout Anglicans, held personal grudges against leaders of the new provincial congress, or who were simply loyal to King and country. The leader of the Bertie conspirators was William Brimage of Bertie, who owned 30 slaves and 10,000 acres of land. The plot was discovered and ended in 1777. Brimage, who was arrested and acquitted of treason, eventually fled Bertie County and was evacuated by the British in Charleston, South Carolina to England in 1782, leaving his plantation, wife, and family in Bertie.[19]

Of those who chose to support the revolution from Bertie, a number would become not only leaders in the new state government, but in the new national government as well. There were several prominent residents who served in the provincial congresses, including John Campbell, who represented Bertie in four of the five provincial congresses. Others who served included David Standley, John Johnston, Charles Jacocks, and Zedekiah Stone, father of future state governor David Stone.[20]

Although there was no fighting in Bertie County nor much in eastern North Carolina during the war, when the British brought the war to the South from 1781 to 1783, the British army under the command of Lord Cornwallis did pass near Bertie County and, in concert with the navy that was enforcing the British blockade of the North Carolina coast greatly impacting the residents of the county, did dispatch an expedition against Edenton.[21]

When the revolution ended, residents wholeheartedly supported their new state and federal government. Although from 1783 until 1787 most of the state supported the Articles of Confederation, Bertie, according to Watson, was a supporter of the United States Constitution due to its dependence on mercantile trade and farm exports. Because of the county's many major waterways, including the Chowan, Roanoke, and Cashie Rivers, which bordered and split the county in two, and its easy access to the Albemarle Sound and the North Carolina Coast, Bertie County's goods were traded to all points along the Atlantic coast and ports around the world.[22] As a result, the county continued to be dependent on intra-state and international trade during the years from 1783 to 1787. Thus, when the state of North Carolina held its first of two state conventions to ratify the United States Constitution in 1788, representatives elected from Bertie led the fight for ratification of the document, noting the benefits to improving trade. However, they failed to convince others in the state of the importance of one national currency and federal regulation of trade, two things they were quite knowledgeable about and which their county had benefited from under British rule.[23]

The state was basically forced to ratify the constitution a year later in 1789 with Bertie County's representatives still making their support for the document clear. The wealthy well-educated delegates who were elected to represent the county and actually attend the conventions were William J. Dawson; John Johnston; Andrew Oliver; David Turner, who attended the Hillsborough Convention; Francis Pugh; and David Stone, who attended the Fayetteville Convention.[24]

Even during the American Revolution, and in spite of the loyalty and military assistance many Tuscarora gave the colonies, whites continued to trick Bertie County's remaining Native Americans out of their land or into long-term leases of their land, for which they were paid very little and sometimes nothing at all. From 1775 to 1777, a total of eight leases were made between the Tuscarora and various well-known landowners in the county, a number of whom were Revolutionary leaders.[25] Among the recorded leasers were Zedekiah Stone, Thomas Pugh Sr., Thomas Pugh Jr., William King, Titus Edwards, John Johnston, and John McKaskey.[26] The conduct of these men during and after the

Revolutionary War in terms of their policies toward the Tuscarora, who lived in Indian Woods and whose nation with the Oneida saved George Washington's army at Valley Forge, is notable. It, at least in their case, seems to give credence to Charles Beard's classic work *The Economic Origins of the Constitution* in which he argues that the founding fathers were really only interested in protecting and preserving their own economic and political interest and had no interest in or intention of creating a true democracy rooted in fairness and equality for nonwhites or poor whites.[27]

In December of 1777, after protest from the remaining Native Americans, the North Carolina legislature prohibited the leasing of any more Native American lands in Bertie County and appointed a commission to supervise their affairs. The commission also legalized the leases already obtained.[28] In 1778, the North Carolina General Assembly acknowledged Chief Withmell Tuffdick as the Tuscarora ruler.[29] Many of the Tuscarora who lived in the county were too old to participate in the Revolutionary War, but pledged their loyalty to the colony of North Carolina. It is plausible that they also supported the cause of those whites living around them, which would have been the logical thing to do. During the war, however, the Tuscarora Nation, along with the Six Nations Confederacy,

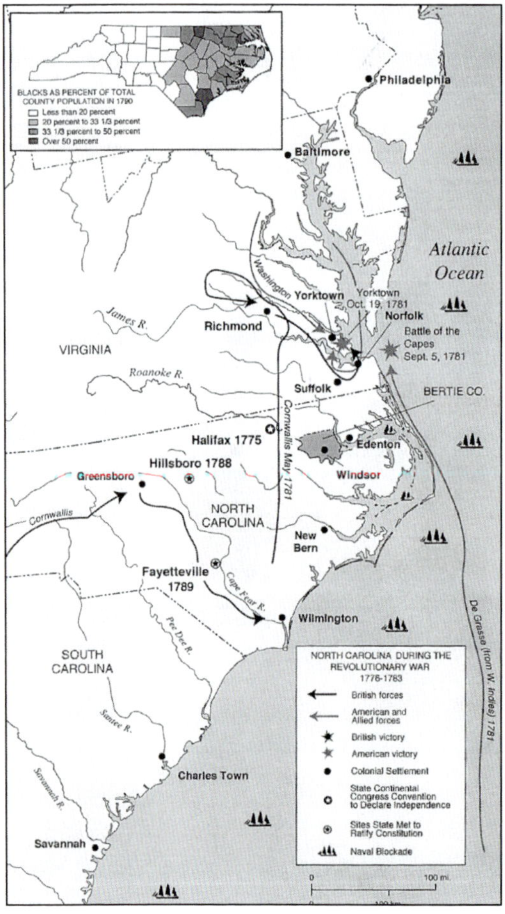

Bertie County is highlighted on this Revolutionary War map of the area. The British naval blockade during the war hurt many plantation owners in the county due to the fact that they were dependent on the mercantile trade exporting tobacco, other crops, and raw materials and importing slaves, guns, rum, and other manufactured goods.

was split. A number of Tuscarora, plus a number of Cayuga, Onidena, Seneca, Onadaga, and Mohawk, under the leadership of Mohawk chief Joseph Bryant, aligned themselves with the British, most probably because they were living in territory controlled by the British near Canada.[30]

Those members of the Six Nations living in the colonies of New York, Pennsylvania, Maryland, Virginia, Connecticut, New Jersey, and North Carolina either chose to remain neutral or joined the Americans since the greater collective part of the Tuscarora Nation had been under the protection of the Oneida since 1715.[31] When the Oneida, whose lands were well within striking distance of American forces, aligned themselves with the Americans, the Tuscarora did so as well.[32]

These Tuscarora, along with the Oneida, played a little known but very significant role in the American colonies' securing independence from England. These Native Americans, and the Iroquois Confederacy of which they had been a part for over two centuries, introduced the concept of democracy, equality, and cooperation between nations of people to the early settlers of Virginia and North Carolina in the South, and Pennsylvania and New York in the North. The notion that all men are created equal was an Iroquois concept in that their entire nation, in fact all six nations, were considered kin and, as kin, all were treated by one another as brothers and sisters. Furthermore, in Iroquois culture, the eldest women (clan mothers) held council amongst themselves and "horned" or "dehorned" the nations' chiefs, referring to practice of Iroquois women crowning their chiefs with deer antlers after their deliberations. Their confederacy was so well crafted that even when they disagreed and split over issues, such as the Tuscarora War and the American Revolution, each nation and each clan respected the right of each chief to, after consultation with his clan, choose his people's path. This did not make him or his people enemies of other nations and clans because they were brothers and, by the Great Law, forbidden to make war on one another.[33]

These concepts were foreign to the whites who settled North Carolina and the rest of the colonies. The absolute monarchies they had left in England and Europe dominated the masses of their people and exploited them for their own gain. Furthermore, the notion of a peasant being kin to a noble and, therefore, his equal was unheard of; even brothers in the same royal or noble family were not treated as equals. And the notion of women selecting leaders, deposing them, or having anything remotely to do with the politics of a nation was inconceivable. One of the things that made the United States unique and the American Revolution unique was that by the end of their first century, they had assimilated much of the culture of the Native Americans they grew to despise, keeping those things they liked and discarding those they did not. Even Benjamin Franklin pointed to the Six Nations as a model the colonies should follow if they were to protect themselves from foreign and Native American threats.[34]

During the Revolutionary War, the Americans used the philosophy of the Iroquois Confederacy with chilling efficiency when the Continental Army commanded by George Washington used a policy of total war, burning Iroquois villages, destroying their crops and property, and decimating what had been for over two centuries the most powerful and influential Indian Confederation in the history of North America. Members of the Six Nations who aligned themselves with Washington escaped this fate. Later in the war, specifically the Tuscarora and Oneida would be responsible for saving General Washington and his men from starvation at Valley Forge when the chiefs of these nations brought food to the starving, freezing soldiers in the dead of winter. When the members of the Six Nations who supported Britain became aware of this, they burned these Tuscarora's homes and destroyed their crops and other property in New York.[35]

At the end of the revolution, George Washington and the new government acknowledged what the Oneida and Tuscarora had done to save their army and perhaps their independence in the Treaty of Fort Stanwix of 1784. In Article Two, the treaty secured the land and possessions of both the Oneida and the Tuscarora. In the generous terms that followed, Washington gave the Oneida sovereign nation status and unlimited hunting, fishing, and access rights to over 6 million acres of land in what today is western New York State, terms that were still in force at the time of the publishing of this book over 200 years later.[36]

Since many of the Tuscarora Nation had been taken in by the Oneida and split into two factions, one supporting the Americans, the other the British during the war, they found themselves not considered a true nation by the United States government and were without land they could call their own. Weakened yet again by their split during the Revolutionary War, the Tuscarora aligned with the United States were not even considered an equal nation by the other members of the Six Nations after the war. The Six Nations were still sizable enough to maintain sovereign nation status. As a result, from 1784 to 1804, the Tuscarora were considered a party to several treaties with the United States, including the Fort Stanwix Treaty of 1784, the Fort Harmar Treaty of 1789, the Agreement with the Five Nations of Indians of 1792, the Canandaigua (Konondaiqua) Treaty of 1794, the Oneida Treaty of 1794, the Genessee Treaty of 1797, and the Buffalo Creek Treaty of 1838. But they held no lands of their own and could not stop the other members of the Six Nations from selling lands given to them.[37]

By 1783, those remaining in North Carolina were so few in number and thoroughly mixed with whites and Africans that they were not treated by Bertie County's whites as sovereign peoples either. In 1784, the North Carolina General Assembly passed an act to conduct a state census that took from 1784 to 1787 to complete. In the census, Bertie County was recorded as having 5,141 slaves and 349 free persons out of a total population of 12,606.[38]

As more African slaves were brought into the county's Tuscarora and Meherrin reservations, interaction between the two groups and slaves increased. This interaction led to the merging of the two cultures in the county. The most convincing evidence of this can be found in their non-Christian religious practices. Both Native Americans and Africans believed in shaman or medicine men, the spirits of nature, and a strong obligation to honor and worship their ancestors. As early as 1669, the colony of North Carolina established the status of Africans as slaves, subservient to white masters in Article Ten of the colony's constitution. It also noted that conversion to Christianity in no way altered the Africans' servitude.[39]

Since becoming Christian did not ease the condition of many blacks, and they were not prohibited by law from practicing their native religions, many slaves who were from Guinea continued to practice their West African faiths. Because of the closeness of Native American and African religion, many slaves began to merge their religions with those of

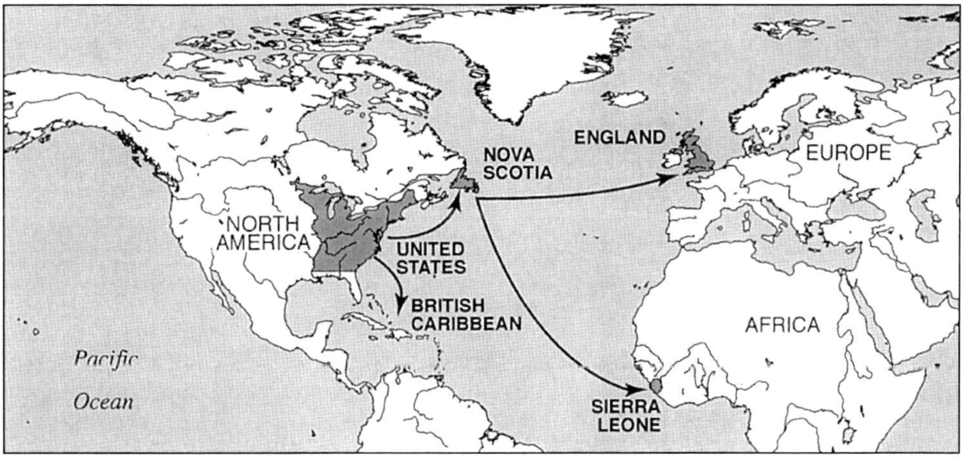

Mapped here are the evacuation routes of Loyalists in 1783. Most black soldiers and their families were taken to Nova Scotia and then to Sierra Leone, Africa. White Loyalists were taken anywhere they desired, including the British Caribbean and England.

the Native Americans, who often married and harbored slaves in eastern North Carolina. The Tuscarora were particularly spiritual. Like Africans, they believed that man had not been given dominion over animals as many Europeans did.

The Tuscarora had high priests, mystics to whom the tribe turned for guidance and protection. There were many slaves in Indian Woods who merged African and Tuscarora religion and became known as great conjurers. These conjurers were both feared and respected by whites and blacks alike. Since both the Native Americans and Africans believed that spirits lived in trees, streams, and animals, it was easy for Africans to learn from their neighbors. Later generations of African Americans would still see and hear Native American spirits canoeing, hunting, and drumming in Indian Woods.[40]

Frank Johnson recounted a most unusual folktale that requires further research. It is about Sallie Rascoe, a black woman who is not designated as slave or free and who turned herself into a white deer. In it he states, "On the west rim of Albemarle, witches turned themselves into white deer to tease the hounds." The story ends by noting that no matter how often hunting dogs followed her trail, it always ended at her door. The most interesting part of this tale is the merging of Native American and African beliefs. Nowhere in West African religion is there any documented reference to a white deer. However, in Native American religion and myths there are references made to this rare phenomenon. There were, in fact, recent sightings of a white deer in Indian Woods in the twentieth century, perhaps a descendant of this famous deer.[41]

There were four recorded conjurers in Indian Woods: Noah Stalling, Daniel Smallwood, Loreenza Smallwood, and Sally Ann, all of whom died before 1930.[42] Interviews with residents do not substantiate these assertions. In fact, few residents remember or are willing to discuss this aspect of their history. Furthermore, in researching this community, several recorded incidents of Tuscarora mysticism during the colonial period were uncovered, as recorded in *The Colonial Records of North Carolina.*[43]

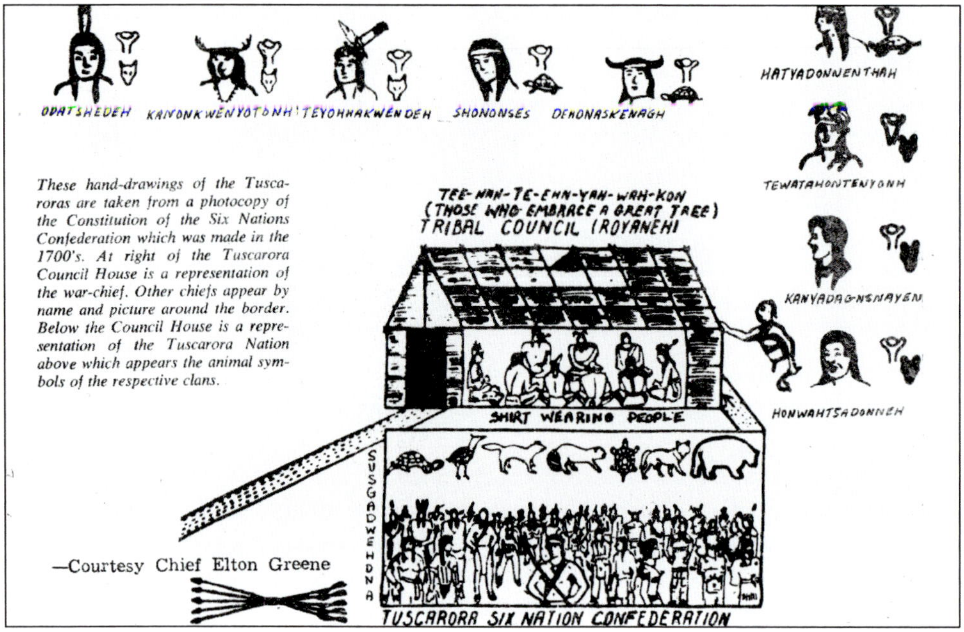

In this drawing the Six Nations tribal council is readmitting the Tuscarora to the Iroquois Confederacy after their defeat in the Tuscarora War in 1711. The Tuscarora war chiefs that relocated to New York are represented along with their clans. (Courtesy of Margaret Johnson and the NCC, UNC.)

In addition to the aforementioned intermarriage and merging of religious traditions, general relations between the Tuscarora and Africans seem always to have been very good. Unlike the Cherokee, the Tuscarora never attempted to adopt the white man's ways. Nor did they ever attempt to own slaves or farm plantations. The Cherokee, however, did in an attempt to gain acceptance by whites.[44]

After the Revolutionary War, the Tuscarora, who had been allied with the Americans, settled in New York at the site of their present reservation on land belonging to the Seneca. This land was purchased from the Holland Land Company when the Seneca negotiated the Genessee Treaty in 1797. The Tuscarora complained for the first time since their arrival in 1715 that land given them by the Five Nations was not really theirs to give and that when treaties were negotiated, it was all ceded without their participation or consent. The Five Nations admitted this was true and, as a result, the Robert Morris gave the Tuscarora, in the Genessee Treaty, 2 miles of their current reservation in Niagara Falls, New York. The Tuscarora, who had fought with the British, settled along the Grand River in Canada with the other members of the Six Nations.[45]

By 1803, many of the last Tuscarora to leave Indian Woods were thoroughly mixed to the point that they appeared black. These mixed-bloods moved on to New York, leaving others behind who had been enslaved like themselves. Although it could not be proven, local whites accused the Tuscarora of assisting slaves on the neighboring Outlaw Plantation in the revolt in 1802 in what became known as the "Great Slave Conspiracy."[46] Following the Great Slave Conspiracy, the North Carolina State Legislature passed a law allowing the remaining Tuscaroras to depart and lease their lands to the residents of Bertie County.[47]

This law and the death in 1802 of the last ruling chief of the Tuscarora in Bertie County, Samuel Smith, helped facilitate their final departure.[48] On February 21, 1803, the Tuscarora Nation communicated to the United States Senate its desire to have the federal government assist in redressing grievances against North Carolina over Indian Woods reservation land given to the Tuscarora after the Tuscarora War in 1717.[49] The United States government appointed William Richardson Davie to supervise the leasing and selling of Native American land as the remaining Tuscaroras prepared to depart Indian Woods.[50]

By 1803, white settlements and plantations had grown and spread throughout Bertie County. Trapped by this growth, the Tuscarora of Indian Woods faced constant threats, harassment, and enslavement by whites. Thus, when their brethren arrived from New York, the remaining Tuscarora left with them without protest. After continued suffering at the hands of the citizens of Bertie County, the delegation of Tuscarora from New York was welcomed. The New York Tuscarora made arrangements to remove them from Indian Woods in 1803.[51]

Upon leaving, several leases were given by the departing Tuscarora to wealthy plantation owners in the county, many of whom had participated in North Carolina's revolutionary and post-revolutionary governments. The leases were for the rich lands in Indian Woods along the banks of the Roanoke River. Among the whites receiving these leases were John Pugh, William Johnston, Thomas Pugh, Ebeneezer Slade, and Jeremiah Slade. These whites leased some land for their own use and the rest for the use of parties they represented.[52]

These leases and several others found in the Bertie County courthouse suggest that large numbers of white farmers and plantation owners were already farming in the area and living on reservation lands owned by the Tuscarora before 1803. Oral accounts passed down by slaves to the current inhabitants confirm this. Polly Outlaw recalled being told by her parents that, for the most part, the Native Americans kept to themselves, but lived side by side on their land with white slave owners and their slaves long before their departure in 1803.[53]

By 1803, the last of the Tuscarora had left North Carolina, leaving the last piece of former reservation known as Indian Woods in Bertie County to whites and a number of mixed-blood slaves. Their departure did not end Native American culture and life in Indian Woods, however, since many of the mixed-blood slaves kept their practices alive. After the departure of the Tuscarora from Indian Woods, white farmers moved onto the fertile lands.[54] With the Native Americans gone and the chance of their returning eliminated, Bertie County began to sell off the remaining lands to those already settled in Indian Woods and those desiring to further their farming interest there. Within a few months, all remaining land was in the possession of white plantation owners. Many of the new residents came from nearby Windsor and Lewiston and took advantage of the chance to acquire farm land. The exact number of people in the community at this time is unclear, but the population continued to rise owing to the growing interest in cotton.[55]

When the migrating Tuscarora reached New York, many were not accepted by the New York Nation as earlier bands had been because many of the New York Tuscarora had become Christian and adopted European ways. Many found the Tuscarora from Bertie County shocking in every way, including religion, language, and the fact that they had become mixed with the Africans to whom they had often given refuge while living in North Carolina. Many of these mixed-blood people eventually found it necessary to move on to Canada where other Tuscarora from Bertie County, who had become separated from the New York Nation because of the American Revolution, had settled.[56]

When the Bertie County Tuscarora reached Canada, they were taken in by Tuscarora already there at the Six Nations Reserve on the Grand River in Oshweken, where their descendants reside today.[57] In fact, one of the Tuscarora from Bertie County who appeared to be African spoke the language and kept the customs so well, he was allowed to join the Long House, the governing body of the Six Nations, which was quite an honor.[58]

Since many of the Bertie County Tuscarora wound up in Canada during the War of 1812, some local whites attempted to use that as a reason to relieve them of their land claims. But most of the Tuscarora living in Canada had grown tired of war and strife, and remained neutral. The recognized nation living in Lewiston, New York actually provided warriors to help defend the state, thus the United States, during the war and continued to support the new government throughout the period.[59] The Tuscarora and their relatives in New York continued to claim their former lands in Indian Woods and regain ownership of the lands taken during the American Revolution. The first recorded attempt by the Tuscarora to regain this land or be paid for it after their departure in 1803 was in 1815 when Chiefs Sacarusa and Longboard sued the heirs of William King for money due on land leased by the Tuscarora upon their departure to New York. The court held that the grant of 1717 by Governor Eden was absolute and did not require the Native Americans to remain on the land, thus forcing the heirs of William King to pay reparations to the Tuscarora.[60]

Shortly after this court ruling in 1820, a religious dispute arose on the New York Reserve. Tuscarora there who had converted to Christianity were opposed by others who believed that it was in the best interest of the nation to continue to practice their traditional religion. The debate over religion split the Tuscarora living on the New York Reserve and caused about 70 anti-Christians to leave and join their brothers with the Six Nations on the Grand River Reserve. This may have also prompted a group that ended up settling in Peoria, Illinois to leave as well. Encouraged to move there by government officials who wanted their land in New York, they settled among the Peoria Native Americans, only to be forcibly removed to Indian Territory (Oklahoma) in the 1830s, along with the other midwestern Native Americans.[61]

The state of North Carolina eventually purchased the Tuscarora lands in Bertie County after receiving a memorial from the chiefs of the Tuscarora Nation in New York on November 12, 1828. This memorial was sent to P.B. Porter, secretary of war, and it stated that two principal Tuscarora chiefs, Sacarusa and Longboard, were returning to North Carolina "for the purpose of adjusting some claims that the Nation supposes itself to have on land within your state from which they formerly emigrated."[62] In 1829, all leased and owned lands claimed by the Tuscarora were put under the supervision of Alfred M. Slade with the consent of the necessary chiefs.[63]

After an examination by a special committee chaired by George E. Spruill from Bertie County, and upon its recommendation, the Tuscarora were paid the sum of $3,250 on

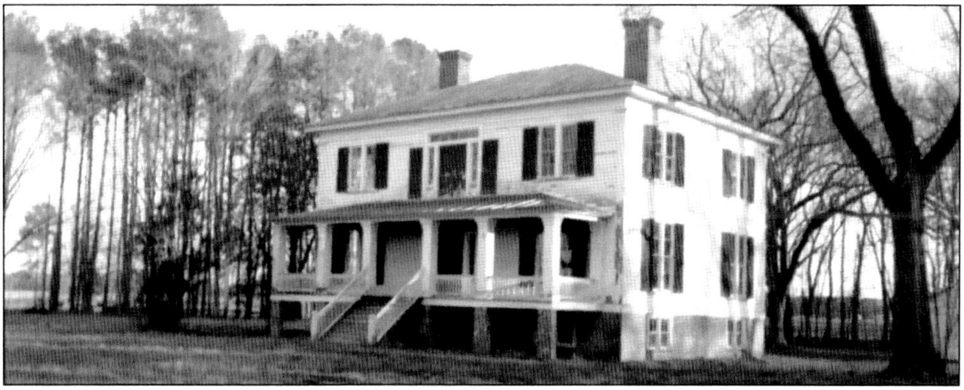

One of the sites of the Great Slave Conspiracy in 1802 was David Outlaw's home in Indian Woods. The son of Ralph Outlaw, David served in Congress from 1848 to 1852. Though destroyed by fire, David's home was located across Indian Woods Road from the home of his son Edward, who was a captain in the Confederate army during the Civil War and sheriff of the county following the war. Edward's house still stands. (Courtesy of SHC, UNC.)

November 19, 1831 for approximately 8,000 acres of former reservation land in Windsor, North Carolina. The agreement was finalized with the consent of Chief William Chew and others and was supposed to end claims by the Tuscarora to all lands leased or owned in Bertie County by the Tuscarora. With the state legally purchasing the land, the white plantation owners who owned or leased land on the reservation were pleased.[64] Even today, however, the Tuscarora still claim the land and with the confusion between the factions in various places, including North Carolina, Canada, Oklahoma, and New York to name a few, it is understandable that the land issue may never be resolved to everyone's satisfaction.

By the early 1800s, the former Tuscarora reservation, which once contained over 40,000 acres, was settled by white plantation owners and their African and mixed-blood part-Tuscarora slaves. These part-Tuscarora, part-African and, in some cases, part-white slaves would continue to work the land and pass on many of the Tuscarora farming practices, religious beliefs, and cooking habits. They would merge Native American, African, and European cultures to create their own culture, which was a combination of all three. The residents of Bertie County would remember their Native American ancestry, but forget their nation. They, however, would not be forgotten by the Tuscarora in other parts of North Carolina, New York, or Canada.[65]

Many of their mixed-blood cousins, like Laura Joseph of the New York Reserve, the sister of Mad Bear, a great Tuscarora shaman, and who, like her brother, is of mixed ancestry (black and Tuscarora), would continue to remember and claim these historic lands. In 1996, Joseph stated that the state of North Carolina was still paying and had been paying the chiefs of the New York clans for lands in Indian Woods.[66]

Chief Leon Lockler of Robeson County, North Carolina, stated that his ancestors, who were also from Bertie County, were away on a hunting trip in 1803, which sometimes took several weeks, when the others departed for New York. Thinking them dead or enslaved, his ancestors migrated to Maxton in Robeson County where they still reside today. Chief

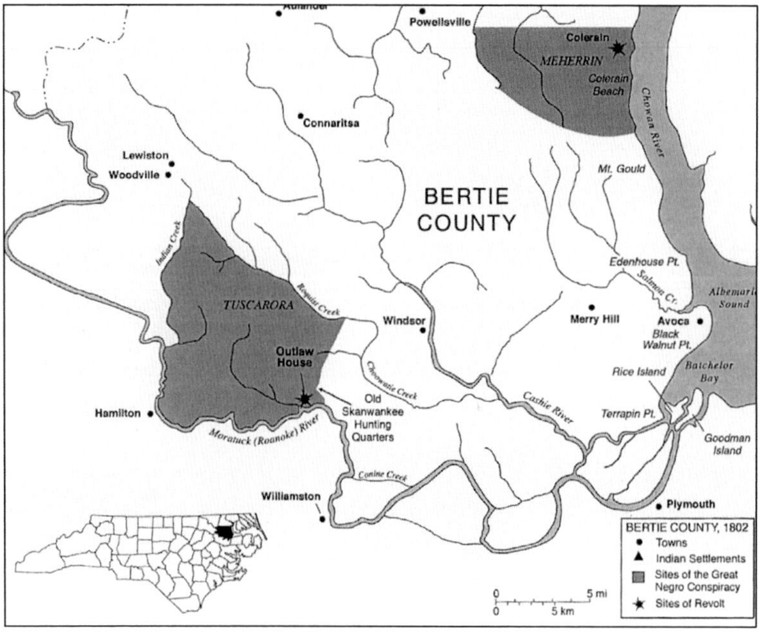

In Bertie County, the Great Slave Conspiracy of 1802 played out on the Meherrin Indian Reservation in Colerain and the Tuscarora Indian Reservation in Indian Woods.

Lockler further stated that his ancestors never agreed to sell the Indian Woods reservation and that he is preparing to sue the state of North Carolina for the return of Indian Woods to his people. Similar claims were made by the Bertie County descendants in New York and Canada.[67]

Very little is known about the Tuscarora by the present mixed inhabitants of Indian Woods in Bertie County. What is known is passed on orally. The older residents of the community relate what they were told by their grandparents and parents. Lucenda H. Hill, 79 years of age when interviewed in Bertie County, remembered her grandfather Charlie Rascoe telling her of his early days as a water bucket boy during slavery. He also related stories about the Tuscarora. She stated that in his telling of the old history of Indian Woods, he revealed that where she lived, in the southern part of Bertie County near the Roanoke River, was once underwater, but the Native Americans built a series of pipes that they used to drain the land for farming. Those pipes are said to still be under various parts of the county. Lucenda went on to state that she became aware of the truth of the story only after modern farm machinery began breaking the pipes up.[68]

Lord Cornwallis Cherry, a farmer and large landowner who is part-Tuscarora, stated that a Native American burial ground was located on Pugh Road. He noted that when the road was being built, the road crews dug up skeletons and many Native American artifacts, including tomahawks, arrowheads, and charms. These statements were supported by other residents of the community. When they were asked where the Native Americans punished those who broke the law, all indicated the same area, the "Indian Gallows," a clearing across from the old Kings Rosenwald school and near the home of Rosetta Bond on Indian Woods Road, where twin gigantic oak trees once stood before being struck by lighting and uprooted around 1892.[69]

5. Religion, Cotton, Tobacco, and Peanuts: The Antebellum Years, 1803–1861

It is ironic that the Tuscarora would leave Bertie County just as it was undergoing a religious transformation that would forever change the county and all of eastern North Carolina. From the end of the 1790s, North Carolina, along with all of the South, underwent a religious awakening. For a state and county in which most people professed no organized or established faith as late as 1752, what occurred from 1797 to 1803 can only be described as phenomenal. Churches began to spring up everywhere in the state and were attended regularly by white and black residents. Fire and brimstone sermons at revivals throughout the county, focusing on sinners in the hands of an angry god destined for eternal damnation in the fires of hell, drove increasing numbers of residents to church. Rich, poor, slave owner, slave—all were driven to repent and rebuke their evil ways.[1]

Although slaves during the early colonial period were allowed to practice their native religions along with Christianity, by 1800 slave owners began to prohibit non-Christian religions. The Great Revival, which began in south-central Kentucky in the summer of 1800, began to convert sinners into devoted Christians. The church of choice for most of these Southerners became the Southern Baptist church. By far, the church of choice in Bertie County was Baptist. Masters throughout the county and state were moved to manumit their slaves on their death bed to save their souls from eternal damnation.[2]

State legislators became so alarmed that they made it a requirement by law that slaves be willed to family members and requested that preachers of established churches instruct their members on the sanctity of being good and saintly masters. After all, we are servants of God, who never mistreats his people. Southern lawmakers and clergy were compelled to develop a religious rationale for the institution of slavery or face a calamity. To ease their collective consciences, slaves were compelled to attend church and hear sermons with their masters. By 1803, churches and, thereby, religion was everywhere in Bertie County.[3]

Slaves and free blacks joined the church and some were even allowed to preach. Whites in the county and region would live to regret this. The Bible studied by black preachers had an entirely different meaning to them than that of their white counterparts. Beginning with Gabriel Prosser in Virginia, black preachers chose to preach on the children of Israel and how God delivered them from bondage in Pharaoh's Egypt. These sermons moved slaves and they became filled with the "holy ghost" and danced, shouted, and sang. Eventually, church members who held a strong believe in God wanted to do "his will." His will, Prosser would tell his Virginia congregation, was for them to be free and for the institution of slavery to be destroyed. In the year 1800, as a result of his teachings, Prosser would assemble 1,000 slaves in preparation for a march on Richmond. Word spread from plantation to plantation by slaves and black ministers.

Although this revolt was discovered and put down by the Virginia state militia, its impact was felt through southeastern Virginia and northeastern North Carolina. In fact, it led directly to the Great Slave Conspiracy of Bertie County in 1802 in which black ministers were also involved.[4] Although both Prosser's revolt and the Great Slave Conspiracy were put down, and slaves forbidden to read the Bible and worship without whites being present, the fear evoked throughout the county and region shook the new religious foundations. As more and more slaves converted and became members of the church, so did attempts by slaves and anti-slavery forces in North Carolina to attack the institution of slavery from within the church. To prevent slaves and anti-slavery whites from plotting against slave owners, whites strengthened slave codes that regulated the movements and sermons of slaves, increased slave patrols, and refused to allow slaves to worship without whites present.[5]

The slaves of Bertie County, however, continued to worship in secret until emancipation, after being forbidden by their masters to worship together. The African-American members of Indian Woods Baptist Church, located in the Indian Woods township, recorded in their church history that their ancestors worshiped in secret at the foot of the great "Gospel Oak," which was still located at Grabtown at the time of the publication of this book. Mrs. Catherine Bond, retired school teacher, life-long resident of Bertie County, and member of Spring Hill Baptist Church, noted that her mother told her that slaves were forbidden to pray and that her grandparents had to place buckets on their heads when they did pray to keep their voices from being overheard.[6]

While Bertie County embraced religion and saw church membership grow, it struggled to reconcile faith with slaveholding. Beyond teaching slaves that even God had servants and when slaves were faithful and obedient God was pleased, it is unclear how slaveholders in the county dealt with the moral dilemma of owning slaves on a daily basis. Nevertheless, by 1850, both slavery and religion were flourishing in the county. The 1850 census reported that there were ten Baptist, four Methodist, one Episcopal, and one Free church in the county. The census also reported that slaves made up 58.5 percent of the county's population of 12,851.[7]

The start of the nineteenth century also signaled the opening of a new age of agriculture in Bertie County. When the first English settlers moved to Bertie County from Virginia, they brought with them their commercial methods of growing and cultivating their main cash crop, tobacco. These were a combination of Native American traditional methods of cultivation and the European method of mass production, which required large amounts of slave labor and large plantations. Because tobacco planters chose to grow tobacco yearly, they quickly exhausted the soil and were forced to clear new land near their plantations or move to new lands that were not being used for farming.[8]

Although cotton was just as labor intensive as tobacco and also exhausted the land after several years of continuous growing, it became less labor intensive than tobacco after the invention of the cotton gin by Eli Whitney in 1790. Prior to the development of the cotton gin, large numbers of slaves were needed to pick the seeds out of enough cotton to make several bales that would bring a good market price. With the invention of the cotton gin, one slave using a machine could do in hours what previously took several days for over 100 slaves. This freed large numbers of slaves to help plant, cultivate, and harvest larger fields of cotton. Not only was cotton no longer as labor intensive as tobacco, but by the early 1800s, it was far more profitable because of the high demand for it by England's growing textile industry.[9]

Generally, growing cotton required seed planting and the periodic hoeing of the field to remove crab grass, which would overtake the seedlings if unchecked. Then, once the crop matured, it could be harvested by even the youngest slaves who, with their parents, filled burlap bags and loaded them onto wagons. This would be repeated throughout the fall until the crop was harvested.[10]

Tobacco, on the other hand, required more labor. Young tobacco plants rather than seeds had to be planted and handled with great care. As the plants matured, they had to be topped, which entailed the breaking off of the top flowering part of the plant. Next, the plants had to be suckered, which involved the removal of small sprouts from between the stalk and more mature leaves of tobacco. Suckering was done several times before harvesting. While topping and suckering, slaves were also required to look for and kill tobacco worms, which destroyed the leaves. At harvest time, slaves would prime the tobacco, which entailed pulling off the lower three or four bottom leaves that had begun to yellow. Every fourth row, there was a gap left for a horse, mule, or ox-drawn wagon. Four slaves were used, two on either side of the wagon. Crouched over all day, these slaves pulled tobacco leaves, periodically rising with armfuls of tobacco that they laid in neat rows on the wagons.[11]

Since most stalks of tobacco stood about 4 to 5 feet high and contained about 12 leaves, at least 3 priming sessions were required for each field. The last of these priming sessions was called striping, and generally all remaining tobacco leaves were removed from the

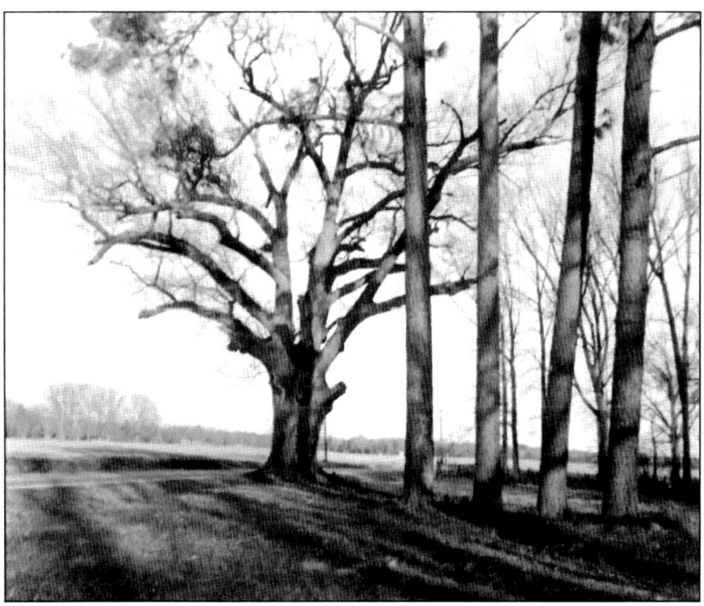

The Gospel Oak, located at Grabtown in Indian Woods near the Outlaw House, served as a trading post for the Tuscarora Indians after 1717. It earned its name when slaves who later founded Indian Woods Baptist Church gathered there in secret to pray and worship. (Courtesy of SHC, UNC.)

stalk. Slaves then loaded mule-drawn wagons with tobacco, which was taken to barns. There, child slaves handed the tobacco leaves to adult female slaves, who tied them with the leaves hanging down onto poles about 1 inch in diameter and about 3 feet long. These poles of tobacco were then given to male slaves, who hung the poles on the inside roofs of the barns. Throughout the nineteenth century, the tobacco was dried using burners powered by kerosene.[12]

After the tobacco dried for about two weeks, it was taken down from the tobacco barns, taken off the poles, which were put away for the next year, and laid on 5-foot by 6-foot burlap sheets. When 60 to 100 pounds of tobacco were placed on these sheets, they were tied by binding the four corners of the sheet together across the pile of tobacco. These bales of tobacco were then loaded onto wagons or boats and taken to Windsor, where they were sold at the tobacco auction.[13]

As cotton began to replace tobacco, Bertie County moved from being a major tobacco producer to one of the state's leading cotton producers. Therefore, the production of cotton dominated the antebellum period in the county. Slave owners, including the Pughs, Williams, Smallwoods, Outlaws, Spruills, Rascoes, and Gilliams, also began to clear and move onto Tuscarora land. In Indian Woods between 1800 and 1840, cotton and the lack of unexhausted farmland also caused more Virginians, North Carolinians, and South Carolinians to move farther west into what had been the Southwest Territory. This migration separated many Bertie County families. Loved ones, slave as well as slave owner, left Bertie County and joined the westward migration.[14]

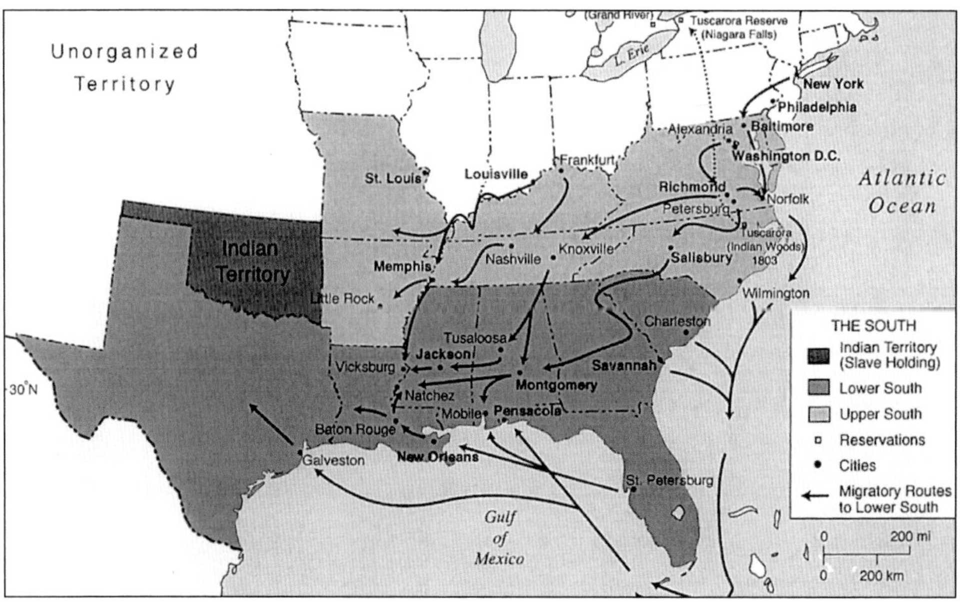

This map shows population movement into the "Cotton Kingdom" during the 1800s. Bertie County saw many of it residents, both white and black, migrate to the Deep South. Driven by the economic importance of cotton and new land made available as a result of Indian removal, many people relocated to Georgia, Alabama, Mississippi, Louisiana, and Texas.

Although many white men went willingly, most white women, white children, and slaves had no choice. Slaves suffered the most as slave women and men were forced to leave husbands, wives, and children behind when slave owner's sons were given a portion of their fathers' estate, including slaves, to start new lives in the Deep South or the Southwest.[15] For those who stayed behind, life on plantations in Bertie County, like other rural plantations in the South, continued to be difficult. Slaves worked in the fields from sunup to sundown while white slave owners enjoyed the comforts and wealth that slavery provided. There were, however, degrees of happiness experienced by those whites living on the plantations. Family was the most important thing to most Southerners in Bertie County and the roles of various family members were well defined and rigidly adhered to.[16]

White women were taught to be good wives and mothers from childhood to adulthood. As a result, they were given a very limited education and were heavily supervised to avoid any premarital relationships that might embarrass their families. White men were taught to be the heads of their households and were expected one day to either take over the family estate or buy their own.[17]

Since the early 1700s, whites in Bertie County, like the rest of North Carolina, were responsible for paying for their education and that of their children. As a result, the level of education varied widely from family to family. For example, David Stone of Windsor and David Outlaw of Indian Woods were very well educated. Stone even had a personal library that was considered one of the best in the state.[18]

Others, mostly poor whites, could afford no education and were as illiterate as the slaves, who were prohibited from being educated by law.[19] Because money and property determined who would be educated and how much education one would receive, some free blacks managed to obtain a basic education for themselves and their children. So bad was the lack of education statewide that, between 1815 and 1817, Archibald D. Murphey compiled a series of reports on North Carolina education, called "Reports on Education," which he issued to state legislators in 1817.[20] The reports called for the establishment of a public education system for the state and state funding for teachers, books, and schoolhouses. As a result of Murphey's report, the North Carolina state legislature passed a public school law in 1839. A year later, the state opened its first public schools. These schools greatly benefited the poor whites of Bertie County, but were not utilized by the large planters, who preferred private education. It must also be noted that even in these new public schools, males were given a better education than females because of societal attitudes in those days.[21]

In typical Southern communities such as Bertie County, young men were also given more freedom than young women. Although young men were not encouraged to be promiscuous, since children fathered out of wedlock were an embarrassment particularly for wealthy Southern families, when it did occur it was almost expected and was not greeted with the disbelief and outrage that a young elite white woman's parenthood would generate.[22]

In spite of the differences in upbringing, there appeared to be genuine love between siblings. When they were separated as a result of marriage, schooling, war, or travel, they often wrote each other and expressed their desire to be reunited. Throughout the antebellum period, the daughters of the planter elite of Bertie County were taught to be

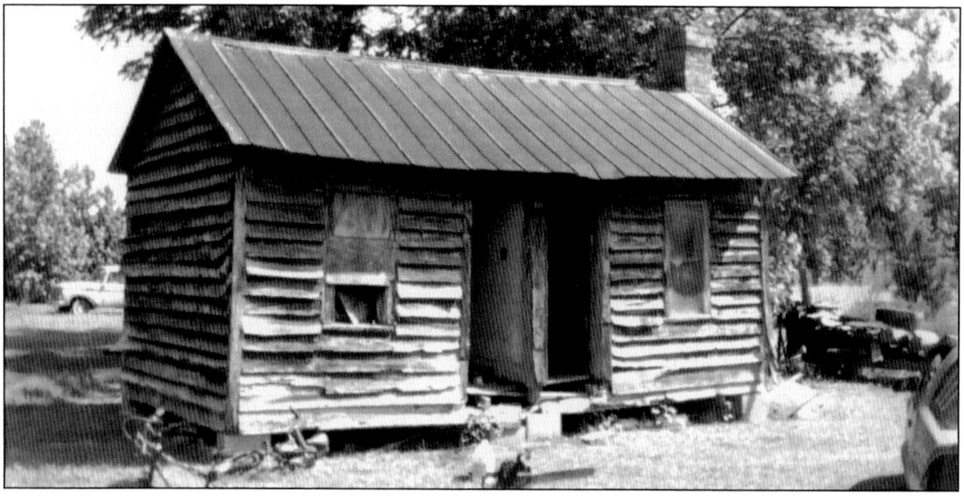

Two families would live in a typical slave cabin in Bertie County, one on the right and one on the left, regardless of the size of the families. As many as 12 people could have shared one room. (Courtesy of SHC, UNC.)

good mothers and wives, with the understanding that black "Mammies" would raise their children and do their domestic chores.[23] Young men in Bertie County were trained to run their father's plantations. This entailed record-keeping, including the numbers of slaves bought and sold, supplies needed to run the plantation, and the securing of luxury items such as furniture, crystal, fine china, and clothes, for themselves and their families. Young men were also responsible for reinvesting and saving the profits from the sale of slaves, cotton, and tobacco.[24]

During the colonial period, this was made difficult by the lack of banks close to Bertie County. The closest reputable banks were located in Virginia and South Carolina during the 1700s and required long and usually dangerous journeys to deposit and withdraw funds. Since Jamestown and Norfolk, Virginia were closer than Charlestown, South Carolina, most depositors from Bertie County chose to bank in Virginia or keep their money on their plantations. As a result, when the Bank of Cape Fear and the Bank of New Bern were chartered in 1804, becoming the first banks chartered in North Carolina, many of the residents of Bertie County, who felt more comfortable placing their money in a North Carolina bank, began to travel to and some even moved to New Bern. When Windsor native David Stone, who lived about 2 miles from the home of David Outlaw, became governor of North Carolina in 1808, he worked to bring banking closer to Bertie County and to make it more secure by establishing a state bank.[25]

As a result of Stone's work, in 1810, the Bank of North Carolina was incorporated. This bank established regional and local branches, including one in Windsor. The bank provided financial services for all the residents of Bertie County. As profits from cotton continued to increase during the 1800s, the planters of Bertie County continued to clear land, buy, and sell slaves, and live a life that was very different from that of the thousands of slaves and poor whites who surrounded them.[26]

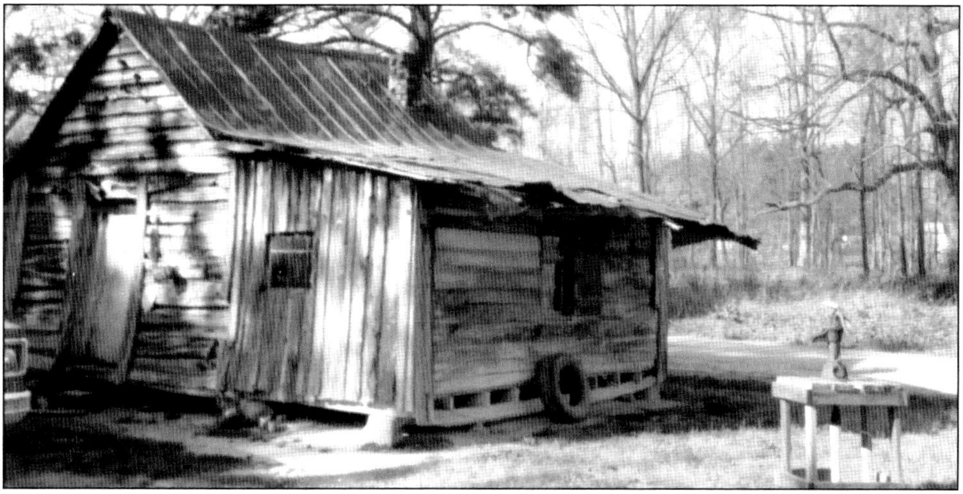

During the antebellum period many poor whites in the county could not afford land, slaves, or even adequate housing. This one-room shack in Indian Woods with an outside water pump was built in the 1800s. (Courtesy of SHC, UNC.)

During the years from 1802 to 1861, the plantations of Bertie County began to produce cotton almost exclusively. Although some tobacco was still being grown and sold, the demand for cotton drove planters to devote more and more acreage to its growth. As a result, Bertie County was as much a part of the Deep South, or "cotton kingdom," as Alabama, Georgia, South Carolina, Mississippi, Texas, or Louisiana. It was, however, a struggle to get the cotton to cotton mills for processing because, before 1818, the closest cotton mill was located in Lincoln County in the western part of the state. Therefore, Bertie County had to send its cotton overland or by water to Virginia for processing.[27]

In 1818, however, the Battle family of Rocky Mount, North Carolina, a few miles west of Bertie County in Nash County, opened a cotton mill and began to receive large amounts of cotton. The ability of planters to get their crops to markets was later greatly enhanced by new and improved roads, rail lines, and expanded navigation of the state's coastal waterways, including the Chowan and Roanoke Rivers, from 1828 to 1861. Before rail lines were built and roads improved, most planters in Bertie County relied on the Roanoke and Chowan Rivers and seasonal roads.[28] In 1828, William Albright began to promote construction of the first railroads in North Carolina. By 1833, the state had built and utilized an experimental railroad in Raleigh, North Carolina. These first railroads opened a new age in transportation in North Carolina. Although there would be no railroads built in Bertie County until after the Civil War, rail lines did stop at North Carolina towns and cities. Many residents also saw the potential for trade if a railroad could be brought through Bertie County.[29]

By 1849, the North Carolina Railroad was chartered by the General Assembly of North Carolina. From 1850 to 1861, new rail lines began to be constructed in the eastern parts of the state in Fayetteville, Goldsboro, Rocky Mount, and Weldon. By 1861, a line was completed from Raleigh to New Bern. In spite of the local interest in having a rail line laid through Bertie County, the county was overlooked until the 1870s.[30] As a result of the lack of good roads and rail service, Bertie County, like the rest of northeastern North Carolina, began to stagnate. The isolation of the county, rural living, and slavery with its restrictions had for generations retarded the educational, economic, and social growth of slaves and its poor white residents. The lack of railroads during the mid-nineteenth century did not help this situation.[31]

In this same time period, many of the young men and women of the educated planter class began to leave the county in search of better economic opportunities in the cotton kingdom. As soil exhaustion and limited inheritances caused the migration of Virginians into Bertie County, the impact of the migration of many whites to the Deep South and the Southwest, searching for more economic opportunities, was being felt throughout the county and northeastern North Carolina by the 1850s. Those who remained in Bertie County found the area increasingly isolated from the economic and urban growth of the other parts of the state, particularly the Piedmont, near the new rail lines that began to criss-cross the state.[32]

The lack of access to rail service in Bertie from 1830 to 1860, and the subsequent economic devastation of eastern North Carolina during the Civil War, helped reduce what had for two centuries been the wealthiest and most influential part of North Carolina to one of the poorest sections of the entire state, which remained the case by the start of the twenty-first century. Although the white population in Bertie and surrounding counties became better educated, due to the development of public education in North Carolina during this period, it also became more isolated. Railroads meant commerce, increased population, growth, and change. Those communities like Raleigh and Durham that had railroads prospered and those without railroads were left behind.[33]

To achieve these internal improvements, the landed aristocracy of Bertie County and the east, which continued to maintain its control of the state General Assembly during the early antebellum period, had to be coerced into action by the more populous and under-represented west. Since the Regulator War of 1771, Bertie County slaveholders and others of eastern

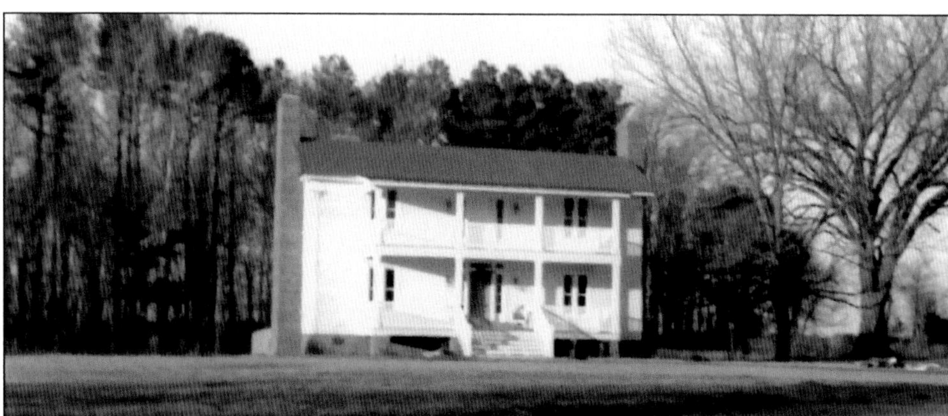

The Spruill house, built in Indian Woods in the 1800s, is an example of a prosperous slaveholder's home in Bertie during the antebellum period. (Courtesy of SHC, UNC.)

North Carolina enjoyed complete control of both houses of the state legislature and the governor's office. These men refused to allow the west equal representation even after the Revolutionary War and the ratification of the United States Constitution by the state in 1789. As a result, resentment in the west for the east festered and grew. Being landlocked, it was imperative that roads and rail lines be constructed and improved.[34]

The westerners, mostly yeoman farmers, were also unhappy with the expense and requirements of maintaining the institution of slavery in the east where the majority resided. Westerners pointed to the years from 1800 to 1836 when eastern North Carolina was directly involved in or impacted by major slave revolts or conspiracies. Those incidents included Gabriel Prosser's revolt in Southampton, Virginia in 1800, which led to the Great Slave Conspiracy in Indian Woods and Colerain in Bertie County in 1802; Nat Turner's Revolt in Southampton, Virginia in 1831; and the rumored insurrection of slaves and free blacks in neighboring Pasquotank County in 1835.[35] These revolts, particularly the Great Slave Conspiracy in Indian Woods and Colerain, and the large slave population of Bertie County kept whites in the east in a constant state of alarm. Slave patrols were increased and slaves suspected of plotting revolts were executed at the state's expense.[36]

All these things were paid for by state taxpayers, including westerners who by and large owned no slaves. These issues and the representation controversy all came to a head in the Convention of 1835. This resulted in several amendments to the state constitution and the granting of more representation to the west. Many eastern slaveholders were not happy with the results of the convention, but bowed to the pressure of the west. With the end of this crisis in 1836, Bertie County turned its attention to cotton production and regulating the institution of slavery.[37]

Bertie County slaves did many things to show their displeasure with the institution of slavery. As discussed, one of the ways was by revolting, but the most common way to rebel was running away. As early as the mid-1600s, slaves began to run away from their captors in Virginia and later in North Carolina, hiding in swamps such as the Great Dismal Swamp.[38] These slaves created large Maroon communities, which served as sanctuaries for the runaways. Because of the nature of the swamp and fierce determination by many of the slaves, recapture was almost impossible. Throughout Bertie County, there were smaller swamps that slaves used to hide in temporarily while they planned their escapes.[39] Many slaves, assisted by friendly Native Americans, Quakers, Moravians, and abolitionists, also made their way north via the Underground Railroad. From 1748 to 1775, 128 slaves were reported to have run away, 114 men and 14 women. The average age was 28.[40] As best as can be determined, these numbers increased during the early nineteenth century. From 1775 to 1865, the numbers of slaves running away from Bertie County continued to increase, with most fleeing during the Civil War. They only returned following the war as soldiers who had served in the Union army.[41]

Slave marriages were not considered legal, but they were allowed to marry with permission from their masters. In a note dated July 24, 1825, a slave owner in Bertie County writes an unnamed slave owner to inform him of his slave James's desire to marry one of his slave women. In the short note, he states that as far as he knows, James is "well disposed," meaning of good character.[42] Slaves were often sold or loaned out in the same manner. If a slave possessed a skill such as carpentry, sewing, bricklaying, or

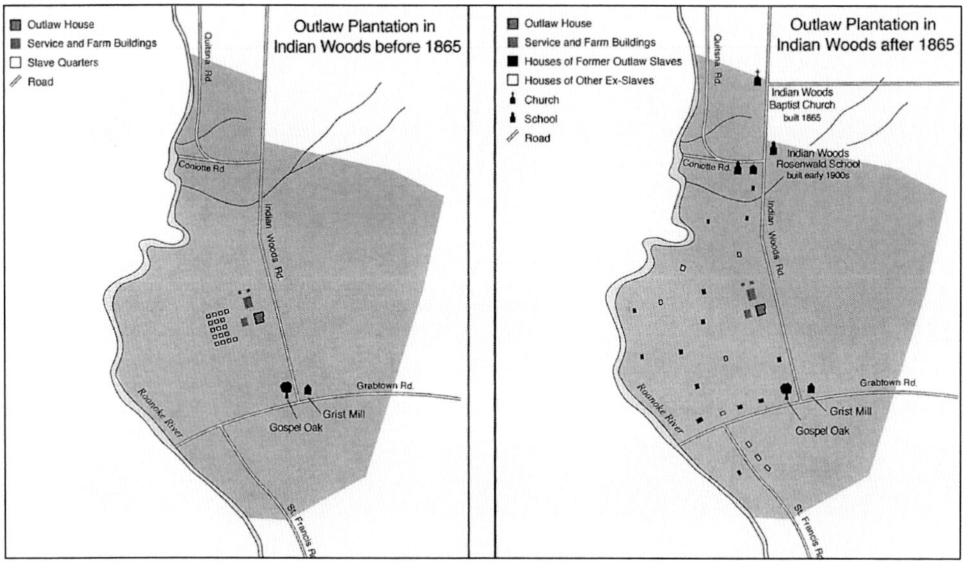

The layout of the Outlaw plantation of Indian Woods, mapped here before and after the Civil War, is typical of most plantations in the county and in the South before and after emancipation.

blacksmithing, he or she was of great value to the owner, and it was not uncommon for the slave to be rented to a neighbor. David Outlaw rented one of his female slaves who could sew to a neighbor.[43] Most plantations were self-sufficient and raised livestock and consumable foods in addition to cash crops like tobacco and cotton. One of the largest and most prosperous plantations in the Windsor township during the antebellum era was the David Outlaw plantation.

During the antebellum period, there were a number of free blacks with families scattered throughout Bertie County. In fact, there had been some free blacks in the county from its beginning in the early 1700s. There were also free blacks who owned slaves in the county. The first census recorded in 1790 that Samuel Jackson, a free black, owned 11 slaves. By the 1830 census, five free blacks, four of whom were women, owned slaves. They included Mary James (1), Sally James (1), Penelope Hill (3), Jane Ash (5), and Willie Tutle (1). As the numbers from the 1830 census seem to indicate, free blacks who owned slaves on paper simply purchased either their children, spouse, or some other family member and were therefore seen as slaveholders, but this was not the norm.[44]

Since free African-American children were not allowed to attend school with whites, in 1818, the Bertie Academy was established by free blacks for their children. The school initially allowed only males, but eventually taught females also. The academy lasted well into the twentieth century. The school consisted of grades two through nine and had a principal who supervised teachers, disciplined students, and taught courses of his own. Free blacks from anywhere in Bertie and the surrounding counties were allowed to attend.[45]

Although some free blacks living in Bertie County showed their dislike for the institution of slavery and their quasi-free position by voting, supporting slave revolts and the Anti-Slavery movement, none supported the colonization movement of the 1820s.[46]

Began by Paul Coffee in 1820, this movement won the support of President James Monroe and other whites who wanted free blacks removed from the United States. At the start of the movement, there were approximately 250 free blacks in Bertie County, ranging in age from 1 to 60.[47] None of these free blacks, unlike those in neighboring counties like Halifax and Hertford, gave money to support sending free blacks back to Africa. Some blacks from neighboring counties even made the trip to Monrovia, Liberia, but those of Bertie, in spite of their hardships in the county, remained. In fact, the only two free blacks in the county that were recorded as giving financial support to the movement did so in 1855. One of those, James L. Bryant, left $534.54 in his estate, which we must assume was paid after his death. The other, James L. Bryan, gave $385.[48] If a slave was lucky enough to gain his or her freedom, he or she often had family members who were still enslaved. As a result, many refused to leave the area where they had been enslaved. They often would attempt to purchase the freedom of other family members and stay and work until their family members were either sold away or they were successful in raising the necessary funds to purchase them. This shows how important family, and what was happening to family members, was to slaves and free blacks in the county during slavery.[49]

Throughout the antebellum period, the state of North Carolina also passed laws denying free blacks the right to vote or move into the state. There were, however, exceptions to the rule, as evidenced by the three registered free blacks recorded in North Carolina. North Carolina also passed stricter laws governing the education and handling of free blacks as a result of revolts in Virginia and northeastern North Carolina. These laws impacted free blacks and slaves in Bertie County in the same way as in other parts of the state.[50] Free blacks and particularly free black landowners in Bertie County before

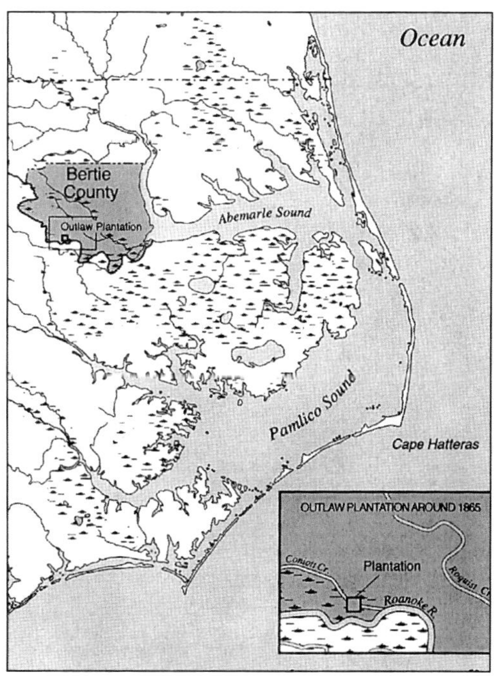

This map shows the location of the Outlaw Plantation of Indian Woods in Bertie County before the Civil War.

emancipation, lived under the constant threat that their property would be taken by whites and that they and their families would be assaulted and sold into slavery. Only having a white guardian protected these blacks from this fate or worse. Although census records from 1800 to 1860 showed an African-American population, including free blacks, which hovered near 60 percent of the county's population, blacks held no power. As slaves, they were viewed only as chattel property.[51] At the end of the Civil War, however, blacks began to purchase more property, own their own land, and many collectively purchased land and materials to build churches for their communities.[52]

Slavery in Bertie County, as best as can be documented, was not unlike slavery anywhere else in North Carolina. Historical writings have dispelled the previous myth that slavery was a benign institution in which the slaves were reasonably content. In fact, slavery has been revealed to be a dehumanizing system of coercion despite the fact that some slaveholders did not brutalize their slaves.[53] Aaron Bazemore of Windsor, who was reared in Indian Woods and was, at the time of his death, more than 100 years old, told stories of how slavery was recounted to him by his grandfather and father. He reported, "In those days a black man had no rights. He had to do whatever he was told; he could not even have a wife."[54] Bazemore also recounted a story (which could not be substantiated) about one black man, whom he did not distinguish as slave or free, who dug a hole in the ground and hid his woman there, and never allowed her to come out for fear of being taken. There she cooked for him and had his children and the whites never found her. Bazemore refused to discuss any details of what he was told about actual day-to-day life as a slave, saying only, "that it was tight and I would rather not talk about it."[55]

It is noted by historians that during slavery most whites owned only one or two slaves. Those slave owners worked the fields along with their slaves. In Bertie County, however, this average was much higher since most slaveholders were wealthy. The county's slaves were used as both field hands and house servants. Most of the male and female slaves worked in the fields, while one or two female and male slaves cooked, cleaned, did laundry, brought in firewood, took care of the master's children, and other personal needs, including caring for the master's horses and buggies. Living and working on isolated plantations caused whites and their slaves to become dependent upon each other. Slaves built houses and barns, repaired broken wagon and farm tools, as well as a host of other jobs. They not only built antebellum Bertie, they maintained and advanced it with their forced labor.[56] The slave master, however, was not as isolated as the slaves because he made monthly or yearly visits to Windsor to pay taxes, attend court, sell crops, and buy supplies, slaves, and manufactured goods.[57]

Like their ancestors, the white residents of Bertie County seemed to maintain a sense of political independence. They, like their ancestors, held a respect for organized assemblies and politics. By 1830, for example, they had managed to form social organizations that kept up with the politics of their day. They expressed support for their favorite political candidates through letters of support and their votes. In one such instance in 1831, six members of the Bertie Social Organization sent a letter of support and friendship to Governor John Branch Enfield, whose character had been attacked by his enemies. He wrote them back responding, "I pray you gentlemen, to accept for yourselves and those you represent, my cordial assurances of respect, esteem and gratitude."[58]

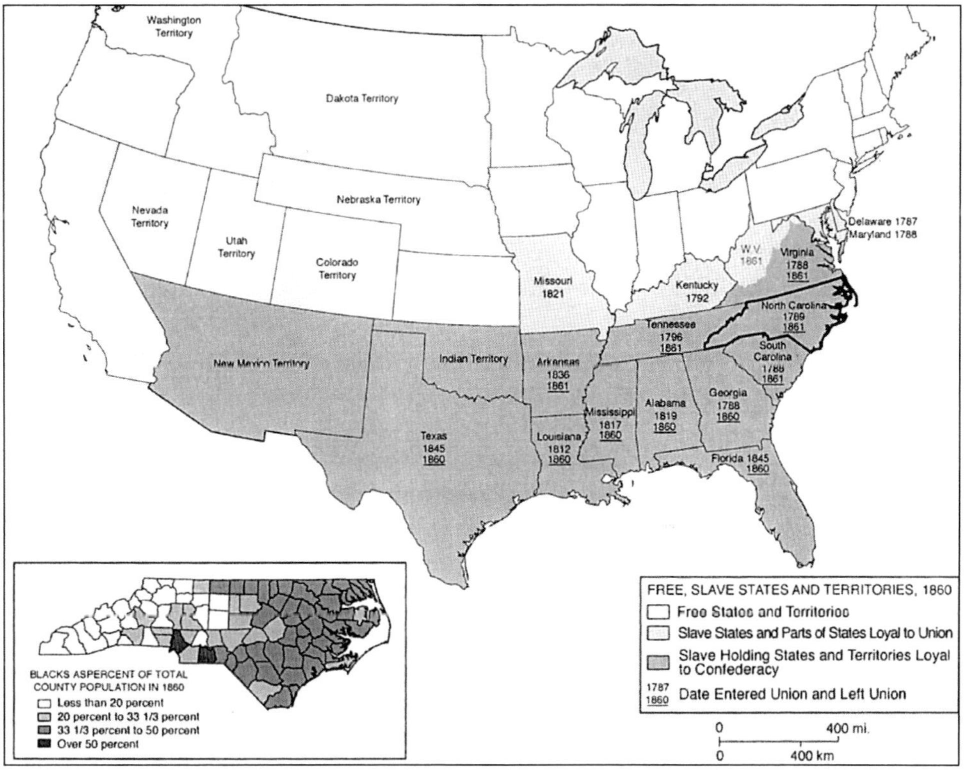

This map shows both slave and free states and territories before the start of the Civil War, along with each's date of admission and secession. Also indicated are North Carolina counties with the greatest slave populations at that time.

A number of residents also became or remained active in local, state, and national politics. One of Bertie County's largest slaveholders, David Outlaw of the Outlaw Plantation, whose father was Ralph Outlaw, was very active in state and national politics, Outlaw was elected to represent North Carolina in the United States Congress from 1848 to 1852. As a member of Congress, he represented the views of many of his family members, friends, and neighbors living in Bertie County. In a speech on the Army Appropriations Bill given on August 3, 1848, Outlaw condemned the Mexican-American War and the acquisition of Mexican territory. He also condemned United States support for the Texas Revolution. He believed that both only increased sectional tensions over whether the land should be slave or free. He also disapproved of the acquisition of the Oregon and Washington territories, which he believed were unjustly given to Northern states at the expense of the South. Outlaw, who was a Whig, refused to discuss the issue of slavery on the floor of the House because he strongly believed that Northerners, who had no first-hand experience with slavery, did not know enough about the institution to discuss it intelligently or judge the South.[59]

Later in 1852, Outlaw again addressed Congress, this time because of concerns over the Compromise of 1850. On June 10, 1852, he stated that Southerners were not only concerned about fugitive slaves, which they had a constitutional right to own, but also the desire of Northern states to repeal the concept of "Popular Sovereignty." During this address, Outlaw warned Congress that when and if the Southern states believed their rights were threatened, they would take action to preserve themselves.[60]

During the presidential election of 1860, the residents of Bertie County, like the rest of North Carolina, continued to support compromise. The election of Abraham Lincoln in 1860, without a single Southern state voting in his favor, was enough however for the lower South to leave the Union. When the lower Southern states of South Carolina, Georgia, Florida, Alabama, Mississippi, and Texas seceded, most white North Carolinians, including many in Bertie County, did not believe North Carolina should join them.[61] Most of the residents of Bertie County were of a similar mind on secession, although for different reasons. Members of the planter class feared what the war would do to trade and the regulation of it. The thought of sovereign Southern states each coining their own money and regulating trade was mind boggling. Furthermore, the cutting off of trade between the county and New England and the mid-Atlantic states, not to mention Britain and the British Caribbean, as a result of war was not something anyone in the county looked forward to. The lower classes in the county, like those in the Appalachian Mountains, saw the coming conflict as not their war, but a war thrust upon them by the planter class. Outlaw was also reluctant to call for secession. In April of 1861, however, all this changed. On April 15, 1861, South Carolina fired on Fort Sumter outside of Charleston, causing its surrender a day later. In response, President Abraham Lincoln called for troops to be raised from each state, including the upper South, to put down the rebellion.[62]

This call for arms impacted the remaining slave states and forced them to decide whether to fight for the Union or against it. As a result of Lincoln's order, Virginia, Arkansas, Tennessee, and North Carolina sided with the lower South, with whom they had kinship ties. Missouri, Kentucky, Maryland, and Delaware, the border states, remained loyal to the Union, but not without strife. Missourians fought a bloody internal civil war over whether or not to secede. Kentucky remained loyal, but not without a secession movement that was quelled by the presence of Union troops. In Maryland, Lincoln ousted the state legislature and the state was placed under marshal law to prevent the nation's capital from being surrounded by the Confederacy.[63] For most North Carolinians and residents of Bertie, it was too much to bear arms against their kinsmen in the lower South; thus, they chose to join them in revolt. Although the future was uncertain, many wealthy families of the county, like the Grimes family, faced it with confidence and resolve.

On May 20, 1861, the state of North Carolina held a special convention in Raleigh at which the state adopted an ordinance of secession.[64] Residents of Bertie County were deeply divided over the war and many poor whites in the county actually joined the Union army and fought against the Confederacy. Large numbers of slaves ran away from their masters' plantations and joined the Union army, fighting throughout eastern North Carolina, southeastern Virginia, and South Carolina. While secession signaled the end of the old social and political order in Bertie County, and as white and slave families chose sides in the coming conflict, agriculture that had sustained the county since its beginning also underwent an amazing metamorphosis.[65]

As tobacco had shaped the colonial period and cotton the antebellum period, a new cash crop that had been around since the late 1500s, peanuts, would shape Bertie County during the Civil War and post–Civil War years. By 1861, peanuts would help many former slaveholders in Bertie County and northeastern North Carolina save their farms during and after the Civil War. The county would build a peanut empire and, by late twentieth century, become one of the nation's leading exporters of peanuts. Prior to the Civil War, peanuts were looked upon as "ground nuts" and, as such, not fit for human consumption or sale. However, they became very popular among the poor and slaves as an inexpensive nutritious supplement to their diets. As the Civil War dragged on and traditional foods became harder to find, peanuts became more and more popular among the elite as well. By the end of the Civil War, with the destruction of the cotton kingdom and the lowering of cotton prices, a few adventurous farmers in Bertie County and other parts of eastern North Carolina began to grow peanuts.[66]

By the end of Reconstruction, a steady market for peanuts had been developed and by the middle of the twentieth century, Bertie County and North Carolina had become one of the nation's leading producers of peanuts. Families like the Outlaws, Gilliams, and Rascoes, who had made their fortunes in the colonial and antebellum periods from the sale of tobacco and cotton and lost them during the Civil War, saw them rebuilt by peanut farms in the late nineteenth and early twentieth centuries. Peanuts would be as much a part of Bertie County's restructuring in the new South as emancipation and Jim Crow.

Bertie County, as Gerald Thomas notes in his book *Divided Allegiances*, was a county torn apart by loyalties to the Confederacy and the Union.[6] Thus, neighbor turned against

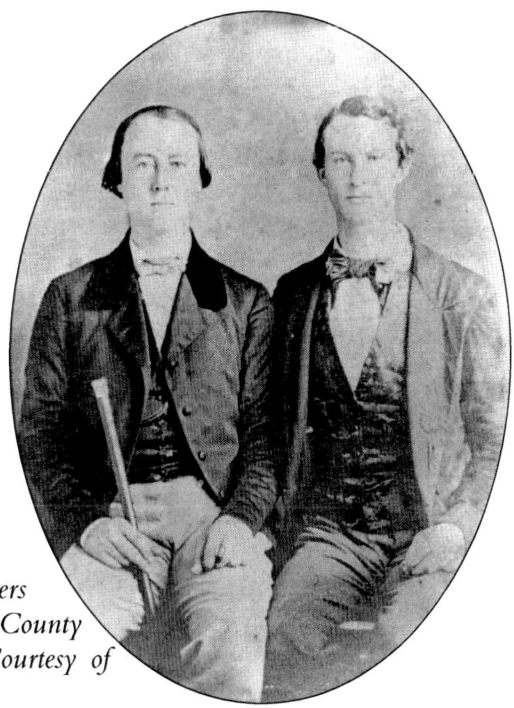

William and Bryan Grimes were members of a wealthy plantation family in Bertie County before the start of the Civil War. (Courtesy of SHC, UNC.)

neighbor as fear and conflict gripped the county during the war. The majority of men from Bertie chose to fight for the Confederacy and were represented in over 37 regiments, departments, and the Bertie County militia and homegaurd. At least 620 men from Bertie joined the Union forces as they moved into eastern North Carolina early in the war. Of the 620 men known to have served in the Union, 222 were whites and 398 were blacks. Of the 222 whites, 214 joined the army and 8 the navy. Of the 398 blacks that served, 349 joined the army and 49 the navy.[67]

Bertie County secessionists and Confederate soldiers referred to North Carolina's blacks and whites who joined the Union army as "Buffaloes." The name was meant to be derogatory in that it was synonymous with thieves, deserters, and outlaws. Buffaloes were also characterized as being ignorant, in need of clothes, and being unable to read or write.[68] Clearly from these statements describing Bertie County's and North Carolina's Union supporters, many were poor or slaves. In Bertie County, these poor whites and slaves most likely chose to support the Union because they were not happy with the economic or social system that was in place in the county before the war. After the Civil War, many of the black troops who remained in the Union army were sent west to fight Native Americans when Congress, on July 28, 1866, authorized the establishment of four permanent all-black military units. Two infantry regiments, the U.S. 24th, which was created from the 38th and 41st Colored Infantry, and U.S. 25th, created from the 39th and 40th Colored Infantry, and two cavalry regiments, the 9th and 10th, were established. These regiments contained eastern North Carolina blacks and were formed from the best of the U.S. Colored Troops (USCT) who were moved by train to Goldsboro, North Carolina and then on to New Orleans before being sent to fight in the west. This is worth noting because, although it is believed that these famed soldiers known the world over as the Buffalo Soldiers got their name from the western Native Americans they fought, it is just as probable that they brought their name with them from eastern North Carolina and Bertie County.[69]

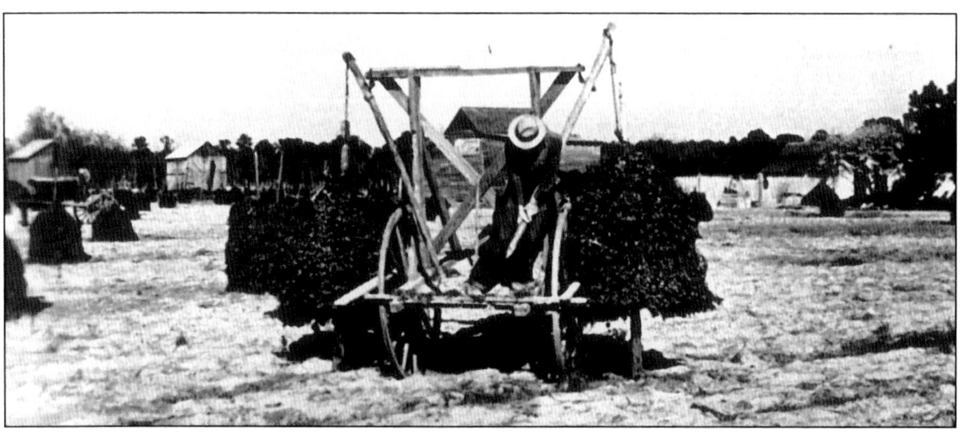

Peanuts are harvested during the late 1800s. Bertie County would, by the twentieth century, help the state of North Carolina become one of the world's leading producers of peanuts. (Courtesy of Frank Stephenson, Chowan College.)

6. A County Divided: The Civil War to the Collapse of Reconstruction, 1861–1877

At the start of the Civil War in Bertie County, as in the rest of North Carolina and the Confederacy, there was no solid South. Blacks both slave and free tended to be pro-Union and, since 59.4 percent of the county's population was black, white supporters of the war, who were in the minority, remained fearful throughout the conflict. Even among the county's whites there was division during the war.[1]

White Southerners who opposed the war showed their opposition in many ways. Some moved north and joined the Union army. Some moved west to avoid the war altogether. Others chose to remain in their home states and counties and wage war for the Union where they were. Pockets of resistance to secession and the Confederacy have been well documented throughout the Appalachian Mountains of eastern Tennessee, northern Alabama, and Georgia, and western North Carolina and Virginia. In fact, West Virginias were so opposed to secession and the "Planters War" that they refused to give up their seats in Congress and seceded from Virginia, earning statehood as a reward after the war.[2] Violent clashes between pro-Union Southern guerrillas and Confederate soldiers are also well documented in these counties. However, in the east, it has been assumed even by local people that support for the war was nearly unanimous.[3]

When the war began, Lincoln gathered his advisors together to come up with a plan to defeat the South and preserve the Union. The resulting plan became known as the Anaconda Plan. This plan held three main objectives: to blockade Southern ports using the navy; to gain control of the Mississippi River and cut the Confederacy in two; and to capture the Confederate capital of Richmond. The first objective, blockading and capturing Southern ports, began by August 1861 in North Carolina. This task became a joint army and navy exercise, carried out by Major Generals Benjamin Franklin Butler and Ambrose Everett Burnside and Commodore Silas H. Stringham.[4]

Their goal was to seize control of the forts on the Outer Banks, which would give them control of the Currituck, Albemarle, Pamlico, Core, and Bogue Sounds, as well as the Chowan, Roanoke, Tar-Pamlico, and Neuse-Trent Rivers that emptied into them.[5] By December of 1861, Butler and his men, with the support of Commodore Stringham and support of loyal whites and blacks living in the coastal counties, won control of Hatteras on the Outer Banks of North Carolina where he declared slaves who were under his control as "contraband." Butler not only refused to return them to slaveholders, but he armed and used the slaves as soldiers and laborers to support his advance. He captured

Hatteras and the Hatteras Inlet in late August of 1861, opening the Outer Banks, sounds, and eastern North Carolina to Burnside's attacks, which included forts on Roanoke Island, the Outer Banks, and ending at New Bern and Beaufort.[6]

Burnside then proceeded to attack, raid, and confiscate materials such as food and supplies from forts and towns from Elizabeth City to Williamston in northeastern North Carolina. As a result, the residents of Bertie County were heavily involved in the Civil War from the start of the conflict.[7] The county, in conjunction with the neighboring counties of Hertford, Northampton and Martin, fought off coastal attacks and defended the Roanoke and Chowan River valleys. Most of the residents of Bertie County supported the Confederacy with money, military service, and labor.[8] Many plantation owners in Bertie feared that the huge Union army, which was camped at New Bern and had control of all of eastern North Carolina by way of the Pamlico and Albemarle Sounds, would raid their plantations for supplies and destroy what they could not use. In fact, there were raids on Windsor, Winton, Washington, Williamston, Hamilton, Plymouth, Edenton, and Elizabeth City during the war.[9]

After 1863, fighting involving both black and white residents of Bertie County took place on the Chowan, Cashie, and Roanoke Rivers, at Winton, Windsor, Plymouth, Williamston, and Hamilton where North Carolina erected Fort Branch. Union troops, including many runaway slaves from Bertie County, battled the sons of slaveholders from

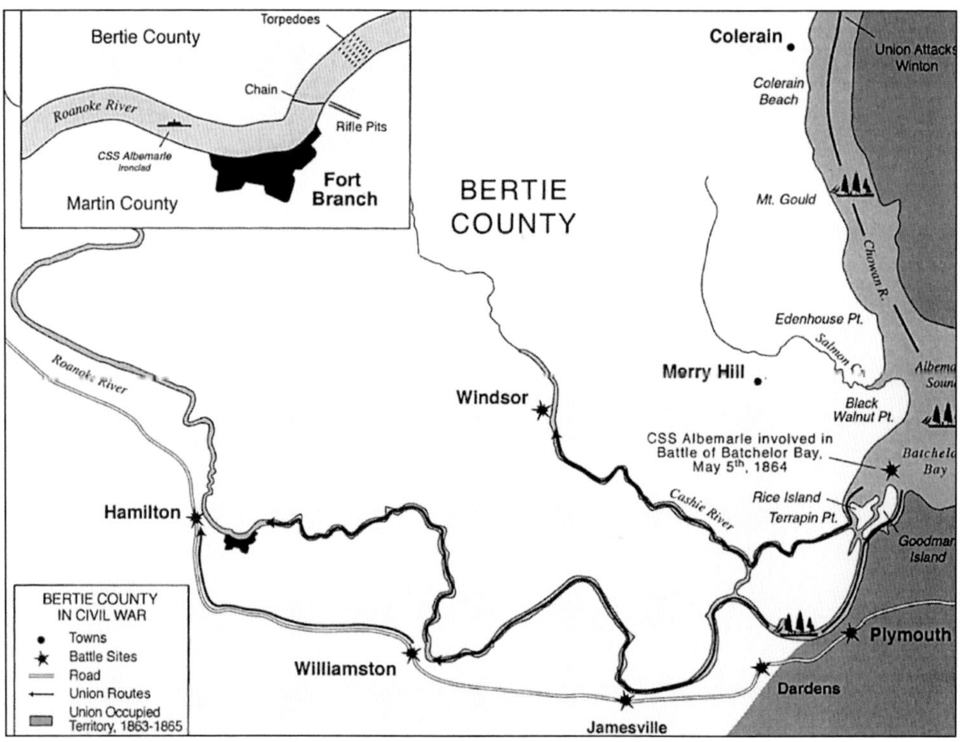

Fort Branch, near Hamilton, was built and staffed with the help of county residents and was used to protect the Roanoke River valley from the advancing Union army.

the county for control of the fertile Roanoke River valley, which supplied Lee's Army of Northern Virginia with vital foodstuffs. To defend the Roanoke River valley, the Confederates in North Carolina constructed Fort Branch on the south side of the Roanoke River in the town of Hamilton. Fort Branch was adjacent to Indian Woods and was built from February to October of 1862. To block Union gun boats from supporting their ground forces attacking Williamston and Hamilton, the Roanoke River by Bertie County was obstructed with a gigantic linked chain, mined with torpedoes, and guarded by a rifle pit with sharp shooters who killed Union soldiers attempting to remove either the chain or the torpedoes. No Union gun boats ever made it beyond this point, but if they had, they would have been met by the heavy guns of Fort Branch, which was staffed by whites from Bertie County.[10] Because many of the Confederate soldiers stationed at Fort Branch were from Bertie County, civilians from there often laundered their clothes, brought them meals, and performed other tasks for them.[11] Fort Branch was maintained until the end of the War in 1865. The fort was then abandoned and the cannons were thrown into the river to avoid confiscation by the advancing Union army in 1865.[12]

North Carolina Confederate soldiers, including some from Bertie County, were involved in the first battles of the war when members of the North Carolina 1st Regiment, on June 10, 1861 in the first battle of the Civil War, soundly defeated a larger Federal army under Major General Benjamin F. Butler at Bethel near Yorktown, Virginia.[13] Later, some were present when three North Carolina regiments were involved in the rout of Federal troops at First Manassas on July 21 of the same year, under General Irvin McDowell. In fact, in spite of the state's reluctance to fight and its position as the last to secede, it lost more men in the conflict than any other Southern state.[14]

At the start of the Civil War, Bertie County's total population was 14,310. Of this number, 59.4 percent were blacks who, along with a number of poor whites, supported the Union during the war by being spies, scouts, and soldiers.[15] In all, the Union raised four regiments of white Union troops wholly or partly in eastern North Carolina, a number of whom were held and died in the notorious Confederate prison in Georgia called Andersonville. These whites who were called Buffaloes by local Confederates made up several regiments, including the 1st Regiment North Carolina Union Volunteers, 2nd Regiment North Carolina Union Volunteers, 2nd Regiment North Carolina Mounted Infantry, and 3rd Regiment North Carolina Mounted Infantry. William David Thomas of Bertie was enlisted in Company B, 2nd Regiment North Carolina Union Volunteers and escaped capture at Plymouth on October 10, 1863. He was transferred to Company I, 1st Regiment North Carolina Union Volunteers and was mustered out of service on June 27, 1865 at New Bern.[16]

Black Union troops served in at least eight regiments, including the 35th Regiment USCT, 34 men; 36th Regiment USCT, 73 men; 14th Regiment U.S. Colored Heavy Artillery (CHA), 172 men; 1st Regiment U.S. Colored Cavalry, 2 men; 2nd Regiment U.S. Colored Cavalry, 22 men; 85th Regiment New York Infantry, 2 men; and 103rd Regiment Pennsylvania Infantry, 2 men. The most well known of these soldiers from Bertie was Parker D. Robbins, who was a free black that enlisted in the 2nd Regiment U.S. Colored Calvary. Parker was appointed a sergeant major and was the highest ranking

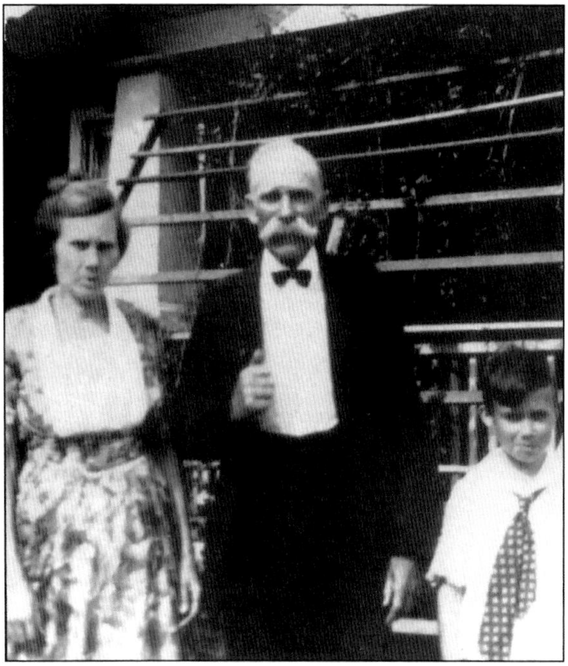

William David Thomas pictured here with his daughter and grandson, joined the Union army along with over 200 whites from the county during the Civil War. These white soldiers along with black soldiers were called "Buffalo Soldiers" by Confederate soldiers and civilians. (Courtesy of Gerald W. Thomas.)

African American from Bertie County to serve in the Union army. He was mustered out of service at Brazos Santiago, Texas on February 12, 1866.[17]

Of the 57 Bertie County men who served in the United States navy during the war, 49 were black and 8 were white. These sailors served aboard over 24 gunboats of the North Atlantic Blockading Squadron, which patrolled the sounds and rivers of eastern North Carolina, primarily slowing and stopping the movement of Confederate arms, men, and supplies. They also rescued runaway slaves, conscription evaders, the families of Union soldiers, and white refugees who were fleeing the fighting by boat. Many of these people ended up in Edenton across the Chowan River from Bertie County. By 1862, the city was under Union control and heavily fortified against Confederate attacks.[18]

The majority of white men from Bertie chose to fight for the Confederacy and were in over 37 departments, regiments, and in the Bertie County militia and homegaurd. Dr. W.R. Capehart, of Avoca on Salmon Creek, whose family after the war would help develop the herring industry in the county, was a surgeon during the war, and David Outlaw's son Edward of Indian Woods served as a captain in the Confederate army, leaving his plantation to be run by his wife and trusted slave. There was also one black from the county who was known for his Confederate service. Benjamin Gray served as a powder boy aboard the Confederate ironclad *Albemarle* and was granted a pension by the state of North Carolina for his service during the war.[19] This is worth noting because, during the war from 1861 to 1865, whites in Bertie County actually placed added restriction on slaves and free blacks living in the county to prevent slaves from revolting or running away. These restrictions limited free blacks' and slaves' ability to travel, gather in groups, even to worship or have contact with loved ones living on nearby plantations.

The restrictions made it easier, however, for the remaining few white men not called to serve in the Confederate army to control the county's huge slave population, which had outnumbered the white population in the county since 1800.[20]

In spite of restrictions on movement and gatherings, slaves were able to maintain contact with one another during the war by using what they called the "Grape Vine."[21] The Grape Vine was a sophisticated system of passing information from plantation to plantation by word of mouth. With this system, information could be passed freely when slaves were sent on errands by their masters or were secretly visiting friends and family throughout the war. As a result, from the start of the war, slaves were very much aware that there was a great war taking place and that they were at the center of it. Slaves in Bertie County, eastern North Carolina, and southeastern Virginia would use the Grape Vine very effectively as spies for the Union and to pass on information about the war to others in the region.[22]

The Union naval blockade and attacks on forts and towns in eastern North Carolina and Bertie and Martin Counties, including Windsor, Winton, Indian Woods, Williamston, and Hamilton, from 1861 to 1863 greatly concerned the slave owners of Bertie. Because most plantation owners were dependent on the Cashie, Roanoke, and Chowan Rivers to transport their tobacco and cotton to the towns of Windsor and Edenton, and then on to European markets, the capture of coastal forts like Plymouth and attacks on these towns caused them to become alarmed.[23] For slaves and white Unionists, however, it meant they

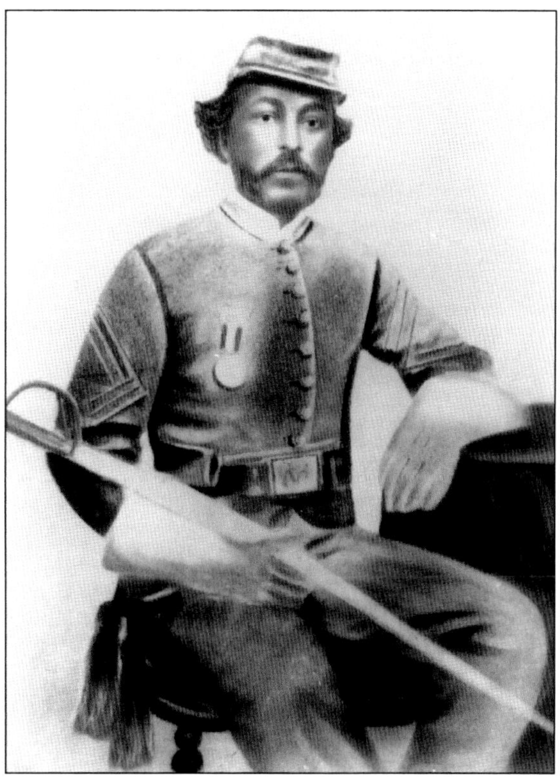

Sergeant Major Parker D. Robbins of the 2nd Regiment, United States Colored Calvary, earned the highest rank of the over 300 blacks that served in the Union army from Bertie County. (Courtesy of Harry L. Thompson, curator of the Port of Plymouth Museum.)

did not have to take dangerous overland routes, avoiding Confederate patrols to Union lines, but could float down the Cashie, Roanoke, and Chowan Rivers to Union lines in and along the Albemarle Sound and the coast. The slaves and Union supporters were encouraged even more when, between January and July of 1862, Major General Ambrose E. Burnside and Admiral L.M. Goldsborough captured Roanoke Island, Elizabeth City, Winton, and Edenton across the Albemarle Sound from Bertie County.[24] By July, General Burnside had also gained control of New Bern, Washington, Plymouth, Havelock, Carolina City, Morehead City, Fort Macon, and Beaufort.[25] With these victories, the Union successfully won control of eastern North Carolina. General Burnside then established his headquarters at New Bern.[26]

During these battles for control of eastern North Carolina and Bertie County, many of the county's residents who served in the Union army were aided by Tuscarora who, along with the other members of the Six Nations, joined the Union army during the war. Many of these Tuscarora, although they could prove their ancestry, were forced to fight with the USCT because many appeared to be black.[27] Other Tuscarora from the state, particularly Robeson County, distinguished themselves during the war as fierce fighters. The most famous, or infamous if you were white, of these Tuscarora was Henry Berry Lowery of Robeson County. Lowery, who was part-Tuscarora, and his men terrorized whites in Robeson County and the state after the killing of his father and brother by local white Confederates during the war. For six years, he and his men, at least one of whom was of Tuscarora-African ancestry, lived in the swamps of the county and hunted down

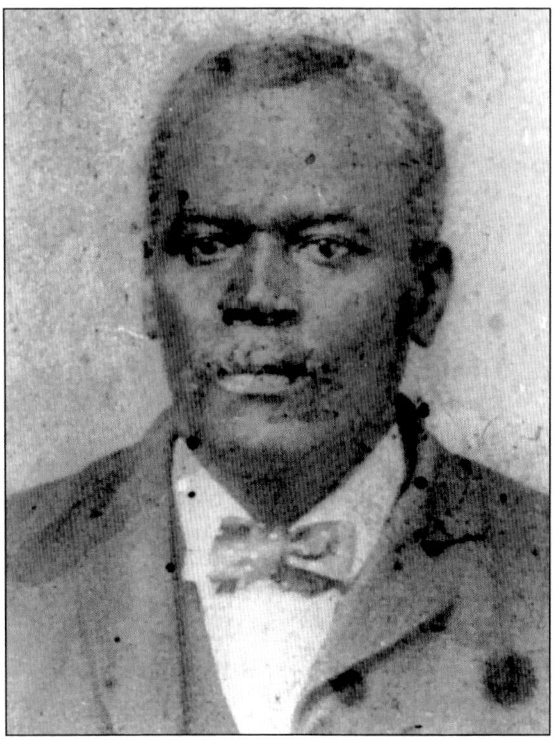

Benjamin Gray, who served as a powder boy on board the ironclad C.S.S. Albemarle, *was one of the more than 200,000 blacks authorized by the Confederate congress to take up arms in defense of the Confederacy. The state of North Carolina paid Gray a pension for his service. (Courtesy of Harry L. Thompson, curator of the Port of Plymouth Museum.)*

and killed nearly all of the men who participated in the slaying of his family or sought the $10,000 bounty placed on his head by the state of North Carolina. Although members of his group, including another of his brothers, were killed, Lowery was never captured and disappeared into legend by the early 1870s.[28]

Wherever Union troops marched in eastern North Carolina they encountered large numbers of slaves. Many of these slaves served as spies or were willing to do anything to assist the advancing Union troops. Although Butler and Burnside were instructed to return runaway slaves by Lincoln, both men felt the policy of returning slaves to the enemy was counter-productive. They also felt that the armies in the field could make better use of the slaves as laborers for the Union cause.[29] Although slaves in Bertie County were aware of Union successes in eastern North Carolina from 1861 to 1862, they remained quiet and cautious rather than escaping to Union lines only to be returned to their angry masters or put in filthy disease-ridden internment camps. However, when Lincoln issued his Emancipation Proclamation on September 22, 1862 following the Battle of Antietam in Maryland, more slaves flooded into Union-held cities or created all-black towns for protection against Confederate soldiers. Blacks also joined the Union army. Once safe behind Union lines in areas like New Bern, slaves from all over eastern North Carolina, including Bertie County, sought protection in African-American communities such as James City.[30]

Black and white union troops from Bertie County were also used to defend New Bern on February 1, 1864 when Robert E. Lee asked President Jefferson Davis to launch an attack on the city to capture much needed supplies stored there by Union soldiers.[31] With the support of these troops from Bertie, this attack was foiled. One of the most well-known battles during the war involving black troops from Bertie County occurred from April 17 through April 20, 1864 at Plymouth.[32] On April 17, over 7,000 Confederate soldiers surrounded Fort Plymouth. One day later, an ironclad christened *Albemarle* steamed down the Roanoke River past Bertie County from Edwards Ferry where it had been constructed. With the help of the ironclad, the Confederates were able to sink and drive off United States naval ships that guarded Plymouth and the mouth of the Roanoke River. Without the support of Union naval artillery, the fort was soon overrun by Confederate forces.[33]

After accepting the surrender of Union troops, a number of whom were Buffaloes from Bertie County, Confederate troops proceeded to massacre black troops, many of whom were from Bertie and surrounding counties. Although there is debate as to whether or not this actually occurred, descendants of black Union soldiers who survived the battle and massacre by escaping into the swamps, as did some white soldiers, insist that it did.[34] With the help of Union naval reinforcements and the crippling of the *Albemarle* at the Battle of Batchelor's Bay on May 5, 1864, Plymouth was retaken and remained under Union control for the rest of the war.[35] The Battle of Plymouth, however, demonstrates the courage and bravery of the county's former slaves who joined and fought in the Union army. Unlike whites, if blacks were caught in Union uniforms, as a rule they were killed by Confederate soldiers throughout the South. The Confederate congress, upon hearing of Lincoln's move to enlist blacks, mandated this action as early as 1863. As slaves were aware of the movement of Confederate and Union forces, they were also aware of this brutal fact, but still signed up and fought for their freedom. Therefore, as with the 54th Massachusetts at Fort Wagner, South Carolina, and black soldiers at Murfreesboro, Tennessee, who were massacred by Nathan Bedford Forrest, there was no surrender for them.[36]

In spite of this, blacks from the county enlisted and fought from 1863 until the end of the war in 1865. Six of those soldiers who served after the war married and settled in the Indian Woods township where they became founding members of Indian Woods Baptist and Spring Hill Baptist Churches. Their graves are marked in the church cemeteries with military headstones, including Robert Smallwood of Company I, 14th U.S. CHA; Luke Smallwood, Company I, 14th U.S. CHA; Sergeant Eli Jones, Company E, 37th U.S. Colored Infantry (CI); Rich D. Whitaker, Company I, 14th U.S. CHA; Lewis Williams, Company C, 14th U.S. CHA; and Corporal Joseph Cherry, who was buried with other veterans of the war in a slave cemetery, Company K, 35th U.S. CI.[37]

Corporal Cherry's grandson Lord Cornwallis Cherry, who still lived in Bertie County when this book was published, stated the following in a tape recorded interview:

> My Granddaddy, Joseph Cherry, was a slave but when the war started he ran away and joined the Union Army to fight to free his family. During the war he was wounded but fought on, and when he ran out of bullets yelled for more to continue fighting. After the war, having been wounded, he was given a pension by the Army and used it to buy a small farm in Spring Hill.[38]

Cherry, who was 78 years old at the time of the interview, continued saying that the white soldiers were so impressed with his grandfather's bravery that they began to cheer together, "A Bullet for Cherry!" After the war, Corporal Joseph Cherry purchased land in the Spring Hill area of the Indian Woods township, which his grandson Lord Cornwallis Cherry still possesses. L.C. Cherry also still has his grandfather's tombstone, which he saved when the slave cemetery containing his grandfather's, other slaves', and Civil War veterans' burial sites was bulldozed for farming land in 1980 by a local white farmer.[39] When the Civil War ended in 1865, over 620 black and white men from Bertie County had served the Union and 142 had died while serving.[40]

Most of the white residents of Bertie County joined the Confederate army during the war. Edward Outlaw, the son of David Outlaw and grandson of Ralph Outlaw, became a captain, and other planters or their children joined the officers' ranks. Other planter families and poor whites deserted or refused to join the army and welcomed the occupying Union troops that moved into the area as early as 1862. However, due to the seizure and destruction of property by Union troops, such as their raids on Winton, Windsor, Plymouth, Williamston, and Hamilton, and the enlisting and arming of runaway slaves from the county, support for the occupying Union armies soon eroded.[41]

For Edward Outlaw of Indian Woods, the choice was simple. He believed, as had his father, that the United States was and always had been a confederacy. His father had even referred to the country as the American Confederacy of States while serving in Congress. The Outlaws firmly believed that the issue was "states' rights" and not slavery, and David Outlaw noted in his letters and speeches that the two were separate. Outlaw did want compromise and hoped that one could be worked out that would save the country—a country that he believed had a bright and promising future.[42]

This map shows Bertie County and eastern North Carolina during the Civil War. Bertie County provided black and white soldiers to both sides during the conflict and experienced the war firsthand as several battles were fought in or near the county and involved its residents.

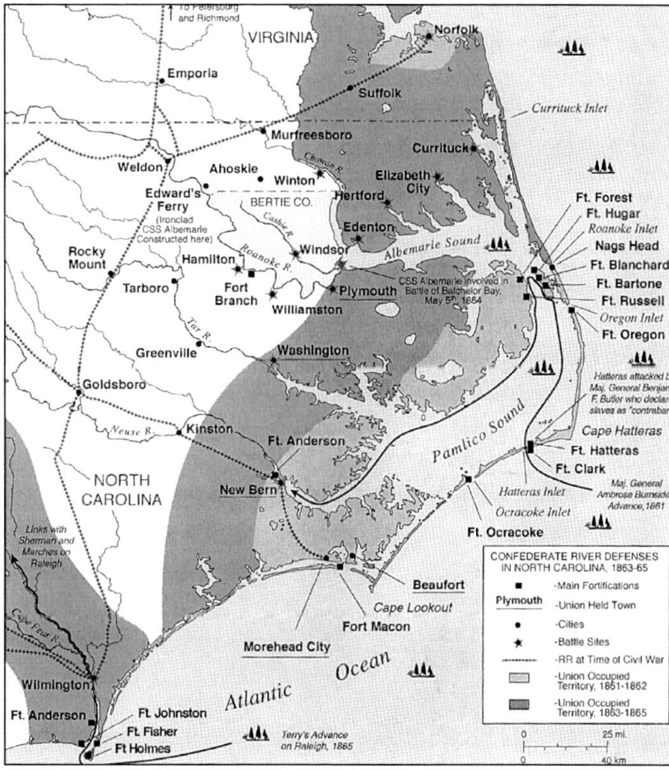

Outlaw and other white slaveholders failed to see the contradiction in believing in states' rights and individual freedom for themselves and their families while denying these same freedoms to slaves, poor whites, and their families. Outlaw did point out quite correctly in his public addresses that white Northerners, who did not own slaves or have large numbers of blacks in their states, condemned the South, while harboring the same ill feelings against the black race.[43]

During the Civil War and throughout slavery, most whites viewed slaves as mentally slow and ignorant. As a result they often openly discussed politics, business, and family problems around them. Slave owners also trusted their slaves to such a degree that many found it hard to believe their slaves could or would plot against them. Paternalism, which was practiced throughout slavery, caused whites to trust their slaves as they would their own children even during the Civil War. For example, when Edward Outlaw left his plantation in Indian Woods, he left his wife and trusted slave in charge and expected that the slaves on the plantation would carry on as if there was no war.[44]

Whites also openly discussed military strategies around house servants and the "Mammies" who cared for their children, never believing that these slaves had the ability or will to forward this information to the Union army. Although most whites in the county were not sure if slaves understood what was taking place, it was clear that slaves throughout Bertie County were very much aware of what was happening and, as they had done since colonial times, they used the information they obtained to help protect themselves and their loved ones on nearby plantations in the county. They also did what they could to undermine the Confederate army in the county by serving as spies, guides, and soldiers for the Union during the war.[45]

By the end of the Civil War, white Confederates from the county had been involved in numerous battles from eastern North Carolina to as far away as Gettysburg, Pennsylvania. Men from Bertie served in companies that fought at Bethel near Yorktown, Virginia, the first battle of the Civil War, where over half of the Confederate troops were a part of the North Carolina First Regiment, as well as at Appomattox, Virginia, and Durham Station, North Carolina where they, along with other North Carolinians, were the last to turn in their guns.[46]

The Civil War, and later Reconstruction, left many white residents of Bertie County dazed. Many, like the surgeon Dr. W.R. Capehart and Edward Outlaw, had served in the Confederate army and saw friends and family wounded or killed. Everyone in the county knew someone who died or was wounded during the war. Although most of the plantations continued to operate by growing cotton during the war, they were beset by work stoppages, runaway slaves, and blocked trading routes by land and water.[47] By the close of the war in 1865, white and black residents of Bertie County had fought and died for both sides.

When the war ended, those former slaves and poor whites who left to participate in the war as Union soldiers returned to their homes in the county. Some, like Joseph Cherry, had been wounded in the war, while others were unharmed.[48] Upon their return, these men helped build churches, schools, and lives for their families and neighbors. They, with

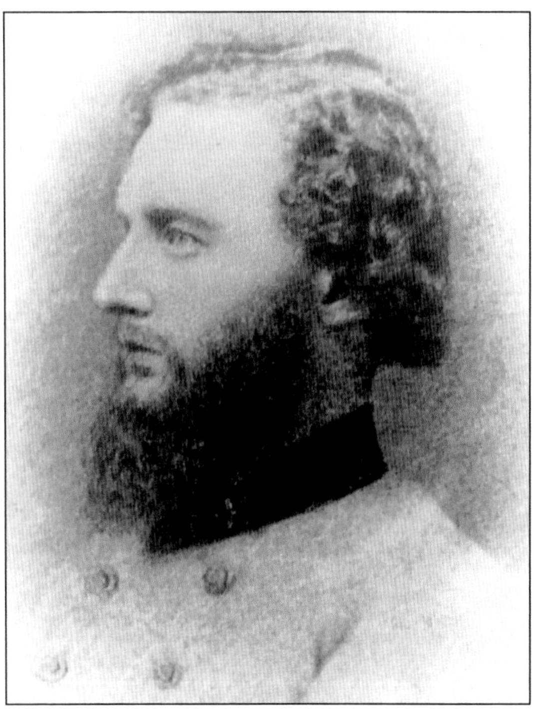

Dr. W.R. Capehart of Avoco was a surgeon during the Civil War. After the war he helped establish Capehart Fishery and became wealthy by selling herring around the world. (Courtesy of NCSAH.)

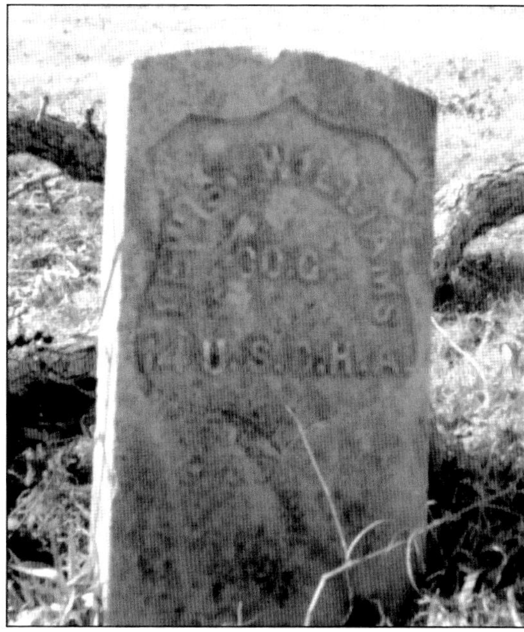

County residents who supported the Union were also honored by their families and kin. This grave stone, located in the Spring Hill Baptist Church cemetery, and others like it in church cemeteries and slave burial grounds all over the county serve as reminders and monuments to those who gave their lives in defense of the Union. (Courtesy of SHC, UNC.)

others in the community, sought to legalize their marriages and purchase land on which they could farm and raise livestock.

Immediately following the Civil War, the African Americans of Bertie County began to construct community churches. These churches were built all over the county from Merry Hill to Roxbel. Spring Hill Baptist Church of Indian Woods, for example, was founded in 1866 by former slaves who wanted to worship together. This had been forbidden before emancipation. After worshipping together for nine years, the deacons of the church, on January 5, 1875, purchased the church and land from James Winslow Copeland for $30.[49] Indian Woods Baptist Church also records its founding following slavery when its founders gathered around the Gospel Oak to worship in secret before building the church after emancipation.[50] As quickly as these former slaves returned to their rural communities and built homes and churches, white plantation owners fled and relocated to the nearby towns between 1870 and 1890, leaving these former slaves to develop their own communities and churches without any direct interference from whites. These churches, nearly all of which were Baptist, would be deeply involved in the Civil Rights Movement by the 1960s.[51]

As the twentieth century dawned, the African-American churches founded in Bertie County following the Civil War began to play a greater role in the everyday lives of the residents. The churches had opened and maintained schools and, in times of economic distress, provided financial assistance for members in need. Little could be or was done about politics or race-based discrimination, however, until the 1960s. The churches, along with their members, tended to be mostly concerned about church affairs and the families of their members. The churches stressed godliness, hard work, and basic education.[52]

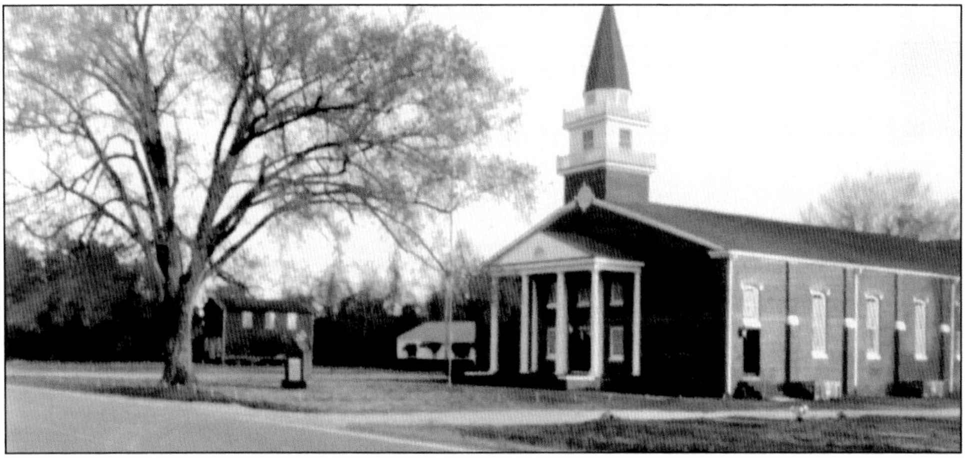

Indian Woods Baptist Church was one of the first black churches built in Bertie County after emancipation in 1865. (Courtesy of SHC, UNC.)

After the war, Bertie County underwent both presidential and congressional reconstruction. The whites of Bertie County, many of whom held political offices in the Confederacy or served as officers in the Confederate army, applauded presidential reconstruction under which both Abraham Lincoln and Andrew Johnson pardoned participants in the war and allowed them to return to their homes to rebuild without any penalties. When Lincoln was assassinated, anger towards the South and Southern whites grew in the North. This anger and a feeling that the South should be punished for Lincoln's death and for causing the war led to the impeachment of Andrew Johnson, a Southerner himself, and to Congress taking control of reconstruction from the President in 1868.[53] This began what has become known as Radical Republican, or Black, Reconstruction. During congressional reconstruction, Bertie County became part of an important political district in the state and nation for the Republican Party, which was a Northern-based party. As a result of the black vote in the county and in eastern North Carolina, blacks elected Parker D. Robbins, who lived in Bertie, to the North Carolina House of Representatives, a position he held from 1868 to 1872.[54]

Newly freed slaves, some of whom helped win their freedom by fighting in the Civil War, were given the right to vote and, as a result, were able to influence local, state, and national elections. While the slaves of Bertie County were enfranchised, many of the whites who previously held political office or were high-ranking military officers in the Confederate government were disenfranchised by Congress, which barred them from voting or holding local, state, or national office. This impacted many of the whites of Bertie County who before the war were some of the wealthiest and most powerful people in the state. They were further crippled by the 15th Amendment which, along with giving blacks the right to vote, forbade former Confederate states from repaying individuals who had invested in the Confederacy through loans to the government or war bonds. As a result, all of the money invested in the Confederacy, along with several million dollars worth of slaves owned collectively by the white slaveholders of Bertie County, was lost.[55]

As a result of all these things, many whites in Bertie County who had been Whigs before the war became devout Democrats. They mourned the loss of their way of life and sought ways to end Northern occupation and "Negro Rule." During Reconstruction from 1868 to 1877, the whites of Indian Woods, with most others in North Carolina, began to join and support terrorist groups such as the Ku Klux Klan. Through these groups and white citizens' groups, both blacks and white Republicans were bribed, beaten, and murdered. Blacks in the state and around the South saw their homes burned, crops destroyed, and daughters and wives raped and beaten. In spite of the Ku Klux Klan Act of 1871, which was supposed to eradicate these groups, they were successful in terrorizing blacks across the South during Reconstruction. Because of this terror, white Democrats regained control of the state as early as 1870.[56]

In spite of their return to power between 1865 to 1877, the number of white residents in the rural areas of Bertie County declined sharply. Although there was also some later drop in the rural African-American population due to the Black Exodus in 1879 and Great Migration beginning around 1914, for the most part, the African-American population remained near its pre-slavery levels during these years. It is not clear why the white residents of the county moved out of the rural areas, but they began their migration after the Civil War, which suggests that the freedom of their former slaves may have been an important factor.[57]

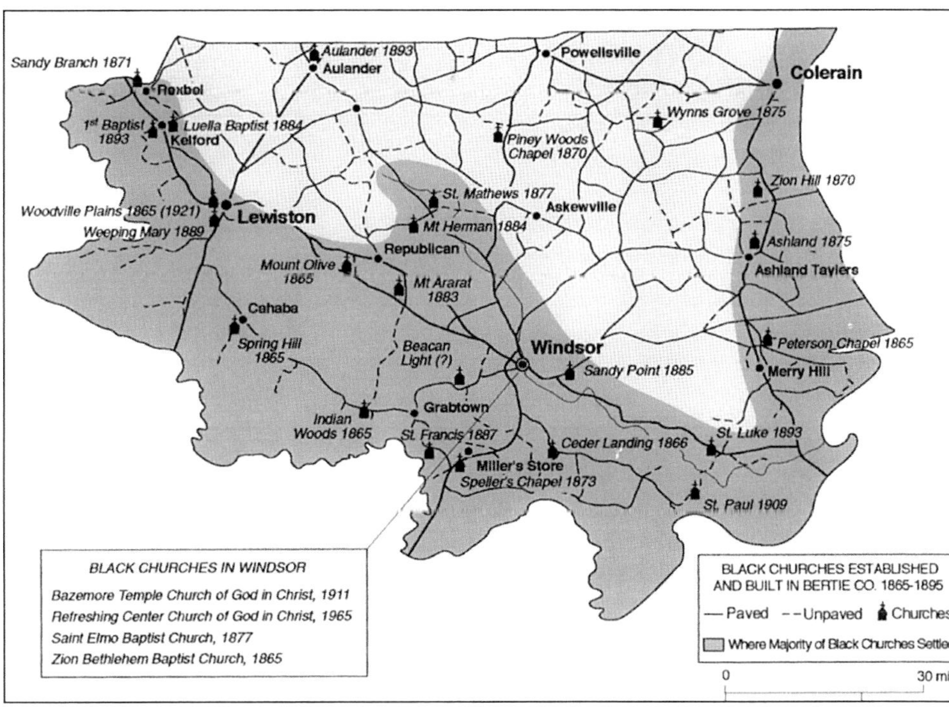

The black churches established in Bertie County after emancipation also often served as schools, teaching former slaves reading, writing, and arithmetic until the Rosenwald schools were built in the 1920s.

When the war ended, most slave owners in Bertie County struggled to rebuild their economy by growing cotton, tobacco, and a new cash crop that gained popularity during the war, peanuts. The days of wealth, prestige, and prosperity in the county, however, seemed to die with emancipation. Although Bertie County remained a major agricultural area, the whites of the county and other rural farming areas in the northeastern part of the state saw their population, wealth, and political power begin to shift to the western and more urban parts of the state.[58]

At the end of the Civil War, Bertie County's black and white population dramatically declined, from 14,310 people in 1860 to 12,950 people in 1870. Bertie County's population actually increased in 1880 to 16,399 people, of which blacks made up 58.4 percent. The most reasonable explanation for this decline followed by such a large increase is that many residents, both white and black, were displaced by the war and, following the war, they searched the state for loved ones before returning to their homes in the county sometime after 1870.[59]

From 1865 to 1870, many slaves were reunited with loved ones who had been sold to other plantations in or out of state. Others refused to work any more for masters who had treated them cruelly. Charles Smallwood, for example, lost nearly all of his slaves in Indian Woods because he severely punished them during slavery. Other former slave owners, such as Edward Outlaw, Whitmell T. Sharrock, and William Grimes, who were respected for their fair treatment of slaves, found huge numbers of slaves asking to work and live on their farms following emancipation.[60]

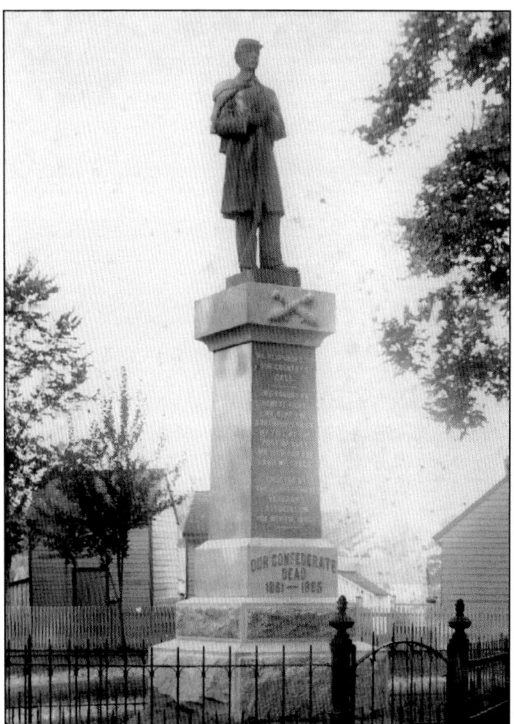

The death toll of the Civil War in Bertie County was horrendous, and many families lost fathers, sons, brothers, and kin. After the war residents of the county who supported the Confederacy honored their dead with this monument erected in Windsor across from the county courthouse. (Courtesy of NCC, UNC.)

As with the rest of the South following the Civil War, many of the plantation owners in Bertie County attempted to reinstate the old plantation system that existed prior to the Civil War. Whites still owned nearly all of the farmable land in the county and controlled the only means through which most blacks could make a living and provide for their families. Through tenant farming and sharecropping contracts, many former slave owners continued to grow cotton, tobacco, wheat, corn, and, by the 1880s, peanuts. Because of the out-migration of whites, many became absentee landlords and merchants, and found "peonage" to eventually be as profitable as slavery.[61]

The abolition of slavery and the end of the Civil War brought many changes to former slaves of Bertie County. One of the greatest was the introduction of a class system among blacks. There had always been differences in slavery in the South. Slavery in the lower South was harsher than slavery in the upper South. Rural slavery was more difficult than urban slavery, and house servants were sometimes treated better than field hands. Added to this was the status of free blacks and mulattos, many of whom had received education. Even during slavery, the slave community was stratified. With emancipation came the opportunity for economic gain and those lucky enough to own their land, rather than sharecrop or tenant farm the lands of their former masters, had an economic advantage.[62]

To own land, however, one had to have money to buy it. Additionally, there had to be someone willing to sell land to blacks. The former slaves who fought in the "African Brigade" did have money. As a result, many were successful in purchasing land from whites leaving Bertie County for nearby towns. Because of their landownership, these African Americans became leaders in their churches and communities. Land-owning African Americans expanded their farms by marrying other landowners. In fact, it was viewed as marrying beneath oneself if one's spouse did not also own property. As stated earlier, the black landowners became leaders in their local churches, around which the communities revolved. There were a number of churches in Bertie County that were established by former slaves. Even today, by comparing the churches, it is clear which had members with greater wealth. Following emancipation, life began to center around these churches.[63]

Blacks were also concerned about legalizing their marriages. On August 30, 1866, the North Carolina General Assembly passed an act allowing blacks to declare their slave marriages, which were not legal, for 25¢. In response, many former slaves in Bertie County went to the county courthouse in Windsor to legalize their marriages.[64]

During Reconstruction, blacks in Bertie County were concerned about five things. The first was freedom and the limits of that freedom, which they tested by relocating loved ones and moving off their old plantations, usually only a few miles away. The second was education, which had been denied them by their masters while they were enslaved. The third was religion, which they had also been denied under slavery due to fear of revolts. The fourth was economic freedom, which many associated with the prosperity that their masters enjoyed. Finally, voting was a concern as Union soldiers and other officials told them they now had the right to vote.[65]

Although African Americans in Bertie County did vote in large numbers and were successful in electing Parker D. Robbins and George Mebane from the county to the North Carolina General Assembly, in 1868 and 1876, respectively, they seemed to be more concerned with the first three issues. In some of the county's rural townships, some blacks lived daily under the fear of violence and the loss of their jobs because of their voting power.[66] As a result, blacks, as well as poor whites, focused on raising and taking care of their families, which they were very capable of doing. They were used to being self-sufficient on their plantations and small farms. They helped feed their families by having gardens, raising livestock, particularly hogs and chickens, fishing and growing foodstuffs like corn and wheat, which could be milled into flour and cornmeal.[67] Flour was used to make biscuits, puddin' bread (a baked mixture of molasses and flour), and several types of sweet breads. Cornmeal was used to make cornbread, hush puppies, and cracklin' bread (a mixture of cornmeal and pork skins eaten with molasses). Since they were not accustomed to being paid for their labor, most continued working, happy for just being able to eat better than they could under slavery.[68]

Reconstruction, particularly Black Reconstruction, helped African Americans most by aiding those who could buy land from their former masters to obtain it and by laying the foundation for a good public education system. By the collapse of Reconstruction in 1877, most African Americans and poor whites in the county were sharecroppers or tenant farmers. However, a surprisingly high number were land-owning independent farmers.[69] After the passage of the Landlord and Tenant Act in 1876, and the County Government Law of 1877, a number of blacks from Bertie County and northeastern North Carolina chose to leave between 1876 and 1894 rather than be cheated and oppressed.[70]

Some African Americans from Bertie County supported the "Back to Africa" movement, which lasted from 1876 to 1894. Others supported the move to Kansas proposed by "Pap" Moses Singleton of Tennessee and Henry Adams of Louisiana in 1879.[71] The migration to Kansas lasted from 1879 until the 1880s. The vast majority of blacks from North Carolina however, moved to Indiana, over 6,000 from Johnston and Wayne Counties alone.[72] None of these destinations seemed to hold much fascination for the blacks of Bertie County. There are several possible reason for this. First, as earlier mentioned, there were large numbers of black farmers in Bertie County who owned their land and would not have been directly affected by the Landlord and Tenant Act of 1876. Second, although the blacks in the county did vote and hold political office, most did not value voting as the most important issue in their lives. They were more concerned with educating their children, building churches, and feeding their families. As a result, they were not as concerned about losing the right to vote for county and local officials, taken away by the County Government Law of 1877.[73]

Because of the need for black labor to grow and harvest cotton, tobacco, and, by the 1880s, large amounts of peanuts, most whites did not want blacks to leave the state. As a result, whites used many methods, including force, to keep blacks from going.[74] This last reason seems not to be much of a factor, however, when considering the large number of Civil War veterans who braved death to fight, only to return to their homes at war's end. What appears a more likely explanation, therefore, is the black population's ties to their churches. The Civil War veterans who lived in Bertie County were deacons in these churches. In 1879, the black Baptist newspaper, *The National Monitor*, urged blacks to "work and pray where they were" and "trust in God for the rest."[75] The African Americans of Bertie County continued to heed the words of the church and its elders and built a thriving, self-sufficient black community throughout the county that still exists today.[76]

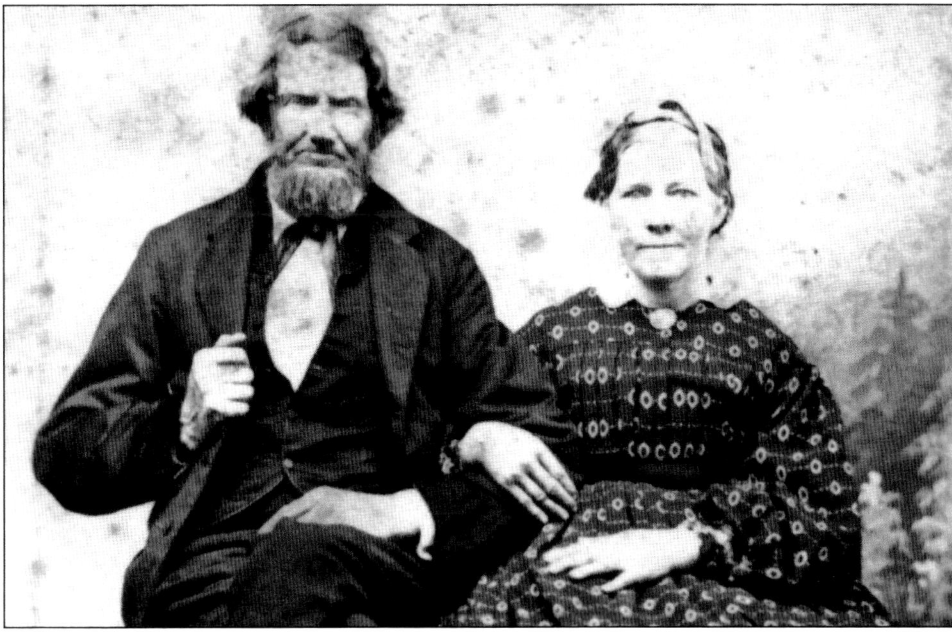

After the Civil War most former slaveholders, such as Whitmel Thomas Sharrock and his wife, Margaret Horne Sharrock, pictured here between 1865 and 1870, negotiated contracts with former slaves to sharecrop or tenant farm their land. (Courtesy of SHC, UNC.)

Many blacks began to take full advantage of their new freedoms as they came together to worship, build communities for themselves, and vote for and hold political office.[77] George A. Mebane, born a slave in Bertie County, was the first African American to be elected to the North Carolina Senate in 1876. In 1989, Rosetta Bond recited the story of how blacks lost their right to vote. It was corroborated by George and Catherine Bond, Lord Cornwallis Cherry, and many other residents of Bertie County. Bond stated she was told by her parents that a black elected official, whose name was not repeated, sold the black ballot box to whites, who did not want the votes counted, for a barrel of flour. When he got home, however, only the top of the barrel was flour. The rest was sand, and so went the blacks' right to vote until 1964.[78]

Before Reconstruction collapsed in 1877, Southern Democrats, predecessors of the "Dixiecrats" in the twentieth century, had regained control of many state legislatures and congressional seats. North Carolina Democrats, with the aid of terrorist organizations such as the Ku Klux Klan, had already regained control of North Carolina's General Assembly by 1870. In northeastern North Carolina, however, where several counties had black majorities, the Union League continued to register and encourage African Americans to vote in local, state, and national elections. As a result, blacks in counties like Bertie continued to be politically active until restrictions such as the State Government Law of 1878 began to limit their voting rights.[79]

During the years from 1865 to 1877, most blacks and whites in the county returned to the cultivation of cotton. From 1870 to 1899, white plantation owners throughout Bertie

County complained about the lack of interest shown by tenants and sharecroppers in the growing and cultivation of the cash crop cotton. The sharecroppers and tenant farmers of Bertie County were no different than many others in the state. Landowners forced them to grow only cotton on all available farm land. This left no time or land to grow foodstuffs. To supplement their diets, many African Americans tended private gardens where they grew cabbage, beets, tomatoes, cantaloupes, peaches, berries, and nuts. They gleaned fields for corn, potatoes, rice, wheat, and peanuts. They also trapped, fished, and hunted deer, squirrel, quail, and duck. Occasionally, someone would get pork from a neighbor.[80]

Vegetables and fruit were canned for the winter months, and meats were salted in wood barrels or boxes after being covered with molasses and spices (usually pepper). Fish and pork were smoked and hung from the ceilings of small smokehouses, which also contained pork sausages when available. All members of the community shared what they had with others.[81] If someone had an abundance of corn or pork, she or he exchanged it for fish or deer. If someone had canned or fresh fruits and vegetables, she or he exchanged them for flour or cornmeal. During Sunday service, if it was reported that someone was sick or doing without essentials, church members attended to their needs and those of their family.[82]

Corn was especially desired because not only could it supplement diets, but it was necessary to feed livestock such as cows, hogs, chicken, and mules, which were used to plow the fields. Sharecroppers and tenant farmers were expected to buy these commodities from the local general store, owned at this time by merchants throughout the county.[83] Sharecroppers were forced to buy fertilizer, which became very popular following the

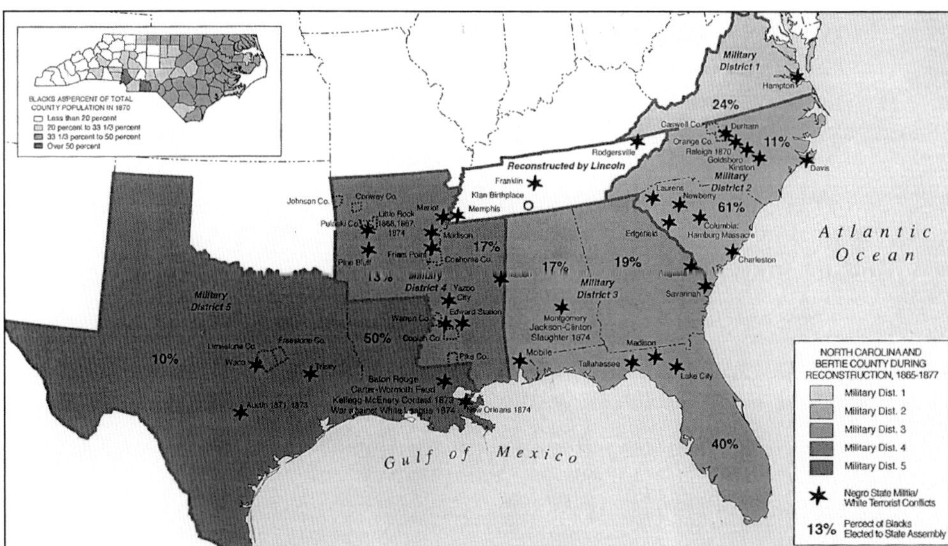

Although the Civil War officially ended in 1865, battles were still waged throughout the old Confederacy between black state militias and white rebel groups, such as the Ku Klux Klan, for political control of state and county governments. This map shows the violence that occurred in North Carolina and the South between 1865 to 1877.

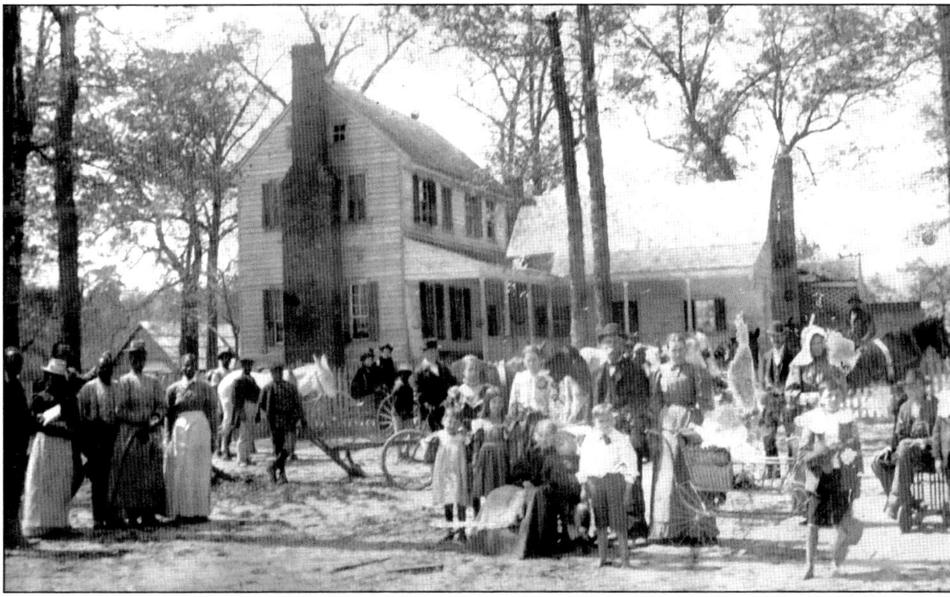

Pictured above is one of several plantations owned by the Speight family of Windsor, North Carolina, the seat of Bertie County, around the time of the Civil War. Both white and black families are shown. (Courtesy of SHC, UNC.)

Civil War, to enable cotton planters to continue growing cotton year after year without depleting and destroying the soil as had been done growing tobacco during the colonial period and cotton during the antebellum period. Buying fertilizer, seed, feed for mules, and farming implements at inflated prices left many residents in debt at the end of the year and without enough money to pay creditors and white landowners, who were generally given half of the crops or the profits generated from the sale of the crops. Thus, many blacks in Bertie County fell victim to the system known as "peonage."[84]

With the end of the Populist movement, life in Indian Woods returned to a state similar to that of the antebellum period. By 1900, African Americans continued to do agricultural work on large cotton, tobacco, and peanut plantations. The residents labored during the week and socialized and worshiped together on Sunday in their various community churches. For blacks in Bertie County, the years following the collapse of Reconstruction were years of stagnation and struggle. Because Bertie County had been a majority black county since the colonial period, whites often feared black domination and passed laws to disenfranchise and control them. This did not, however, stop blacks from showing their dissatisfaction by attempting to register to vote.[85]

There were carpetbaggers who moved to Bertie County during Reconstruction and decided to stay. Some attempted to improve political, economic, and educational opportunities for blacks and poor whites in the county. Others became a part of the culture of the county either because they feared terrorism if they spoke out or because they agreed with the unfair system in the county.[86] By 1877, Bertie County was still recovering from the trauma of the Civil War and the confusion and instability of Reconstruction.

7. The Collapse of Reconstruction through the Jim Crow Era, 1877–1954

The election of 1876 and the Compromise of 1877 that followed brought an end to Reconstruction in the South. Although former Confederate leaders had regained control of the North Carolina legislature by 1870 following the Holden War, Bertie County and other counties in northeastern North Carolina with large freedmen populations remained under the influence of Republicans supported by former slaves until 1877. With the election of Rutherford B. Hayes in 1876 and the removal of federal troops and officials from North Carolina after his election, many blacks who had been active in county, state, and national politics as Republicans found themselves disenfranchised. Without federal troops and officials to police the county the rights extended and protected during Reconstruction were quickly lost. The loss of political representation and the right to vote, along with an increase in threats and assaults, caused many former slaves great fear and anxiety.[1]

In response to this increase in oppression and violence beginning in 1879, thousands of blacks left the South in what has become known as the "Black Exodus." Led by "Pap" Singleton, blacks headed west to Kansas to escape the racial oppression of the South. Most North Carolina blacks, however, moved north to Indiana. This exodus caused a great deal of alarm among local white farmers in Bertie County and around the South, for although they were unhappy with the large numbers of former slaves living in their county, black farm labor was still a necessity to the agricultural economy. White farmers began to worry about who would plant and harvest their cash crops. Although some blacks did leave, most preferred to remain in the only homes they had ever known, while others were encouraged to stay by whites offering them larger shares of crops if they stayed.[2]

While whites were encouraging blacks to stay on their rural plantations and work, most whites in the county had begun leaving their rural plantation homes and migrating into the county's small towns, leasing, renting, and sometimes selling their old houses to their sharecroppers and tenant farmers. This white migration seemed to at least in part be caused by the number of former slaves living nearby. The greater the number of freedmen the greater the out-flow of whites. By the 1880 census, the majority of the county's population was still rural, but the size and number of towns began to grow. The county seat of Windsor, for example, contained the county courthouse, a hotel, and, by 1888, growing business and residential areas.

The 1880 census recorded eight townships and two major towns, Windsor and Colerain, with significant populations in the county. Others would follow between

The steamer Bertie *moves down the Roanoke River near Jamesville on December 22, 1888. (Courtesy of NCSAH.)*

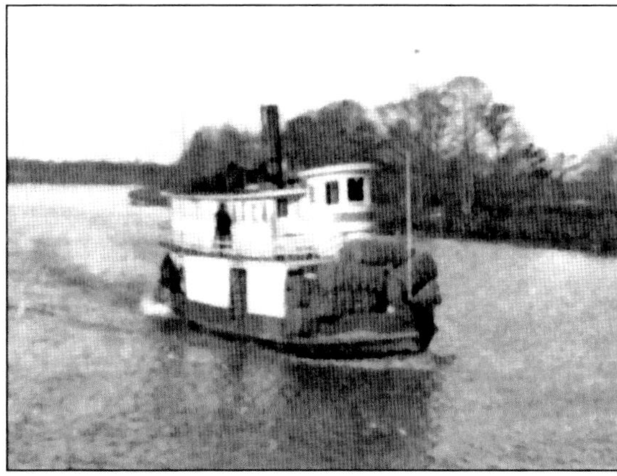

1890 and 1950, including Aulander, Lewiston-Woodville, Roxobel, Kelford, Askewville, Midway, and Merry Hill. Windsor was recorded as having a population of 461, while the town of Colerain recorded a population of 94. These were the only two urban areas noted and their combined populations totaled only 555 compared to the rural townships, which contained a total of 15,844 people. The townships included Colerain township with a population of 2,424; Merry Hill township, 1,580; Mitchell's township, 1,358; Roxobel township, 1,702; Snake Bite township, 1,291; White's township, 1,154; Windsor township, 4,224; and Woodville township, 2,111.[3]

Since most of the county's residents lived on or near rural plantations, most of them relied on this land to make their living and take care of their families. Living on rural isolated plantations such as those in Bertie County following the collapse of Reconstruction had both advantages and disadvantages. Two of the disadvantages for African Americans during and after slavery were the harsh work and isolation from others. During the Jim Crow years, however, the residents' familiarity with hard labor and their isolation from white racism actually became advantages. To blacks, the labor system known as "sharecropping," which was put in place during Reconstruction, was no different from the slave system of their parents and grandparents with one positive change: there were no longer any overseers or masters to whip, rape, and otherwise abuse them and their children.[4] Also, unlike blacks living in Southern cities and towns, those of Bertie County were not confronted with the daily humiliation of segregation.[5]

Since most blacks and poor whites in Bertie were accustomed to farming, they continued to make their livings off the land by being tenant farmers or sharecroppers. The land that these individuals farmed, however, remained in the hands of wealthy white landowners throughout the Jim Crow era. Most of these landowners became merchants or absentee landlords.[6]

To farm the land, the residents, like their former masters, required a large dependable labor force. To fill these labor needs, residents began to have large families, some as large as 18 children. The average family contained around 9 children who were put to work as early as 10 years of age planting gardens and cultivating fields of cotton, tobacco, and peanuts, feeding livestock, harvesting crops, and cooking, cleaning, and caring for younger

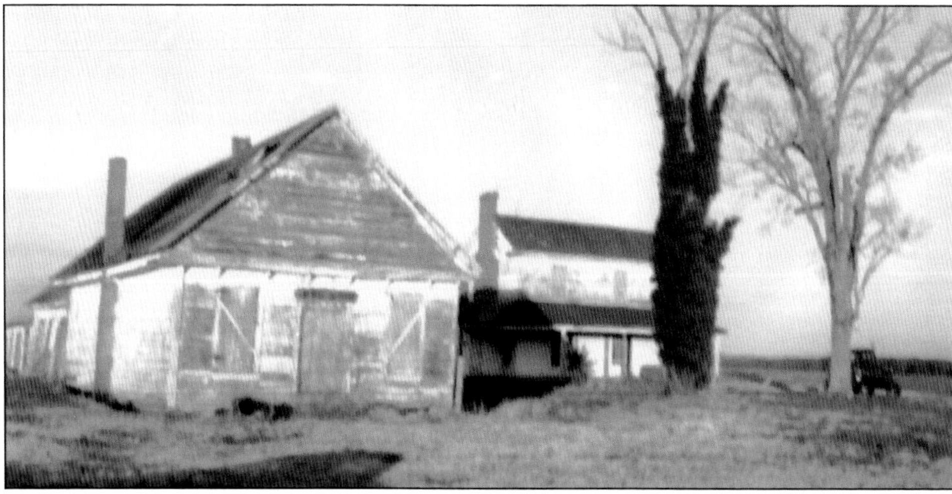

Spruill, a former slaveholder, negotiated labor contracts with freedmen to farm his land and sold seed, fertilizers, and farm implements to freedmen in Indian Woods. Spruill's store, at left, operated until the late 1970s. (Courtesy of SHC, UNC.)

siblings. One of the more unfortunate results of this is that many of the families began to function as mini plantations. This included the fathers playing the roles of masters, and wives and children as slaves.[7]

During the Jim Crow years, the lives of both black and white residents of Bertie County were spent making a living and very little else, except worshipping on Sunday and some schooling during the winter months. Crops were planted and harvested in much the same manner as they had been during slavery. These crops, lumber, and people were transported to markets and port cities by a combination of steamers and rail lines, such as the old W&P Railroad, or "Walk and Push" as it was known, from Windsor to Ahoskie by way of Askewville and Powellsville. Steamers like the *Bertie* were frequently seen on the Cashie, Roanoke, and Chowan Rivers.[8] In fact, three of the leading companies were the Cashie Steam Navigation Company, which was formed by the Seaboard & Roanoke Railroad, and its connecting rail and steam companies in Baltimore, Philadelphia, New York, Boston, and all places in North and South Carolina.

There was also the Roanoke, Norfolk & Baltimore Steamboat Company, which ran a direct line from the Roanoke River to Norfolk, Virginia. And finally, the Roanoke River Transportation Company had three steamers, the *Astoria*, the *Rotary*, and the *Vesta*.[9] Few residents, black or white, with the exception of large landowners and merchants, could afford luxuries like fine clothing, china, or furniture. Instead, they, like earlier generations, made and repaired their own clothes, quilts, and furniture from pieces of cloth, denim, burlap, and wood found in and around their homes. Also, supplies like seed and fertilizer could be purchased at the general stores located in rural parts of the county, such as Spruill's store in Indian Woods. Most of the residents of Bertie County's rural areas rarely went to nearby towns. With the added lack of transportation, most poor blacks and whites were content to remain in their communities where they were not bothered.[10]

In these rural areas, the sense of community became very intense. Community residents rarely spent much time in contact with residents who lived in other parts of the county unless they had kin living in a particular area. In fact, life everywhere in the county tended to center around family, work, and church.[11] Most communities and the families that comprised them behaved more as clans than modern communities. All residents living in a particular community tended to be related by blood. Cousins, aunts, uncles, grandparents, and great grandparents all lived within walking distance of each other. The elderly of the communities maintained a special status and were often visited and cared for by everyone who claimed the person as a common ancestor.[12]

Because of the large size of most families, children grew up with plenty of opportunities to socialize at home while doing chores, at work in the fields, at church on Sundays, during prayer meetings, at baptisms, weddings, funerals, or revivals. From the 1880s until 1954, this would be the norm for the residents of Bertie County. For African Americans, the isolation and devotion to family, work, and church kept their children from the daily sight of signs saying, "whites only" and conflicts with racist whites living in towns. In areas of the county where numbers of poor whites and blacks lived closely together, such as in Beaching Light, children did play together and families treated each other as good Christians would.[13] They did not, however, attend church together, nor encourage dating or marriage. They were respectful of one another without violating the Jim Crow laws of the state. In fact, relations between blacks and whites throughout the county were very individual. Some whites and their families were known to blacks throughout the county to be fair, kind people while others were known for their unfairness, meanness, and treachery. Whites of the latter sort were avoided and, thus, the county endured the Jim Crow years with few racial incidents.[14] This is not to say that the black residents of the county were totally immune to the effects of segregation or that they were not aware of life outside of the county. Rural life did, however, have its advantages. With no need for an education beyond basic reading, writing, and arithmetic to conduct farm business, most residents were satisfied with their under-funded and inadequate educational facilities. In fact, in comparing them to the facilities that many parents and grandparents experienced under slavery, they were seen as quite an improvement. What the residents may not have realized until the 1950s was that Jim Crow and segregation meant more than just signs, but economic and educational opportunities that they were entitled to but denied.[15]

During the period from 1890 to 1920, which historians have termed the progressive era, Bertie County, North Carolina, the South, and the nation saw many movements that impacted them. These included the Populist movement and Farmers Alliance, the Women's Suffrage and Feminist Movement, and the education and social reform movements.[16] Although whites also instituted and expanded segregation in Bertie County and North Carolina during this period, progressives were successful in convincing the people of the importance of education for whites and blacks as well as women. As a result, North Carolina saw an increase in the number and funding of state colleges and universities, as well as primary and secondary schools during the period. The funding for black institutions was usually about half what it was for whites, but the state's emphasis on education had a positive impact on the county during the period.[17]

Educational reform gave poor residents of the county access to a better education than was possible at any other time in the county's 300-year history. Rich and poor, whites and blacks, boys and girls, men and women were encouraged and allowed an education in large numbers for the first time, though the professions such education could be used for were limited for many in the Jim Crow South.[18]

During the progressive era, Bertie County built a number of schools called Rosenwald schools for its black residents. The brain child of Booker T. Washington and the Tuskegee Institute, and funded by local residents and philanthropist Julius Rosenwald, president of Sears, Roebuck, and Company, the Rosenwald schools covered the county, state, and entire region. With Rosenwald's financial assistance, over 5,300 schools were built in the South between 1910 and 1930. North Carolina led the South with over 800 schools built under the direction of W.F. Credle, the supervisor of the Rosenwald fund in North Carolina. By the time the funds ran out, 19 schools had been built in Bertie County. After 1931, another seven were built in the county, using the Rosenwald plan, by Credle, as the new director of School House Planning for the state of North Carolina.[19] Although the Rosenwald schools helped blacks in the county learn basic reading, writing, and arithmetic, segregation and the lack of blacks, women, and poor white men who could not pay the poll tax or pass the literacy test to vote hindered the development of these groups in the county until the 1960s.[20]

Teachers included Sadie Ruffin, Catherine Bond, Lucy Bazemore, Evelyn Little, Sahara Williams, and Maude Philips.[21] At all the schools, students were required to pledge allegiance to the flag and say a morning prayer before classes started. If students misbehaved or did not complete assignments, they were spanked by their teachers. In the winter, teachers used pot-bellied stoves, which used coal as fuel after kindling was used by

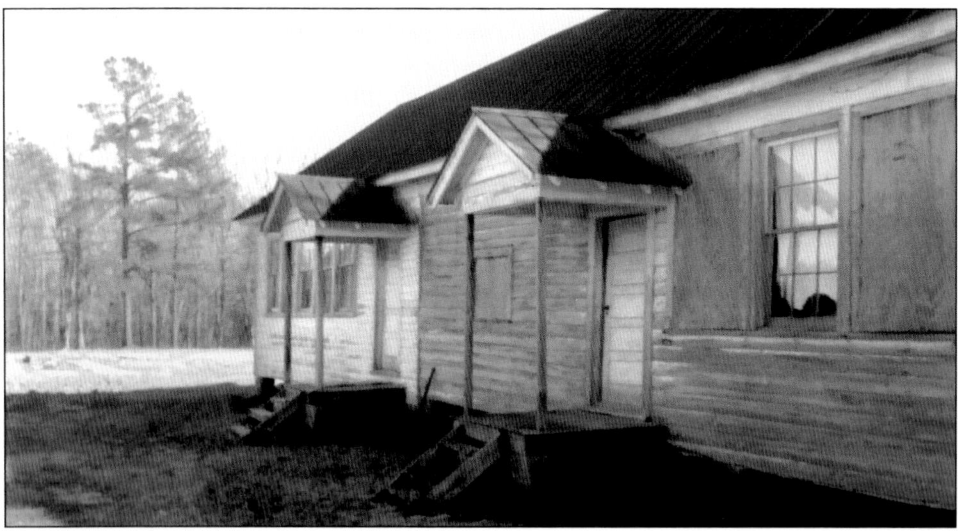

The Spring Hill Rosenwald school was one of 26 in Bertie County and one of more than 800 built in North Carolina from 1910 to 1930 under the direction of W.F. Credle, supervisor of the Rosenwald fund in North Carolina. (Courtesy of SHC, UNC.)

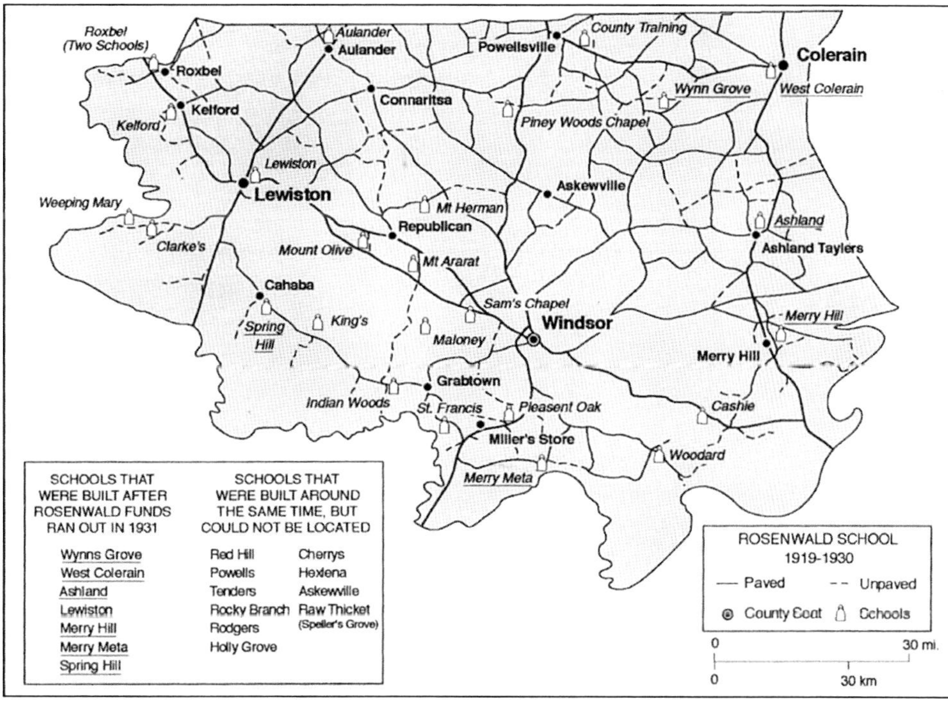

Rosenwald schools were built with funds raised by local residents and money donated by philanthropist Julius Rosenwald, president of Sears, Roebuck and Company. Through Rosenwald's efforts, over 5,300 school were built in the South from 1910 to 1930.

the teachers to start the stoves burning. It was the students' job to bring coal and kindling in to keep the fires going. These schools, along with the rest of the county's schools, were consolidated in 1959. This consolidation eliminated the all-black school system in Bertie County and created one county public school system for all children. Students from Spring Hill were bused to the town of Lewiston to the John B. Bond School for grades one through seven, and those in Indian Woods, Saint Francis, Caine, and Beacon Light were bused to the town of Windsor and attended W.S. Etheridge School. Eighth and ninth graders from all over the county were sent to Bertie Junior High School, and students in tenth through twelfth grades were sent to Bertie Senior High School. Prior to bus service, a parent would have to pay for a child to travel or board while he or she attended W.S. Etheridge High School. This bus service began in 1936 and continued from then on.[22]

The inability of poor white men and women to understand that their interests were connected to those of black men and women also hindered the educational, political, and economic development of all these groups in the county. The establishment of the Farmer's Alliance and the rise of the Populist movement in the 1890s joined poor white and black tenant farmers, sharecroppers, and yeomen farmers to create a viable third party in the state and nation, take control of the state assembly, and threaten the presidency. In spite of support for both the Farmers Alliance and the Populist movement, because of segregation, little political interaction took place between whites and blacks in the county.

As late as 1935, poor whites still saw blacks as competitors for jobs and as a threat to their families, rather than as allies against the wealthy landowners and merchants who kept them in an economic form of slavery.[23]

Although the county continued to be one of the state's leading producers of cotton, tobacco, and peanuts, it would also become a world leader in producing herring. Herring fishing had been part of Bertie County's culture and life since the time of Native Americans. Due to the Roanoke and Chowan Rivers being major breeding areas for herring, for centuries during the spring, fishermen with nets and baskets have harvested the fish from these rivers by the thousands. During the colonial period, residents smoked and packed them in salt to preserve them throughout the summer months. They were used to supplement their diets throughout the winter. Slaves who lived on plantations near the rivers were allowed to fish when work was slow and looked forward to the spring runs in which enough fish could be caught to feed the whole plantation for months. Spring fish fries were begun and, by the 1890s, communities organized groups of men either in boats or on the shore to catch fish, while women known as cutters cleaned, scaled, smoked, and packed them. As the popularity of the fish grew, local whites began to pack and sell them. By the antebellum period, herring fishing was becoming a major industry for the county. Disrupted by the Civil War, it began again in earnest at the close of the war and, by the 1890s, was well on its way to becoming a worldwide enterprise. The wealth generated, for example, helped the Capeharts of Avoca to rebuild their family's fortune lost with the emancipation of their slaves in 1865 and offered other former slaveholders along the Chowan and Roanoke Rivers the same opportunity.[24]

The first seine fishery in Bertie County was established by Joseph Blount Skinner of Edenton at Eden House Beach in 1807; the second at Lawrence's Point on the Chowan 6 miles south of Colerain in 1815. Throughout the mid-1800s, seine fishing was practiced by Bertie fisherman on the shores of the Chowan, Roanoke, and Cashie Rivers and in the Albemarle Sound. As advanced nets were developed and deployed further up the sound, seine fishing in Bertie County waters became less profitable and, by 1915, had disappeared altogether. The last seine to operate in the county was Capehart's Fishery at Sutton Beach, owned by Dr. W.R. Capehart who had served as a surgeon in the Confederate army during the Civil War. After his death, his son George W. Capehart ran the seine until it stopped operating.[25]

There were a recorded total of 18 fisheries in Bertie County, but there may have been more, particularly on the Cashie River. These fisheries not only provided work for male and female residents, but they helped many former slave owners maintain a standard of living they had enjoyed before the Civil War. The Chowan fisheries included Lazy Hill, Point Comfort, Colerain, Goose Pond, Bull Pond, Mount Gould, Hermitage, Willow Branch, Eden House, and Bal Gra. On the Roanoke, there were Kitty Hawk, 2 miles above Plymouth; Calm Point, 6 miles above Plymouth; Willow Point at Jamesville; and Slades near Hamilton. The Cashie fisheries included Terrapin Point, Hopewell, Wood Island, and possibly others. And on the Albemarle were Scotch Hall or Capehart's fishery which, by the 1960s, had been closed, and the Avoca farm sold to R.J. Reynolds Tobacco Company.[26]

One of the only remaining fisheries in the county by 2002 was the Perry-Wynns Fishery based in Colerain. This fishery survived by buying fish from fishermen and processing

This herring fish haul could have been at any of the more than 18 fisheries in Bertie County along the Chowan and Roanoke Rivers and the Albemarle Sound from 1865 to the early twentieth century. This picture was taken in early 1900s. (Courtesy of NCC, UNC.)

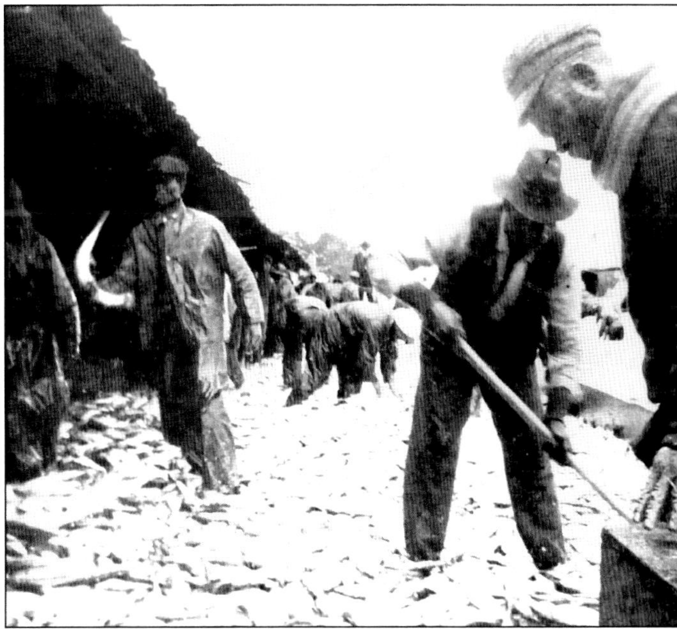

them. All of the fish brought to the fishery were used for food except "down-runs," which were fish that had spawned upstream and were floating back down again. These fish were sold to farmers as feed for livestock. In 1962, the fishery was recorded to have processed 13 million herring, 2 million of these were (pickled) vinegar-cured and the rest were salted or corned. All parts of the fished were used as either livestock feed, food, or, as was the case for the scales, costume jewelry. Perry-Wynns exported herring and other fish around the world and remains one of the county's major industries.[27]

By the early 1900s, life in the county was not unlike anywhere else in the Jim Crow rural South. Poor whites and blacks worked tobacco, cotton, and peanut plantations in the county. Blacks feared lynchings and mob violence if they did not abide by Jim Crow laws, and they and poor whites were exploited for their needed labor. Whites and blacks also continued to hunt, fish, and raise domesticated animals for food as they had since colonial times. Poverty or near poverty, however, was the condition for most residents throughout the 1900s. There were, however, still prominent whites who sat on the judiciary or served in the state legislature like Reverend T.T. Speight, who served in the North Carolina Senate. Speight lived in Windsor and was well respected and well thought of, as was the rest of his family.[28]

Throughout the early 1900s, church also remained a central force in the lives of all the residents of the county, rich or poor, white or black. Residents flocked to church on Sunday and enjoyed the fellowship it provided. Although most residents by 1915 still walked or rode horse- or mule-drawn wagons to church, some of the wealthier residents of the county purchased automobiles. The invention of the automobile revolutionized the United States and beyond. It was another marvel of a rapidly mechanizing world. In spite of the county's and region's lack of good roads, it was home to one of the pioneers

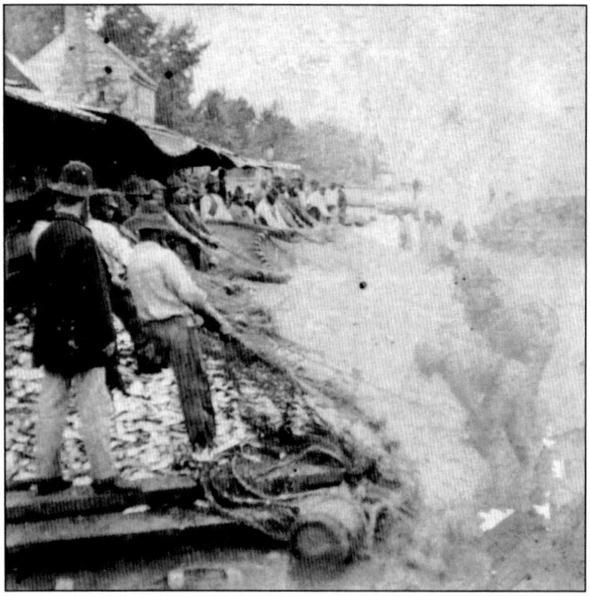

Fishermen secure a haul of fish at the Capehart Fishery in the 1890s. (Courtesy of NCSAH.)

of automobile transportation, Charles H. Jenkins and Company of Aulander. Jenkins brought automobiles to Bertie County by having them driven 75 miles down from Norfolk, Virginia, a torturous all-day trip on narrow dirt roads through miles of forest and swamps with no paved roads, bridges, or service stations to stop for gas or repairs. For those who could afford them, they were a necessity and, by 1916, quite popular.[29]

When World War I broke out in 1914, most residents of Bertie were isolationist. As the war dragged on, the Germans began to threaten international shipping and a number of residents became supporters of United States intervention. When the United States entered the Great War in 1917, a number of whites and blacks from the county joined the Marines, Army, or Navy and served during the war. Blacks from the county who joined the armed services eventually served in France, some under French commanders because the federal government did not want them to fight. But with the support of General John Pershing, who had commanded black troops during the Spanish-American War, they were allowed to serve and did see combat by the end of the war. The soldiers who served would never forget its horrors. Those that survived were changed forever.[30]

For most residents in the county, it was a faraway war in a faraway place that did not seem to be their war, but for those who frequented the waters off the North Carolina coast, German U-boats that attacked ships along the coast brought the war closer to home. As Bertie residents had done in previous wars, both blacks and whites answered their nation's call to service. When the war ended in 1919, many returned home with mixed feelings. Many of the whites who had served were convinced of the need to stay out of Europe and its conflicts. The African Americans who served were amazed at the seeming lack of racism in Europe, particularly France, where many served and received high praise and military honors. They returned to Bertie County, which was firmly entrenched in segregation and peonage, and those who returned to live understood, but never truly accepted these issues. These men were the first to see what life in the county could be like without segregation and racism. Nevertheless, as the events of what historians call the "Red Summer" showed (with over 30 violent racial clashes, nationally causing the loss of hundreds of lives and the destruction of millions of dollars worth of property), neither their nation nor their county was ready for change. As a result, at the end of the war, many of the soldiers returned home and, as their grandfathers had done, used the money they earned during the war to purchase the land their families had farmed for generations or added to their farms if they already owned them.[31]

Because of limited economic opportunities in the county, some of those who stayed at home began to leave when jobs opened up in the war industries elsewhere. Because of the war in Europe, many poor whites and blacks left the county, if they could, in search of these high-paying industrial jobs in port cities in Virginia—Norfolk, Portsmouth, and Hampton—and northern industrial centers like New York, Philadelphia, and Baltimore, becoming part of the Great Migration. Some residents were lured by the promise of better wages and living standards to these port cities where they could work in the shipbuilding and other war industries. But most residents remained in Bertie County and continued to farm or work as farm laborers.[32] With plenty of work to do and close family and religious ties, these residents found it hard to leave their home. Those who did leave enjoyed the freedom, anonymity, and entertainment of large cities like New York. For African

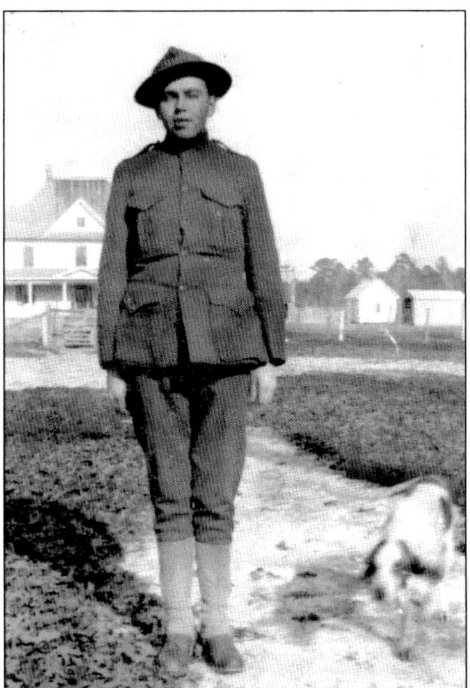

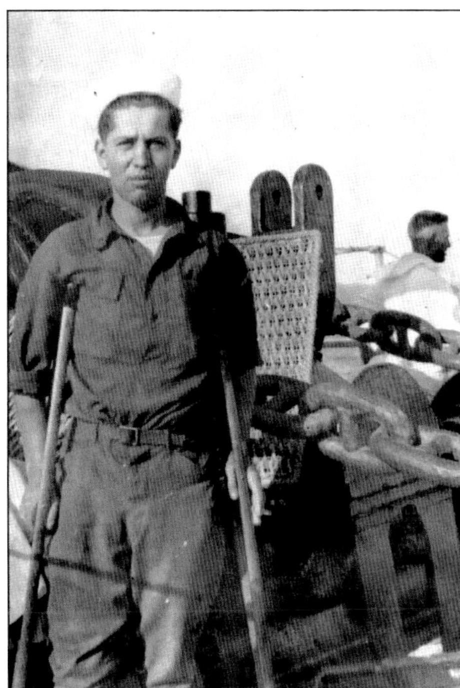

Pictured at his home in Windsor in 1918, James Alexander Speight (left) joined the Marines during World War I. Lloyd Wood Speight, also of Windsor and pictured (right) in 1918, served in the navy during the same war. (Both courtesy of SHC, UNC.)

Americans, it was the beginning of the "Harlem Renaissance" and the Marcus Garvey Movement; for whites, it was the speakeasies and fast life of the Roaring Twenties.[33]

For most of the poor residents that remained in the county, there was no memory of such noted events as the Harlem Renaissance or the Roaring Twenties. In the rural, isolated farming environment, these things were unimportant to poor farming folk, who understood only basic reading, writing, and arithmetic, and were devoted to their work, churches, and families. Most had neither the time or interest to devote to the intellectual or social movements during this time. There were, however, Garveyites in Bertie County. Marcus Garvey, who preached race pride, self help, and independence from whites, was well liked and well received by blacks throughout northeastern North Carolina. Although blacks in Bertie held little interest in returning to Africa as he advocated, they did join Garvey's organization and support it financially. Thus, from 1919 to 1929, they were ardent supporters and followers of Garvey. During this period, there was also an increase in Klan activity. Whether whites saw black involvement in the Garvey Movement as a threat, or blacks joined the movement in response to the increased threat of racial violence, is unclear, but until the start of the Great Depression in 1929, there was an increase in tension between whites and blacks in the county.[34] Most blacks did not trust authorities such as the county sheriff, elected officials, or the courts.

By the start of the Great Depression, most poor whites and blacks were still making their living off the land. During the Great Depression from 1929 to 1939, life in Bertie County remained basically the same as it had for over 300 years. Most rural families were living in houses that were constructed in the late eighteenth and early nineteenth centuries. They had no running water or electricity and still heated their homes and cooked on wood stoves in the winter and outside during the hottest months in the summer.[35]

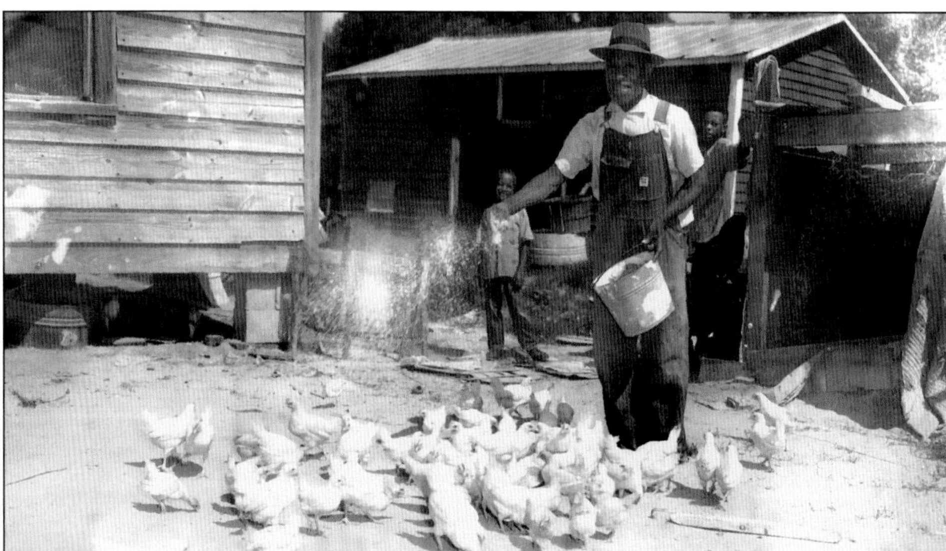

Daniel Smallwood feeds chickens in his swept yard in the early 1960s as two of his children look on. (Courtesy of Frank Stephenson, Chowan College.)

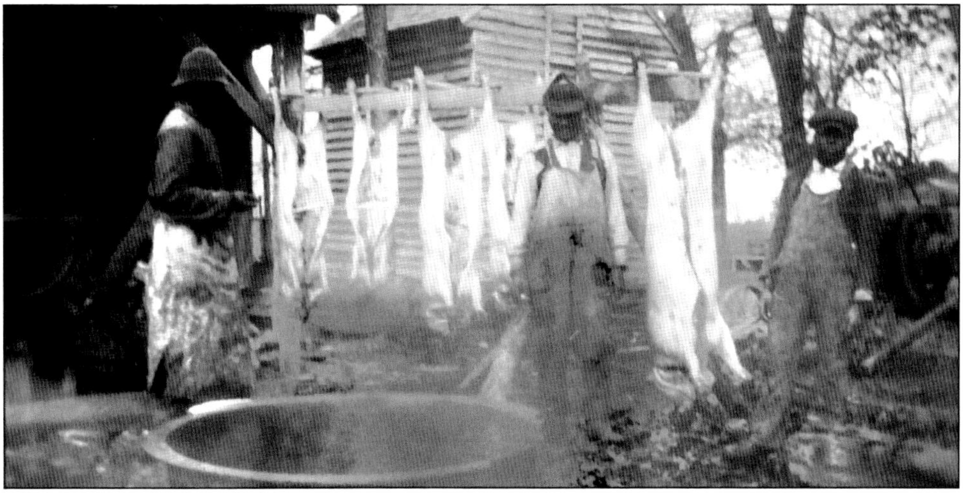

This 1920s scene shows hogs being prepared for salting, smoking, or becoming the region's famous pork barbecue. (Courtesy of SHC, UNC.)

Because families were accustomed to doing without money and tended to, at least, keep their money in mattresses and jars hidden in walls or buried in the yard, they were not as adversely affected by the stock market crash. In fact, many were amazed to hear that people were committing suicide, the worst sin according to their religion. Most residents enjoyed an abundance of foodstuffs, which they had managed for years to grow, hunt, and raise, and some even owned their small farms.[36] As a result, they weathered the hardship of the Depression well. Lord Cornwallis Cherry, who was a young boy during the Great Depression, remembered that although money was scarce, they had plenty of food to eat. He remembered raking leaves for 10¢ per hour from 1929 to 1934 and remembered making only $6 for an entire winter's worth of work.[37]

In spite of the hardships of the Great Depression, the residents of the county demonstrated remarkable loyalty to their churches, families, and community. Although economic changes forced the residents of Bertie County to migrate out of the area and become more exposed to racism, they continued to maintain their faith in God. In 1935, C.W. Bazemore reported, "In church membership per square mile, or per thousand population, Bertie County, in the eastern section of North Carolina, leads the hundred counties of the state for both white and colored races." Bazemore stated that only Charlotte, which was considered the "church goingest" town in North Carolina, was close to it. He went on to state, "The Negroes of Bertie County are regarded as the most religious of any in eastern North Carolina, and their devotion to their churches is amazing." He further noted that blacks would sell chickens, hams, eggs, corn, potatoes, and work at day labor to pay their preachers and other church obligations—surpassing the whites in the county in their loyalty. He concluded his observations by stating that no community or person in Bertie County was beyond reach of a church and that practically every child, upon reaching ten to twelve years of age, joined the church of his parents and grandparents.[38] When asked, many residents of both races quickly point to God, church, and family as the most important things in their lives. They credit God with giving them the ability to endure adversity and to carry on. This unbreakable faith in God and family would serve the residents of the county well throughout the Great Depression

That very little attention was paid to political and economic empowerment was fine with the white local and county officials. Social development, however, was encouraged. When residents were not working, they enjoyed attending church, particularly church socials. During these events, called fish fries, food would either be prepared at home and brought to the church or prepared at the church. One dish that was often served was fried herring and cornbread, and the gatherings were usually held in the spring during the spawning season. Church members with small fishing boats would fish, netting herring by the thousands. Once dressed, the fish were deep-fried in large iron pots that would be filled with lard and heated by wood fires. Pork was also served at these socials. Unlike herring, which was seasonal, pork was served year round. Pork barbecue, which was unique to eastern North Carolina, and appears from the colonial records to have originated with the Tuscarora, normally involved a freshly killed hog that, once dressed, was split in two and grilled on an open wood fire. Oak was the primary choice because it was believed to season the pork as it cooked. Finally, once the pork was done, it was chopped up into very fine pieces and seasoned with salt, black pepper, red pepper, and vinegar and served with cole slaw. Eastern North Carolina barbecue is unique and appears to be an example of the merging of European, African, and Native American cultures in the region. Europeans introduced vinegar and pork and Native Americans and Africans introduced the preparation and seasoning. Two favorite dishes served with barbecue—cole

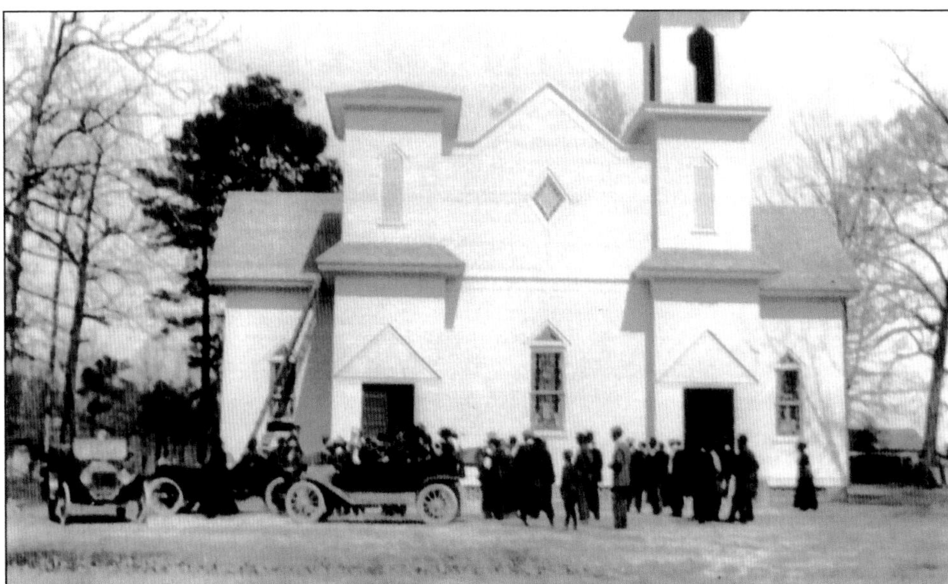

Members of the Republican Baptist Church pose in front of the church in the early 1900s. Reverend T.T. Speight served as a member of the senate in the North Carolina General Assembly. (Courtesy of SHC, UNC.)

William Outlaw waters his mule at lunch time on his farm in Bertie County, c. 1938. (Courtesy of SHC, UNC.)

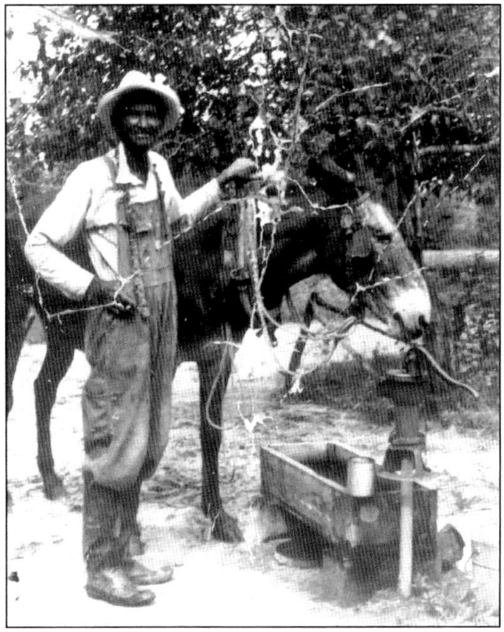

slaw and hush puppies—also appear to be a merging of ethnic tastes. Hush puppies are a mixture of cornmeal, onions, and spices that seem to originate in West Africa. Cole slaw, on the other hand, is a cabbage-based dish that originated in Europe.[39] Church and church socials provided residents on nearby farms an opportunity to worship God with family and friends and to socialize with people who were otherwise unable to see much of each other because of distance, lack of transportation, and work.[40]

Daily life for most African Americans living in Bertie County revolved around work, family, and the church. With the exception of the spirituals sung at the various African American churches, no evidence has been uncovered to indicate that the black residents of Bertie County have retained their African culture in a pure form. Instead, the evidence tends to support a meshing of African, Native American, and European cultures, which is evident in the various homes and churches that are present today in the county.

By the presidential elections of 1932, many of the eligible voters had grown weary of the inaction of the Republicans. Bertie County still was dependent on farming and trade. Low farm prices were driving most sharecroppers and tenant farmers further into debt as landowners and merchants tried to pass on their economic troubles to the poor laborers. Unable to afford seed, fertilizer, or other farm supplies, many found themselves with no share or little share at the end of the growing seasons. As a result, most whites in the county voted enthusiastically for Franklin D. Roosevelt, a Democrat. With the support of the South, Roosevelt won the election of 1932 and immediately set out to jump-start the economy. Although programs such as the WPA had little positive impact on the county's black population, the county did receive over $14,000 in loans and grants for school improvements from 1933 to 1937, most of which were allocated to improve the white public schools in the county.[41]

The Roosevelt years meant radical changes in both the politics and daily lives of the residents of Bertie County. Because Roosevelt appeared willing to listen to the concerns of blacks, he gained a great deal of respect and political support from blacks, who had been loyal Republicans since emancipation. Evidence of this includes 700 blacks from North Carolina, calling themselves the "United Negro Democrats of North Carolina," who endorsed Roosevelt in June of 1940. Later, in the election, Roosevelt received three-fourths of the state's black vote. This trend continued as blacks all over the nation began to join and vote as Democrats. The Roosevelt years would also see the rise of the National Association for the Advancement of Colored People (NAACP) in Bertie County, as membership in the organization grew throughout the state.[42]

Unfortunately, it was not the depression that adversely affected many of the poor farming families of Bertie County, but the New Deal policies introduced by Franklin D. Roosevelt and enacted by Congress between 1933 to 1945. When the Agricultural Adjustment Act (AAA) was passed by Congress in 1933, it was intended to pay struggling farmers whose crops, such as cotton, tobacco, wheat, and corn, had become too expensive to grow. They were, therefore, paid not to grow certain crops. In Bertie County, as in the rest of North Carolina and the South, landowners paid these subsidies, promptly asked their tenant farmers and sharecroppers not to farm, but expected them to continue paying rent for living on their lands. They even fired some, forcing them off the land since landowners made more money from the federal government for allowing land to sit idle. This forced many whites and blacks not fortunate enough to have landlords who allowed them to stay and farm for their families to leave their farms and the county in search of work. Only independent small black and white farmers survived this ordeal. As a result of this situation, which was happening all over North Carolina and the South, tenant farmers and sharecroppers attempted to organize unions.[43] All of these were violently broken up by landowners and anyone who had joined or attended meetings was run off their land. These people joined others from all over the South who moved north in search of better economic opportunities.[44] The impact of this migration can clearly be seen by examining the Indian Woods township of Bertie County from 1940 to 1950. In 1950, the United States census recorded that the Indian Woods township contained a population of 1,349, a decrease of 336 people from 1,685 in 1940. The 1960 census recorded the population of Indian Woods to be 1,183. Of this number, only 76 were white. There were 600 males, 583 females, 76 whites, and 1,107 blacks.[45]

The start of World War II in Europe in 1938 and the preparation for war saved many of these families from the depths of the Depression. Most found jobs when they arrived in northern cities in the war industries that were mass producing tanks, planes, guns, and munitions for the Allies. Others from Bertie County and the South would join them from 1938 to 1941 in the Great Migration, lured by the high wages offered in these industries. The South lost over 3.2 million blacks to northern cities, many of whom were from Bertie and other parts of North Carolina.[46]

When the United States entered the war in 1941, Bertie County's men and women were again called upon to serve their country. Residents did what they had done in other wars and joined the Army, Navy, Marines, and Air Force. By the end of the war, hundreds of the county's citizens had served and some had given their lives either fighting the

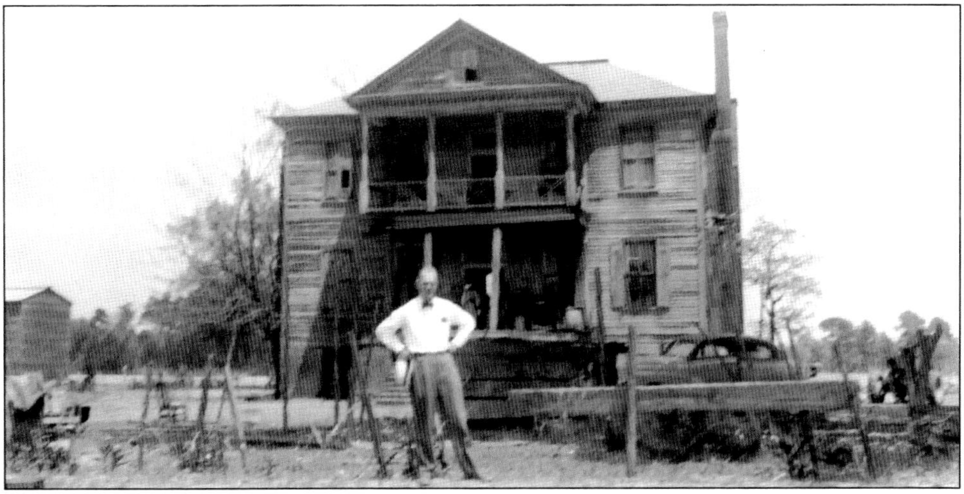

Phillip Russell stands in front of the Hope House in Windsor before its restoration. The Hope House was home to former governor David Stone who served North Carolina from 1808 to 1810. (Courtesy of NCC, UNC.)

Germans and Italians in Europe and North Africa or fighting the Japanese in the Pacific. This war was not seen by residents as simply a faraway war like World War I. This new war was brought home by German U-boats, which constantly torpedoed ships headed for Europe off the North Carolina coast during the early years of the war. Residents of eastern North Carolina could often see the fires of burning ships off the North Carolina coast.[47]

Those who did not serve in the armed forces began to join thousands of North Carolinians who were leaving the state for jobs in the war industries in port cities to the north. Many from the county found jobs nearby in Norfolk, Virginia as earlier residents had done during World War I. More adventuresome people took buses to Baltimore, Washington, D.C., Philadelphia, or New York. Some residents returned after the war, but most did not. World War II marked the beginning of a mass exodus from Bertie County that took place between 1940 and 1980. The continuation of this migration out of Bertie County had a tremendous impact on the county.[48] The population of Indian Woods, for example, would continue to fall, as would that of other townships and, by the 1970 census, a decline of 26 percent (1,183 to 874) was recorded, a decrease of 309 people.[49]

As the migration continued, it increasingly involved young college-age men and women leaving to join the military, go to college, or seek employment outside of the county, particularly in Norfolk, Virginia, where jobs were plentiful at the naval shipyard. Few of these young people ever returned to Bertie County, except to visit family and friends who remained.[50] Things began to change in Bertie County. Tractors replaced horses and mules. Corn, peanut, and cotton pickers began to do the work that previously required manual labor. Furthermore, pesticides and weed killers were being used instead of the hoe. Machinery was finally changing Bertie County as nearly everywhere else in the world. Because of the changes brought on by farm mechanization in Bertie County, many residents began to lose the only jobs they had ever known. However, the fishing

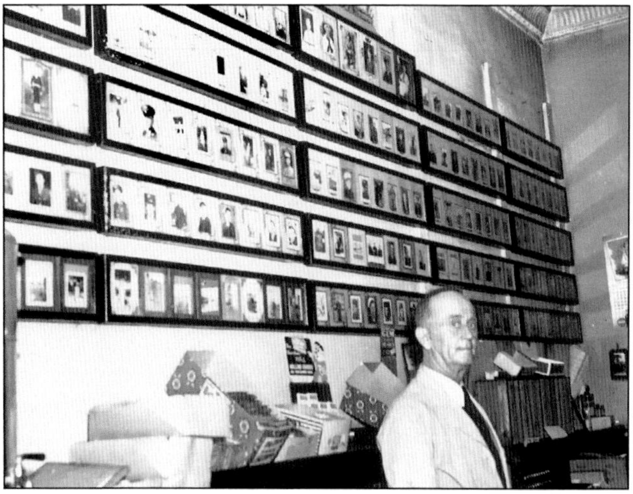

In this 1945 image, A.B. "Pop" poses in his store in Windsor in front of a photo gallery of Bertie County men who served their country in World War II. (Courtesy of NCSAH.)

and lumber industries had always been as important to the economy of Bertie County as farming. Because of the residents' desire to stay near their birthplaces and an abundance of work in the township, there had never been any reason for many to leave.[51]

Farm mechanization permanently altered the lives of the farming families of Bertie County. Although a number of independent farmers still existed, they were rapidly disappearing as they lost their family farms due to financial problems brought on by the rise of technology. The children of sharecroppers and tenant farmers, whose fathers had remained dependent on agriculture for their livelihood, were no longer needed in the same numbers as before farm mechanization. Other small, independent farmers either could not afford the new farm machinery or, once purchased, could not afford to pay for it.[52]

For most middle- and upper-class whites in the county, the end of World War II brought prosperity and a desire to return to normalcy. With the financial assistance of the G.I. Bill, residents built new homes, attended college, and began to raise families. They enjoyed the county's beaches, fishing, and boating in the rivers. Many residents felt as they had during World War I—that the war was not their war. Many segregationists, unhappy with the recruitment, training, and deployment of black troops during the war and outraged by the desegregation of the armed forces in 1948 by Harry S. Truman, vowed to maintain segregation in the South and enforce Jim Crow laws. Segregationists in the county were determined to stop any changes to their way of life.

As a result, for those who remained in Bertie County, life changed very little. Farms were still tended in spite of displacement due to rapid mechanization. Residents still attended church on Sundays and children still helped in the fields during the summer months and attended school during the winter months. Nevertheless, the war really had changed the United States and the millions of blacks living in this country, including those in Bertie County. Although local blacks continued to avoid direct confrontation with segregationists, most blacks in the county were armed. As Timothy Tyson points out in his article on Robert F. Williams in the *Journal of American History*, rural blacks throughout the South during the Jim Crow era were armed and used their firearms to hunt for food. Thus, most were skilled at using their weapons and, when threatened, even by whites, blacks, and Native Americans in North Carolina, were known to use their guns for protection as was the case when the Lumbee of Robeson County routed the Klan in January of 1958. White and black ministers from 1945 to 1954 encouraged their congregations to refrain from violence, while also preaching on the horrors of racism as revealed in Hitler's Germany and the Jewish Holocaust. Blacks and many whites were determined not to allow a similar event to happen in this country.[53]

By 1954, the county, the state, and the entire South would experience its greatest challenge yet in the form of the Civil Rights Movement. This movement and the laws passed as a result of it would empower poor whites and blacks in the county and change the old social, economic, and educational order of the entire state. Although the movement was successful in changing the county without loss of life, it was not without protest and defiant action. The success of peaceful protests in Williamston and Windsor, United States Supreme Court rulings in 1954 and 1955, and new laws enacted by Congress in 1964 and 1965 to integrate schools and businesses and to protect blacks' right to vote were met with the closing of some schools and the opening of private Christian academies throughout eastern North Carolina. Many poor whites who had suffered just as much under peonage and Jim Crow as blacks, allowed racism to infect them and joined forces with the same affluent whites who had mistreated them in opposing integration. In spite of this, change did come by the mid-1960s, and religion and black churches, established from 1865 to 1895, were the catalysts for that change. They would inform, educate, inspire, and raise funds that would be used to uplift the poor all over the county.[54]

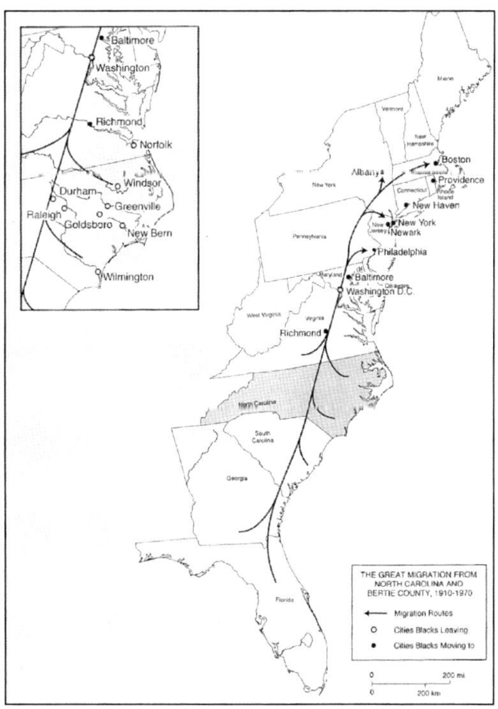

This map shows the routes and destinations of the people who joined the Great Migration out of Bertie and the surrounding counties. The migration had a tremendous impact on Bertie County, North Carolina, and the rest of the South. From 1910 to 1970 thousands of whites and blacks left Bertie County for northern industrial cities like New York, Philadelphia, and Boston.

8. Life in the Rural "New South": During and Since the Civil Rights Movement, 1954–2002

The Civil Rights Movement began in the final days of World War II as the United States emerged from the war as a superpower and the strongest democracy, both economically and militarily, worldwide. Europe and the rest of the world looked to the United States to lead them and protect them from the second great superpower, the Soviet Union, whose political ideology (Communism) was seen as more evil and destructive than Nazism. With the world's eyes upon it, America was forced to deal with segregation in the South and its treatment of millions of its African-American citizens. To the world, the lynching, beating, raping, and outright murder and intimidation of blacks that happened daily in the South was no different than what the Germans had done to millions of Jewish and non-German people in Europe, and was precisely what the Soviets were doing in areas of Europe under their control.

To be seen as the leader of the free world, it was important that the United States be seen as free itself. Blacks were United States citizens and most were descendants of the first Africans brought to colonial Virginia in 1619 and the rest of colonial America by 1660. They had built the country and fought in all of its wars, but by 1945, were still seen as less than human. In Bertie County, most were still living a hard life in spite of the fact that, by 1950, blacks made up 59.8 percent of the county's population of 26,439.[1] They were unable to vote, hold local, state, or national political office or any county government positions such as sheriff, county commissioner, or register of deeds. Nearly all lived without running water or electricity on rural farms where they had unpaved roads and few cars, and continued to grow cotton, tobacco, and some peanuts working with horses and mules. In spite of their courageous service to their county, state, and country, during World War II in the 1940s and in Korea by the 1950s, neither the county nor state had made any effort to change its attitudes or its Jim Crow laws. Whites in the county were comfortable with segregation and the privileges the laws granted them and their families.

By 1954, however, African Americans in the county and all over the South were not only prepared to fight for freedom abroad, but were also prepared to lay down their lives for their civil rights in the cities and towns of their home states. As a result, during the 1950s, the county, state, and the entire South would have their social systems challenged in the courts, on the streets, in the national media, and all over the world. The Civil Rights Movement

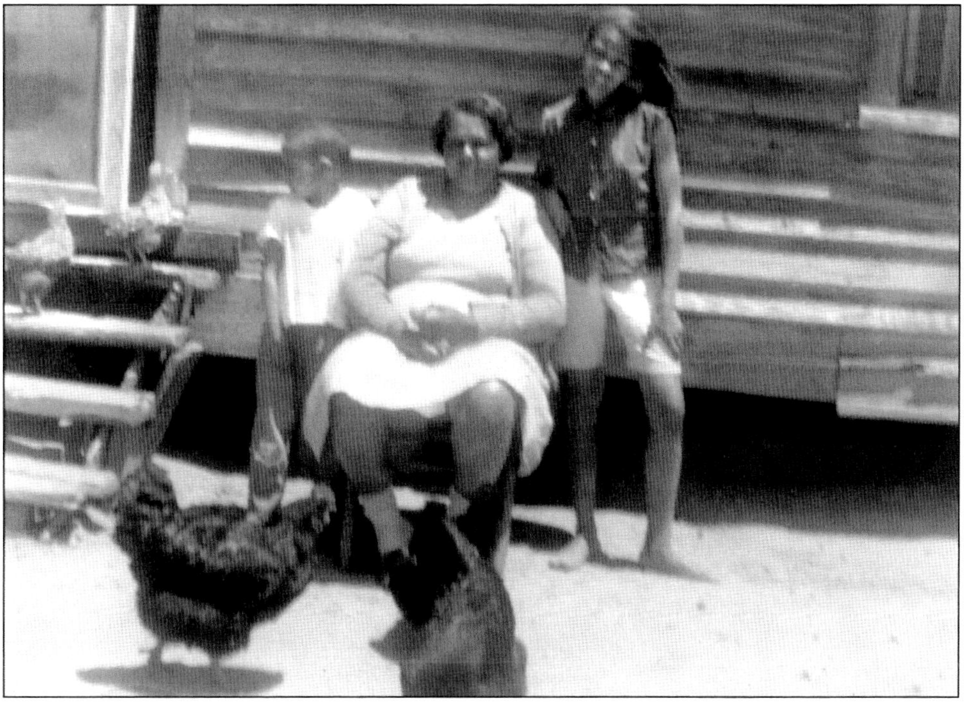

Lottie Beatrice Walton Cherry and her children, Jacqueline and Reginald, are pictured on their farm in Indian Woods in the mid-1950s. Like many poor people in the county, their home had no electricity, running water, or indoor pluming. (Courtesy of SHC, UNC.)

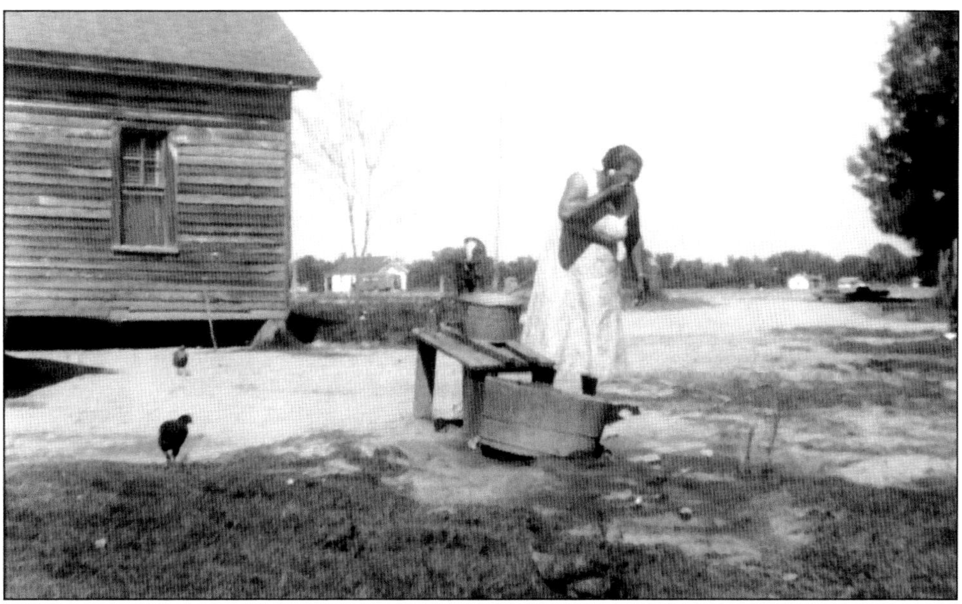

Lottie Cherry pumps water on her farm in Indian Woods in the mid-1950s. (Courtesy of SHC, UNC.)

and the laws passed as a result of it would empower poor whites and blacks in the county and change the old social, economic, and educational order of the entire South.

The Civil Rights Movement caused many changes throughout the country, particularly in Southern society. The effects of this movement on many large urban areas in the South and North are well documented, but little is known about the impact on many rural Southern communities like those in Bertie County. This chapter examines the impact of this movement, the black Baptist Church, and local civic leaders on Bertie County, especially the Indian Woods township, which is representative of the movement's impact on the rest of the county's townships.[2] The chapter also looks at activism in the Indian Woods township to document how rural people personalized and tailored the rhetoric of the Civil Rights Movement to suit their community and county needs.

The movement would have both positive and negative effect on rural African-American communities in the county. During the years between 1950 and 1980, the lives of the African-American residents of the county were greatly improved by political, educational, and economic empowerment. But, at the same time, because of the success of the movement, there was an acceleration of the Great Migration, draining these rural black communities of their young gifted men and women who chose to move away for college or better economic opportunities in larger cities around the country. In Indian Woods, two organizations that helped encourage and train these young men and women were the Blue Jay Ball Club and the Blue Jay Recreation Center.

Bart F. Smallwood founded the Blue Jay Ball Club in 1965 and the Blue Jay Recreation Center in 1972. They were supported with grants created under President Lyndon Johnson's "Great Society" programs and helped keep youth in the community out of trouble by giving them fun, constructive things to do with adult supervision after school.

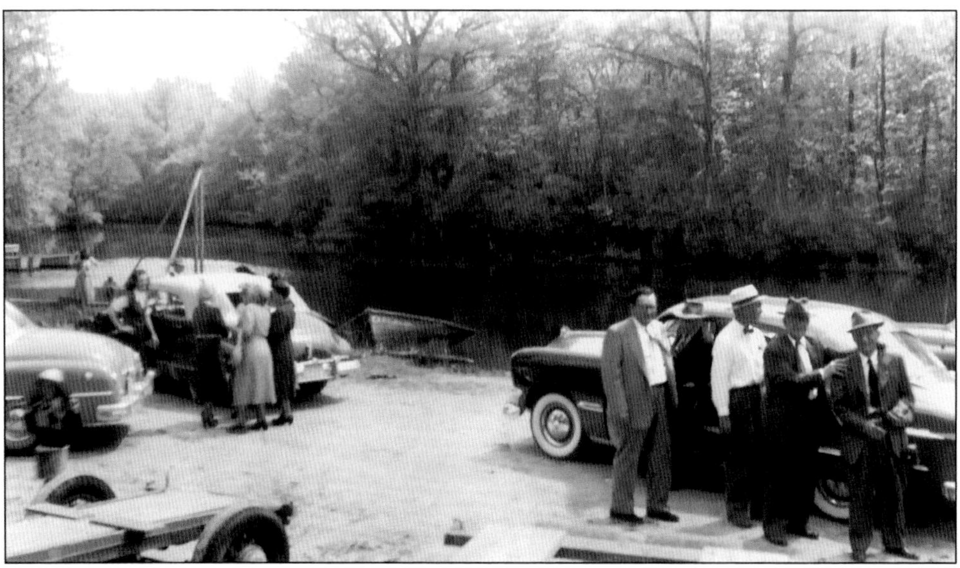

A social gathering takes place along the Roanoke River in Bertie County in the mid-1950s. (Courtesy of NCC, UNC.)

These organizations would be replicated throughout the county by blacks and whites and supported by donations from community residents, corporate, or small business sponsors, and grants from the county.[3]

While the Great Migration drained the county of its young men and women between the ages of 18 and 30 from 1950 to 1980, the rest of Bertie did not languish, but entered the 1960s, 1970s, and 1980s with new vigor and cohesiveness. The loss of people in the 1950s, 1960s, and 1970s began to end the clannish behavior of many of the county's residents. For example, African Americans from various townships began to organize and fought to provide more opportunities for their young people. These residents became closer, sharing a common sense of loss as their young men and women left for war in Korea or Vietnam, or military training, better employment, and advanced educational opportunities. In an effort to create more opportunities for their young people closer to home, many of the Baptist African-American residents of Bertie began to join the civil rights struggle through their churches. The Baptist churches scattered all over the county began to work together for the economic, educational, political, and social betterment of all residents of Bertie County. Since their creation during Reconstruction, these churches remained powerful influences in the lives of their members and, from the late 1950s to the 1990s, they would combine their efforts to work for the good of the entire county.

When Martin Luther King Jr. established the Southern Christian Leadership Conference (SCLC) in 1959, the pastors of many of these churches immediately joined the organization and encouraged their members to do so as well. The ministers and residents became greatly interested in the SCLC and its program of community empowerment. Residents became motivated by the sermons of their pastors, who encouraged them to become better educated, more politically active, and more involved in their community. By coordinating their efforts, four church pastors in and around Indian Woods—C. Melvin Creecy (Indian Woods), Andrew Jackson Cherry (Spring Hill), Brady Carmichael (Saint Francis), and Johnnie Rascoe (Beacon Light)—were able to teach residents the importance of cooperation in improving their condition. These pastors continually preached sermons about self help and racial unity, and a number of residents from their churches went out and attempted to improve their communities. They in effect created groups of civic leaders who volunteered their time and gained county and statewide recognition for their community service.[4]

Church leaders, community leaders, and residents formed the core of the Civil Rights Movement in the county. One of the most well-known and popular leaders among whites and blacks in the county was Bart F. Smallwood of Indian Woods. Church and community leaders began to encourage and promote agitation for economic, educational, political, and community development. From 1965 to 1990, Bertie County experienced a flurry of legal, social, and political activity by its African-American residents. The new leaders that emerged made contributions that improved the quality of life for all the residents of Bertie County, and relations between whites and blacks throughout the county. One of the first issues these leaders addressed was education.

By 1965, many African Americans believed that the Civil Rights Movement needed a new approach to ending the poverty and ignorance that contributed to discrimination. It was believed by many that for the Civil Rights Movement to continue to be a success, it

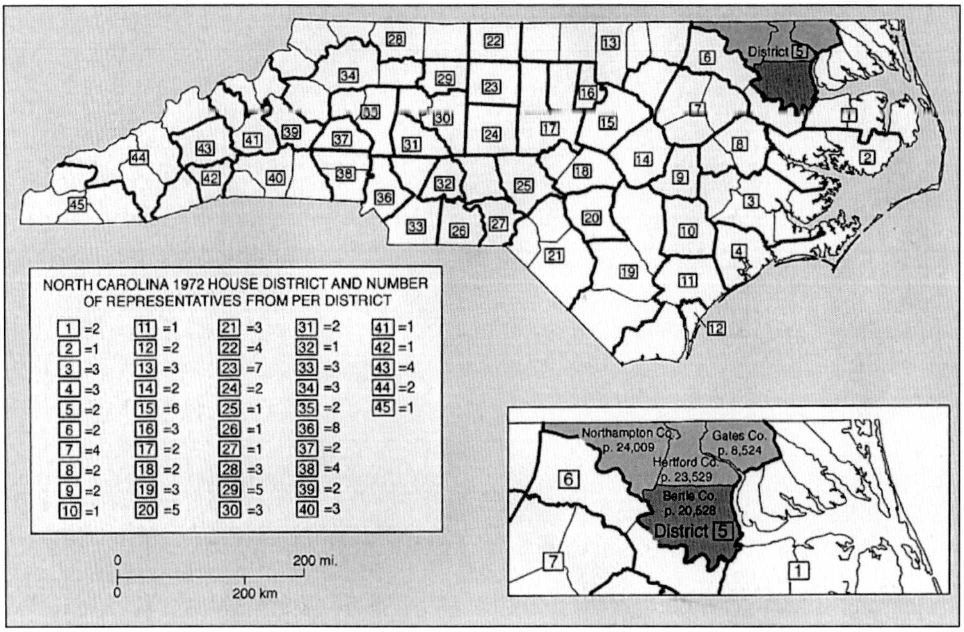

This map shows how Bertie County, along with Northampton, Hertford, and Gates, made up the District 5 of the House of the North Carolina General Assembly in 1972.

would have to come from the bottom up. Many civil rights activists believed the movement had to become focused on survival issues, including education, jobs, housing, and health care.[5] These survival issues, particularly education, were of great concern to the residents and community leaders of Bertie County. Many of the county's African-American residents lacked even basic reading, writing, or mathematical skills needed to improve their conditions. Reverend Andrew Jackson Cherry recalled that when he first became pastor of Spring Hill Baptist Church in 1954, "most of the members were uneducated, a few had a high school education, and only one or two had high school diplomas. Most could neither read nor write very well."[6] Cherry added that he began to encourage members of his church to finish school and to keep their children in school, thus inspiring many members and their children to finish high school. And by the mid-1970s, many were even sending their children on to college with the assistance of financial aid. Pell and SEOG grants were provided for low-income families, of which Bertie County had a significant number. African Americans also filed lawsuits to force integration of the public schools in the county and were successful in electing a number of African Americans to the county board of education, including Reverend Cherry and Mrs. Cora White, by the 1970s and 1980s.[7]

As more residents became aware of college and the fact that they could afford to send their children, Bertie County began to lose more of its young men and women to the continuing Great Migration. The rising level of education in Bertie County among parents and their children also brought about a rising interest in politics and community development. In the late 1960s and early 1970s, a plan was developed by the county's black churches to educate African-American residents on how to vote effectively in local, state, and national elections. This plan also informed residents about the candidates that would support their interests and how to use their growing political power, which began to rise in the late 1970s and early 1980s. Church pastors and community leaders in the county encouraged residents to register and vote in all local, state, and national elections. Polly Holly Outlaw registered voters in the Indian Woods township from 1970 to 1990. She was also a member and the secretary of the Indian Woods Baptist Church from 1967 to 1981. Outlaw stated that the community churches played a crucial role in getting residents to register and vote.[8]

By the mid-1970s, blacks helped to end unfair legislation, such as the poll tax. As more blacks began to vote in Bertie County, they also ran for and held public offices at the local and state level. Among them were Andrew Jackson Cherry, who served two terms on the Bertie County school board, and Cora White, a resident of Indian Woods, who also served two terms on the school board. Black political activity reached its peak in the 1980s when C. Melvin Creecy, pastor of the Indian Woods Baptist Church, ran for and was elected to the North Carolina state legislature. He became the first black to represent the fifth district, of which Bertie County was a part, since Reconstruction. Creecy campaigned as "a candidate in touch with the people."[9] His church, other community churches, and blacks from all over Bertie, Gates, Hertford, and Northampton Counties supported his candidacy. As a result, Creecy won the election and, less than seven months after his election, began

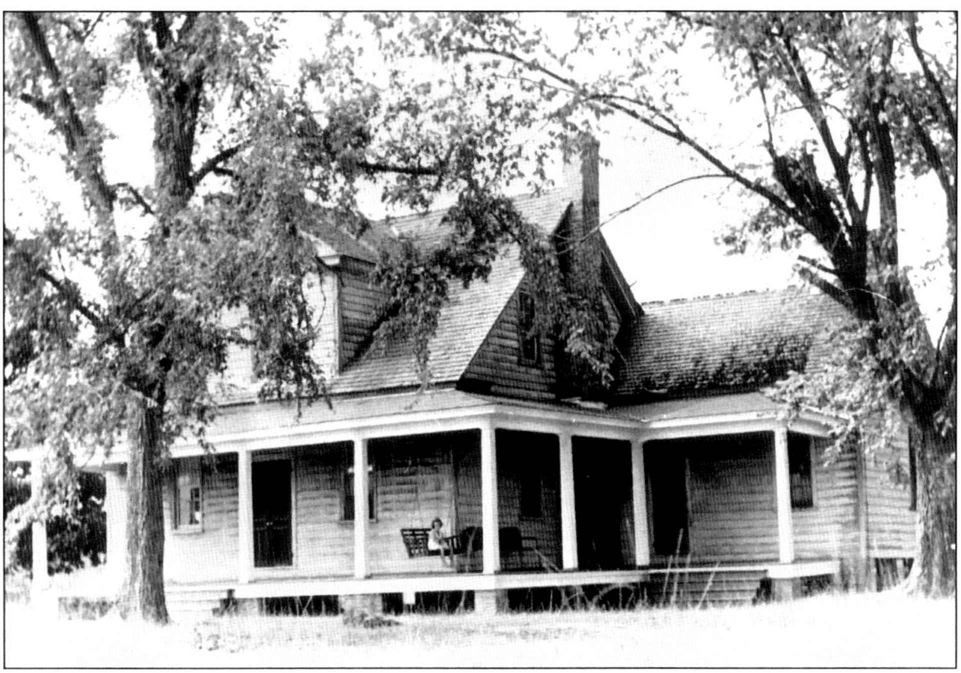

A young girl sits on the porch swing of the Hempstead-Fletcher-Giggetts house in the summer of 1954 while lawyers argued before the U.S. Supreme Court over whether it was constitutional or not for her to attend a whites-only public school. (Courtesy of NCSAH.)

lobbying Governor James B. Hunt for financial assistance for his constituency. The *Bertie Ledger-Advance*, the county newspaper, reported his lobbying with the Northeastern Caucus for economic development, which included Bertie and the surrounding counties.[10]

To win elections, political leaders in Bertie County developed a four-point strategy. First, campaign workers held voter registration drives to register as many voters as possible before the election. Second, campaign workers personally went to various churches to meet with and listen to residents before the election and to assure them that, if their candidates were elected, their concerns would be addressed. Third, campaign workers explained to potential voters the importance of voting and how to vote on election day. Finally, campaign workers drove voters without transportation to the polls. This type of concern for residents not only helped to increase voter registration, but also voter turnout. On election day, follow-up letters were sent to various community churches outlining candidates to vote for and reminding residents of where polling places were located.[11]

There were many other community leaders in Bertie County who were active politically. One such resident was James S. Pugh, a member and deacon of Spring Hill Baptist Church. Born and reared in Spring Hill, he is credited with starting the Bertie Association of Concerned Citizens, of which he served as president from 1981 to 1990. As president of this organization, Pugh traveled throughout the county, encouraging residents to speak out against economic and political discrimination by voting. Pugh, with the support of pastors and residents, fought for economic and political changes in Bertie County throughout the 1980s.

While the African-American residents of Bertie County were concerned with gaining political influence and educational and economic opportunities, they, along with whites, were also concerned about community development. By 1965, residents also worked on developing their recreational needs. One of these needs in Indian Woods was for some type of community recreation center for children between the ages of 5 and 18. In response to their need, a group of residents, led by Bart F. Smallwood, created a Little League and, later, a Big League baseball team. They later built and chartered the Blue Jay Recreation Center as well. Although in the early stages of development Bart Smallwood acted alone, by 1967, he had solicited the support of area churches and interested residents. The pastors of these churches encouraged their members to donate time and money to developing the recreation center just as they had for the Civil Rights Movement. This set the stage for more community involvement and cooperation. By working together to establish the recreation center, residents began to look beyond their church and local concerns and began to be concerned about what was happening to blacks all over Bertie County. They became interested in things like good roads, quality education, and economic opportunities.

The recreation center proposed by Smallwood represented an opportunity to improve the community and the lives of area children. Smallwood began to look for ways to help fund this center. The two methods he pursued were, first, asking for donations from the community churches whose members would directly benefit from its establishment and, second, seeking county and state funds earmarked for parks and recreation. After working exclusively with donations from area churches from 1966 to 1972, Smallwood and a new board of directors made up of local residents drafted a proposal in 1973 and submitted

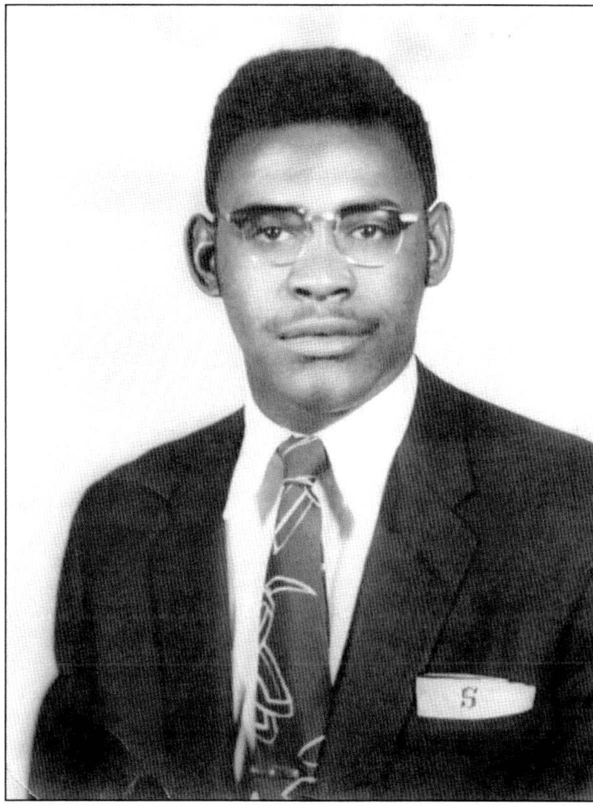

Bart F. Smallwood of Indian Woods was a county activist and the founder and president of the Blue Jay Recreation Center, its baseball team, and the Blue Jay Volunteer Fire Department. This picture was taken in the late 1950s. (Courtesy of SHC, UNC.)

it to the Bertie County Recreation Committee for funding. In it, the board presented a long-term plan and worked with county and state representatives to secure monies for the recreation center.[12]

Smallwood became well known throughout Bertie County for his volunteer work with the children of Indian Woods. Under his leadership, the five communities that made up the Indian Woods township were brought together in unity for the first time. Smallwood was noted not only for founding the Blue Jay Ball Club in 1965 and the Blue Jay Recreation Center in 1966, but also the Blue Jay Volunteer Fire Department in 1976, which was the first and only all–African-American volunteer fire department in the state of North Carolina. Both the ball team and the recreation center served all five communities that made up the Indian Woods township. The fire department, however, served only the communities of Cain, Spring Hill, and Indian Woods. This was because of its distance from the two closest fire departments, one in neighboring Windsor, located in the Windsor township, and the other in neighboring Lewiston, located in the Woodville township.[13]

The Blue Jay Ball Club was started in 1965 by Smallwood and 18 young men from the Cain community. The first team was called the Cain Blue Jays and played on a 6-acre lot rented by Smallwood from H.B. Spruill. Smallwood's wife, Lois Marie, recounted why her husband started the baseball club and, later, the recreation center:

> While returning from work one afternoon in 1965, my husband saw a number of young boys playing baseball, in a cut out forest. They were running to stumps for bases. He asked the children why they were playing in such a dangerous area, and they replied they had nowhere else to play. At that point, he began the development of the Blue Jay Recreation Center and Ball Club.[15]

Since baseball was such a popular sport among the young and old, Smallwood began to talk to his church pastor, C. Melvin Creecy, about developing some type of community park where baseball and other sports could be played. He then talked to an area farmer about securing a piece of land. To gain community support for his idea, Smallwood traveled to the four churches in the Indian Woods township and asked members for their economic and physical support in building the center and team. The response of the area churches was overwhelming. Reverends Cherry, Creecy, Carmichael, and Rascoe all endorsed Smallwood and the idea, bringing along their congregations.[16] The churches collected weekly donations to help purchase building supplies for the center and church members volunteered time to help construct the first structures. The four churches began announcing, every Sunday, the status of the work that Smallwood and residents were doing and urged the community to continue to aid them.[17]

With the financial and physical support of area residents, the Blue Jay Recreation Center and Ball Club began operation in 1966. Once the land was acquired, Smallwood,

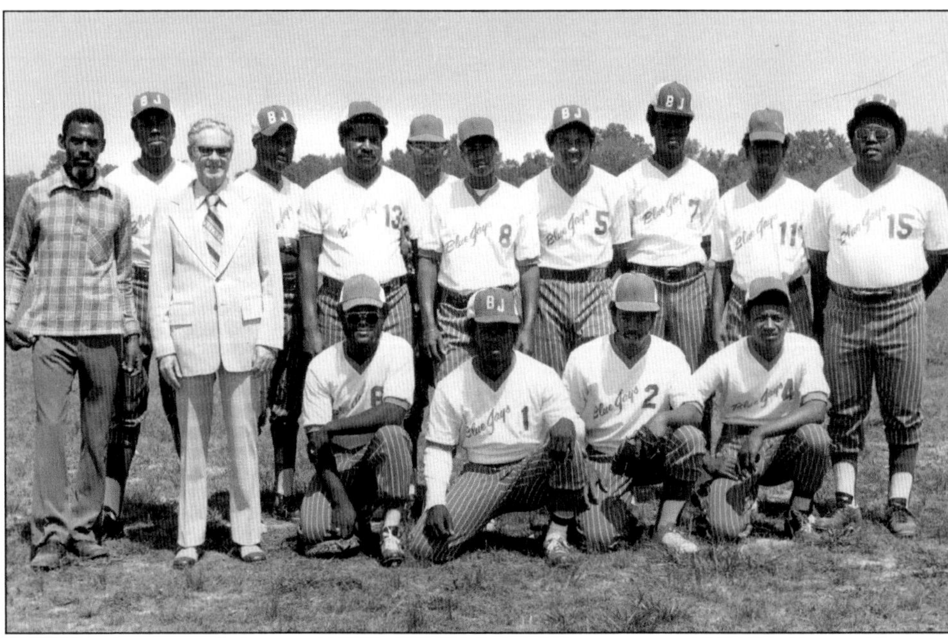

One of the Blue Jay Ball Club's big league teams poses in 1974 with sponsor Hoke Roberson Sr., president of R&W Chevrolet of Windsor, and Bart F. Smallwood, manager and president of the team. There were a number of black and white teams in the county that played one another throughout the late 1960s, 1970s, and 1980s. (Courtesy of SHC, UNC.)

using his tractor, prepared a suitable playing field by cutting the grass and grading the lot.[18] Next, efforts were made to recruit young men who were interested in playing. It was not long before 18 players were recruited and the first Blue Jay Ball Club began.[19] The team was originally named the Kings Blue Jays after the location of the new playing field in the community of Kings. The team was so successful that, the next year, the young women of the community began a softball team.

From 1965 to 1973, Smallwood dedicated himself to the ball club and center. He traveled throughout the various communities asking residents, businesses, and friends to give money and time in support of the community's youth. Very often, due to lack of funds, he would pay for the team's travel out of his own pocket. He used his pickup truck to carry the team to their games. Getting sports equipment was also difficult for the team. Smallwood, however, was successful in convincing many businesses to sponsor his teams and provide uniforms, balls, bats, gloves, and safety equipment. The largest sponsor was R&W Chevrolet Company of Windsor, North Carolina, which supported the team from 1970 to the late 1980s.[20]

As interest in the project grew, a need for some type of community building to conduct park business became apparent. In 1971, Smallwood asked Henry B. Spruill for the use of his abandoned barn adjacent to the ballpark. Spruill agreed on the condition that if the barn was destroyed by fire, the Blue Jay Ball Club would pay him the sum of $600. This was outlined in a letter to Smallwood on March 31, 1971.[21] The interest that the young people in the community showed caused Smallwood and the residents to desire a wider range of recreational activities. Residents also began to realize the benefits of owning the property rather than leasing it. To accomplish these objectives, it became necessary to become more structured and organized and also to develop goals. The first goal set by the center was to purchase the property they were leasing. To own the property, the residents had to first ask Spruill if he would be willing to sell the leased land. Spruill agreed on the condition that the center pay him $2,000 down, $750 per year for six years, and $1,000 the seventh year, which would be the final payment.[22] Unable to raise this much money from donations, Smallwood and the center wrote a grant proposal to the newly established Bertie County Recreation Committee. On July 11, 1973, after a meeting with the county officials, the grant was funded for $2,500. The amount of $1,500 of this grant was to be used to purchase the center's leased land and the rest was to be used to expand the recreation center by adding swings, slides, and other recreational facilities. It could also be used to aid its existing little league, big league, and girls' softball clubs.[23]

The grant received from the county would be the first of many that averaged more than $2,000 per year from 1973 to 1980. So successful was the center at both writing and administering their grants that, in 1979 when the county's grant monies were cut, it still received a grant of $1,200. This was significant because it was the only rural African-American grant funded. Of the 11 organizations receiving monies that year, all were located in towns. Furthermore, nationally noted organizations such as the Boy Scouts of America were not funded.[24]

To celebrate the grant award, an "Appreciation Day" was held at the center in the summer of 1973. Smallwood and the newly created Recreation Committee thanked all the supporters of the center for help in making it a reality. Among the supporters listed were John E. Whitehurst, county manager; C.H. Edwards, chair of the Bertie County Commissioners; James C. Kearney, chair of the Bertie County Recreation Committee; Hoke Roberson Sr., owner of R&W Chevrolet; and most notably State Senator J.J. Monk Harrington of the North Carolina state legislature.[25] What is interesting about all these men was that they were all white, quite wealthy, and none lived in the township.

With the grant also came more structure, including a new constitution, rules governing the center, and an executive committee. This committee was made up of president Bart F. Smallwood, vice president Roy Bond, secretary Evelyn T. Outlaw, and treasurer James R. Outlaw Jr. It also had a seven-member board of directors, including Irving Coggins, Oscar Rascoe, Joe Frank Hyman, Joe W. Thompson, Garland Outlaw, Esther Allen, and Catherine Bond.[26]

With the grant secured, the group began to discuss its long-term plans. Their principal goal was to continue to provide wholesome quality recreation for both youth and adults from the five communities. Their long-term plans also included two baseball fields, a well-equipped playground, and a community building. With the county grant, they began putting their plans into action. With the grant, the center purchased the following items:

Purchase of land	$1,500.00
Playground equipment	369.18
Wire fence	300.00
Rent for land before purchase	50.00
Wire for ball screen	30.82
Little league football (25) boys	250.00
TOTAL	2,500.00[27]

It should be noted that all of the improvements made with the funds raised were carried out by residents in their spare time.

By 1974, baseball games were held every Sunday afternoon during the summer months. While adults enjoyed the baseball games, their young children enjoyed the swings, slides, and seesaws of the center. There were now three ball teams. These included the little league baseball team, which played its games on Saturdays, the girls' softball team, which also played on Saturdays, and finally the Blue Jay Ball Team, which played on Sunday afternoons. The Blue Jay Ball Team became the main attraction for the adults in the community. It brought residents from miles around who loved baseball. The little league team helped to instill good sportsmanship in the children who participated. The players were required to recite and adhere to this pledge: "I trust in God, I love my country and will respect its laws. I will play fair and strive to win. But win or lose, I will always do my best."[28] With these values in mind, the team would travel throughout the county playing other teams, black and white, for the love of the sport and social interaction. As the little leaguers grew older, they began to play on the adult team. As a result, the center soon had enough young men to maintain a successful baseball program.

Although baseball was very successful, the directors of the center continued to try new programs to enhance the lives of their young people. In the fall of 1974, Smallwood organized a little league football team after receiving an invitation to a meeting at Bertie

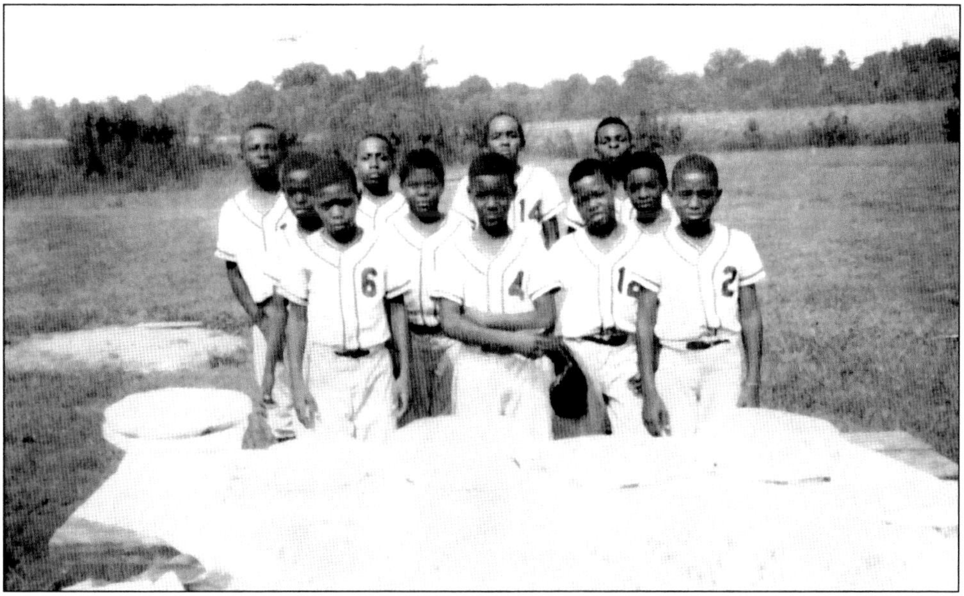

This group, one of the Blue Jay Ball Club's little league baseball teams that played in the county from the late 1960s to the early 1980s, was one of a number of black and white teams around the county that competed with one another and learned sportsmanship and good citizenship. This photograph was taken in the late 1960s or early 1970s. (Courtesy of SHC, UNC.)

Senior High School asking him to consider starting a team to enter into the new Bertie County league. The meeting was called by Jerry Smith, coach of a little league football team in Windsor.[29] Smallwood took the idea back to the center's committee and asked whether Indian Woods should participate in the program or not. The committee unanimously agreed and the football team was formed. The new team was named the Red Devils and began play in September of 1974. This venture, however, would not be as successful as baseball and would be dropped the next year.

By the end of 1974, attendance at the recreation center was averaging 45 children per day, whereas more than 450 attended baseball games. With the number continuing to rise, the recreation center petitioned the county for more money, giving as their objective improving the services offered. To do this, they required money to purchase additional equipment.[30] They outlined their proposal in September of 1974:

Land	$1,000
Equipment	1,200
Water pump	200
Fence	500
Building	500
Bathroom	1,300
TOTAL	$5,000[31]

It is not clear from the records reviewed whether the entire amount was obtained by the center, but it is clear from newspaper accounts and site visits that all of the aforementioned items were installed at the facility during the years that followed. From 1974 to 1976, the center sponsored dances, raffles, fish and barbecue dinners, and all kinds of creative contests, such as the Little Miss Blue Jay Pageant, to raise money to continue to expand the park.[32] As the center continued to grow, it established rules to prevent problems on the grounds. The rules included no alcoholic beverages or drugs on premises, no profane language, and no weapons.[33] In late 1976, baseball regulations, which previously had not been needed, were developed and expanded to settle disputes over baseball revenue and how the ball team should operate. Baseball had grown to be so well liked by the residents that some players desired to be paid for their services. This was never intended. It was only to be a game for fun between various communities within the county. Therefore, it was quoted, "We the recreation committee shall redefine the role of baseball in the Blue Jay Recreation Program to settle unrest among the players."[34]

The new regulations introduced by the recreation committee were not well received by the players and, in fact, resulted in a strike of sorts. A number of players decided not to play until they shared in money raised at the games. The committee explained, however, that any funds gathered during a game were not used as profits, but put back into the upkeep of the park. In fact, since the center received state and local funds, it could not by law operate as a profit-making institution. Therefore, the players could not be legally paid even if this was desired. In the end, the members of the center simply asked area youth

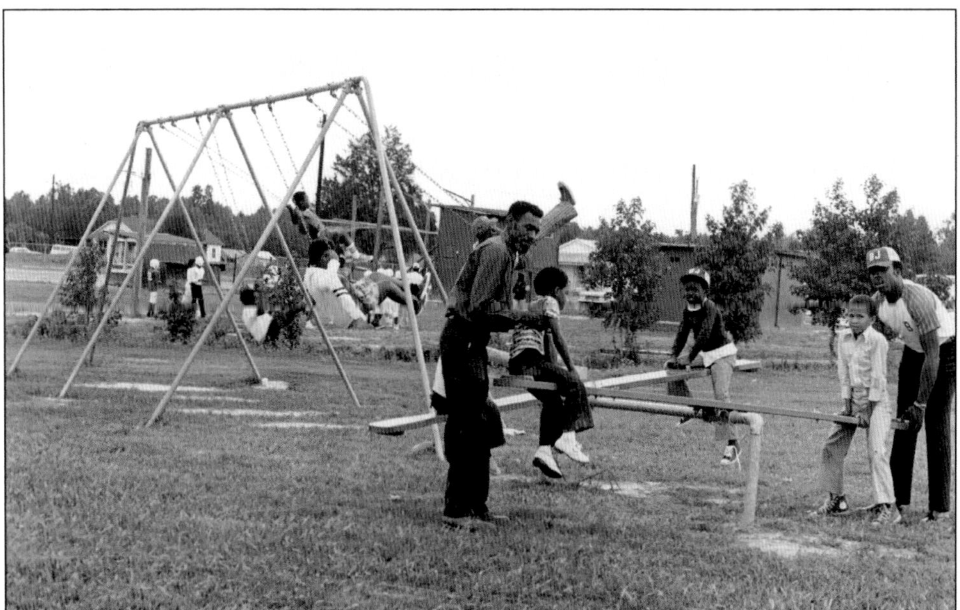

Local children, like these at the Blue Jay Recreation Center in Indian Woods, enjoyed recreation centers that were built throughout the county in the 1970s. (Courtesy of SHC, UNC.)

if they wanted to start playing on a new team in order to continue the sport. Eventually, some of the players who had left the original team returned to play. The resulting controversy did bring into focus how successful the center had become.

In the summer of 1980, the Blue Jay Recreation Center made its final payment of $1,000 to H.B. Spruill. To celebrate, they held a "Mortgage Burning" on Saturday, July 5, 1980.[35] During this ceremony, all present recited in unison:

> We now dedicate ourselves, our services and our substance anew to the work of our beloved project and to the recreational concerns throughout this community, this nation, and the whole world that the character and fitness of all may be enhanced.[36]

The center continued to prosper and, with state representatives such as J.J. Monk Harrington and C. Melvin Creecy supporting it, services continued to expand. The center remained true to its commitment to improving the quality of life in its surrounding communities.

Smallwood was relentless in his attempts to bring new services to Indian Woods. On August 29, 1976, at Indian Woods Baptist Church, Smallwood presided over the Blue Jay Fire Department Development Program. Among the residents, community leaders, and county officials present were area pastors, including Reverend Andrew J. Cherry of Spring Hill, Reverend W.A. Moore of Beacon Light, C. Melvin Creecy of Indian Woods, and Reverend Eugene Watson of Saint Francis, and two county commissioners, Windsor fire chief Pete Alston and James Kearny. The county commissioners stressed the benefits of having a fire department within the community and discussed how it could be accomplished.[37] Thus, again with the community's support, plans were made to raise money to acquire a truck and fire fighting equipment. The first recorded members and officers were Bart Smallwood, president; James S. Pugh, secretary; Robert Cherry, treasurer; Lloyd Cooper, fire chief training officer; Roy Bond, assistant training officer–captain, tank division; Robert T. Smallwood; and George Bond. Together, there were 45 members.[38]

The Blue Jay Volunteer Fire Department joined the ten existing fire departments in Bertie County as the only African-American department servicing the newly created Blue Jay Fire District. Less than two months after the organization of the Blue Jay Volunteer Fire Department, the Windsor Fire Department donated an old, but maintainable, fire truck to the department. At a ceremony held on October 17, 1976, the mayor of Windsor, Lewis T. Rascoe Jr., presented the fire truck to Smallwood for the department. Among the guests present who gave remarks were Windsor fire chief E.E. Alston; Lewiston fire chief Cecil Parker; E. Rawls Carter, president of the Bertie County Fire Association; C.H. Edwards, chairman, Bertie County Commissioners; and a consistent powerful supporter, State Senator J.J. Monk Harrington of the first district.[39] The new Blue Jay Fire District extended from the end of the Spring Hill community to the edge of the Indian Woods community. The fire station was located at the Blue Jay Recreation Center.

The fire department served two positive functions. The first is obvious. It gave the community greater security in case of fire. The second was not as obvious, but just as significant. To operate a fire department safely and efficiently took training and, because the Blue Jay Fire Department was the only African-American department in the county, that training had to be done with other white departments. This fostered cooperation, for the first time, by the communities with whites living outside the Indian Woods township for the approximately 45 men who, at various times, volunteered to work with the department. An example of this cooperation could be seen as early as 1977 when a letter was circulated among the churches of Indian Woods that asked for donations to purchase equipment for the fire station. The letter stated that donations for the department could be left at any of the 11 fire stations that made up the Bertie County Fire Association.[40] This cooperation with area fire departments created lasting professional as well as personal bonds that would strengthen throughout the 1980s.

By 1980, Smallwood decided that leading both the recreation center and fire department was too much, so he resigned as president of the center on January 12 to dedicate more time to the fire department.[41] He continued, however, to work with the baseball program and with the children of the community as a volunteer. On November 1, 1983, he received the Governor's Volunteer Award for establishing the Blue Jay Recreation Center and the Blue Jay Volunteer Fire Department.[42]

Smallwood continued his efforts to find funding for the fire department and on August 27, 1985, received a letter of encouragement from Senator J.J. Monk Harrington, former president pro-tempore of the North Carolina General Assembly. Senator Harrington, the owner of a lumber mill in Lewiston, was one of two state senators from District 1, of which Bertie and 13 northeastern counties were a part. In the letter to Smallwood, Senator Harrington wrote: "Bart . . . I want you to know that in 1986 Representative Creecy and I want to get some money for your Fire Department and Blue Jay Recreation Center but this will have to come in 1986. Be sure and keep in touch."[43]

Although Smallwood had the influence and will to continue his work, he no longer had the strength. By August of 1985, Smallwood was suffering from terminal lung cancer that was getting progressively worse. On September 4, 1985, the residents of Indian Woods held a ceremony to honor Smallwood and the first baseball team. A marker was erected at the gate to the center that read as follows: "In Honor of the 1965 Baseball Team & Founder Bart F. Smallwood."[44] By this time, Smallwood could no longer work either with the fire department or the community as a volunteer. Bedridden and suffering from shortness of breath, yet another honor was bestowed upon him: the Bertie County Involvement Council, on December 12, 1985, recognized Smallwood as volunteer of the month and held a dinner prepared by the Windsor Cook's Club to raise money to help pay for his mounting medical bills.[45] It is clear from his letters, honors, and awards that Smallwood was highly regarded among both white and African-American residents of Bertie County. On December 18, 1985, six days after the Involvement Council's award and fund-raising dinner, Smallwood died of lung cancer. The suddenness of his death stunned the community. He had become synonymous with the organizations he founded and people wondered what would happen to these organizations. His funeral, held at Indian Woods Baptist Church, brought white and black residents and leaders from all over the county.[46]

By 1990, the successes of the residents of Bertie County in improving education for their children had taken a toll. Its population had fallen from 26,439 in 1950 to 20,388 in 1990 and, by 2000, to 19,773.[47] The exodus of young people that began in the 1950s and lasted through the 1990s left very few children or teenagers in the communities in the county to enjoy the recreational centers. The teenagers who remained became more interested in driving to the nearby towns of Williamston or Ahoskie, located in neighboring Martin and Hertford Counties, if they or their friends had access to automobiles to go shopping or to movies. By 1990, as a result of the Great Migration, there were only three groups remaining in the county: children under the age of 18, the elderly over 65, and married couples with children under 18. By 1990, the county had effectively been drained of many of its 18- to 30-year-olds.

In spite of this, the quality of life for the black and white residents of the county continued to improve. New and better homes were built, schools were maintained and improved, and large numbers of the residents' children began to attend college at either North Carolina or Virginia schools. In North Carolina, they primarily attended North Carolina Central University, North Carolina A&T State University, Saint Augustine College, Shaw University, East Carolina University, Fayetteville State University, Elizabeth City State University, University of North Carolina at Chapel Hill, or Winston-Salem State University. In Virginia, they attended primarily Norfolk State, Hampton Institute, Old Dominion, and William and Mary. Many of Bertie County's young people left to attend one of these colleges between 1975 and 2001.[48]

From 1990 to 2002, Bertie County, like the rest of eastern North Carolina, would remain rural and poor. The economic boom of the 1980s and 1990s that transformed the piedmont and cities like Charlotte, Greensboro, Winston-Salem (the triad), and Raleigh, Durham, and Cary (the Research Triangle Park) into thriving metropolises, bringing hundreds of thousands of people to them and millions of dollars, did not reach Bertie

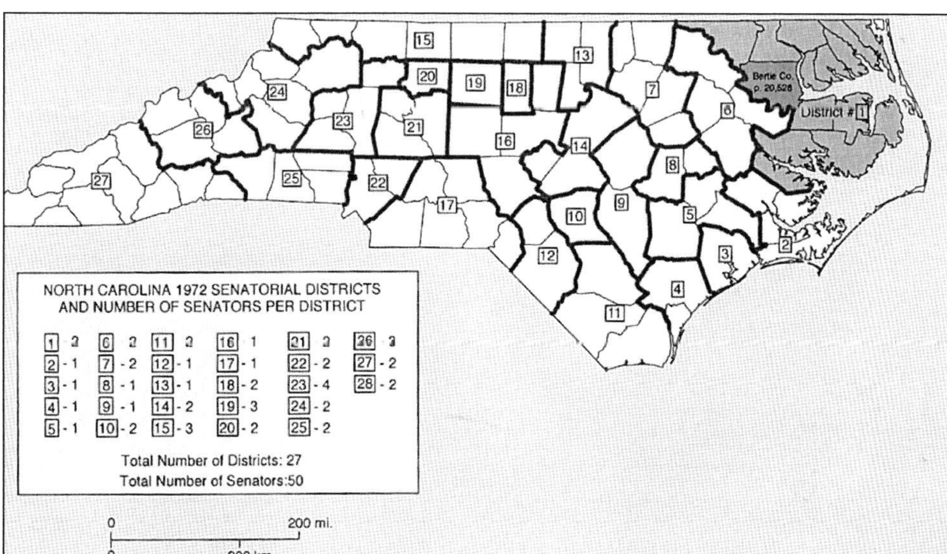

As this 1972 map shows, Bertie County, along with several other northeastern counties, made up District 1 of the senate of the North Carolina General Assembly.

County or the northeastern coastal plains. By the 1990s, however, the county did see some of its young people join the return migration that was happening all over the South. Many young people who had left the county for better-paying jobs or college began to return to it to become school teachers, lawyers, and other professionals. They also ran for public offices, such as county commissioner, and helped organize county voters, including those who would help elect Representative Eva Clayton to the United States House of Representatives from the first district.

The county and region were dealt a massive economic blow with the arrival of Hurricane Floyd in September of 1999. There had been other hurricanes and floods—the Flood of 1940, Hurricane Hazel in 1954, the Flood of 1958, and Hurricane Ginger in 1971—but Floyd and the flooding it brought caused millions of dollars in damage to Bertie County and billions to eastern North Carolina. All of the major rivers of eastern North Carolina and Bertie County overflowed, causing what many residents have called "The 500-year Flood." Never in the history of the state had there been a storm so violent and destructive. County residents noted that the storm, in two days, had "changed their lives forever!"[49] The Cashie River covered the town of Windsor, the county seat. The homes of prominent families and businesses were under water, as were Main Street, the county courthouse, the post office, and a number of restaurants, including Bunn's Barbecue. The Cashie, Roanoke, and Chowan Rivers, along with the creeks and streams

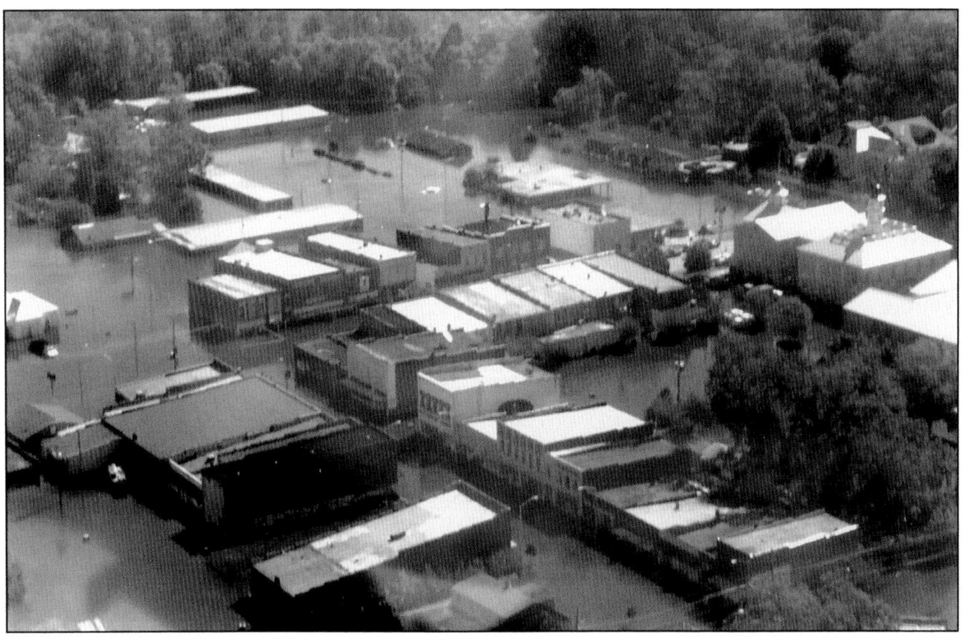

Downtown Windsor, the county seat, was flooded by Hurricane Floyd in 1999. The hurricane, and the flooding it caused, was the worst natural disaster in North Carolina's 400-year history; it cost the state billions of dollars and Bertie County, alone, millions. Floyd has become known among county residents as the "The 500-Year Flood." (Courtesy of J.W. "Russ" Russell Jr.)

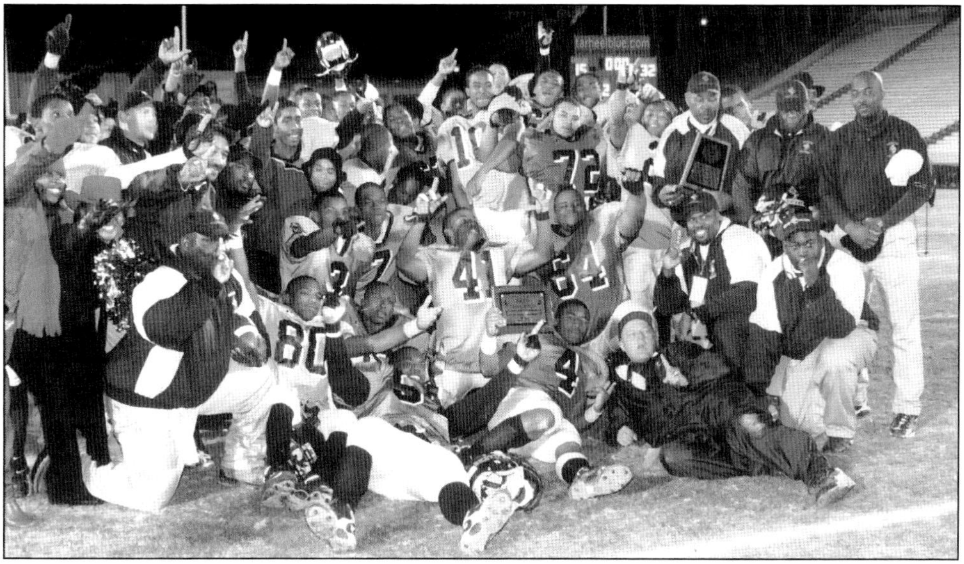

Bertie High School's football team celebrates its second state championship in the fall of 2000. (Courtesy of J.W. "Russ" Russell Jr.)

that flow into them, spilled over into peoples homes, fields, and churches, destroying crops, livestock, family businesses, and much of the county's history. In the words of then-governor James B. Hunt, the flooding in the region was of "biblical proportions." Never in the long recorded history of the region had an event so catastrophic occurred. The flood waters, which caused at least two deaths, also caused bodies to float from their graves. With state and national help, the region began to rebuild once the waters receded and, by March of 2000, was starting to recover from the tragedy.[50]

By the fall of 2000, the county's residents had something to celebrate when Bertie High School, the only public high school in the county won its second state 3A High School Football Championship against Jamestown Ragsdale. Although there had been other championships, the first in football in 1995 against High Point Central, in track in 1975, and in basketball as a 4A high school in 1970, the 2000 championship was especially rewarding. This championship helped to instill the beleaguered county with a sense of pride in knowing that, in spite of its limited resources, it still was viable and capable of doing great things. By the spring of 2002, Bertie County and the state continued to move forward with road building projects through the county that expanded Highway 17 and extended Highway 64 in neighboring Martin and Washington Counties from Roanoke Island to Raleigh. When completed, the road would give the residents of the county access for the first time to a major east-west highway.

Much has changed in Bertie County over the past 400 years, but even more has remained the same. Whether Native American, European, African, or a combination of all three, the residents of the county have been shaped by and continue to shape the county's landscape. In the words of the *Bertie Ledger-Advance*, in its special issue on the floods, theirs was and is "a story of tenacity, survival and optimism.[51]

Bibliography

Endnotes

See preface for the locations of archived endnotes containing additional information on Native American, African-American, American, European, and Southern history related to this work.

Archival Materials/Manuscripts

Buffalo and Erie County Historical Society Library, Buffalo, NY

Wheeler, Frank Storer. Papers.

Historical Society, Philadelphia, PA

Philadelphia Yearly Meeting of the Religious Society of Friends. Indian Committee. Records.

Main Library at the Ohio State University, Columbus, OH

Dearborn, Henry Alexander S. Papers.

National Archives and Records Administration, Record Group 109 (War Department Collection of Confederate Records). Wash., D.C.

Compiled Service Records of Confederate General and Staff Officers and Non-Regimental Enlisted Men. (Microcopy 331). File: Walter G. Bender. Service Records of Confederate soldiers who served in the Roanoke Valley and defended "Fort Branch" on the Roanoke River, 1862–1865.

New Jersey State Library, Newark, NJ

Shute, Samuel Moore. Journal.

North Carolina Division of Archives and History, Raleigh, NC

Anderson, John Huske. Collection.
Biggs, Kader. Papers.
Bryan, John. Papers.
Clark, David. Papers.
Clark, William J. Papers.
Coombs. Manuscript.
Devereux, John. Papers.
Div. of Negro Education. Rosenwald Schools.
Div. of School House Plans. Rosenwald Schools.
Eason, William. Papers.
Hawks, Francis Lister. Papers.
Heckstall. Papers.
Holloman, Charles R. Collection.
Jacocks, Charles W. Papers.
Johnson, F. Roy. Collection.
Kilgore, Benjamin Wesley. Papers.
Miscellaneous Papers.
Nicholls, Benajah. Papers.
Palatine. Papers.
Peele, Josiah. Papers.
Pollock, Thomas. Papers.
Schooner Franklin. Logbook.

Sharrock, Whitmell T. Papers.
Slave Collection.
Smithwick, Edmund, and Family. Papers.
Spotswood, Alexander. Papers.
Stone, David. Papers.
Surginer, John. Papers.
Taylor, John Douglas. Papers.

SOUTHERN HISTORICAL COLLECTION, UNIVERSITY OF NORTH CAROLINA AT CHAPEL HILL, NC

Alston, William. "Stud Book."
Armistead, Stark. Papers.
Bentley, Gordon. "Common Place Book."
Bertie County, North Carolina Materials.
Brimley, Herbert Hutchinson. Papers.
Britton, William. Papers.
Bryan Family. Papers.
Capehart Family. Papers.
Confederate Hospital. Records.
Cotten, Bruce. Papers.
Edenton (NC) Port Book.
Florida (Ship Log).
Grimes, Bryan. Papers.
Gilmer, Jeremy Francis. Papers.
Hoke, William Alexander. Papers.
Hill, Whitmel. Papers.
Jacocks, Jonathan. Papers.
Jones, Margaret Hathaway. Papers.
Kaplan, Ann. Collection.
Lawson, John. Letters.
Manumission Society of North Carolina. Records.
Mebane and Graves Family. Papers.
Morattock Primitive Baptist Church. Books.
Norfleet Family. Papers.
Norman, Ellie C. Correspondence.
North Carolina Geological Survey. Papers.
Outlaw, David. Papers.
Planters Club. Papers.
Pugh, E.W. Records.
Revolutionary War. Papers.
Skinner Family. Papers.
Smallwood, Bart F. Papers.
Smallwood, Charles B. Diary.
Smallwood, Charles B. Papers.
Speight, Sarah and Francis. Papers.
Southern Education Board. Records.
Southern Tenant Farmers Union. Papers.
Thompson, Lewis. Papers.
Valentine, William D. Diary.
Walker, Thomas. Papers.
Washington, George. Order Book.
Wheeler, Samuel Jordan. Diaries.
Williams, Edmund Jones. Papers.
Winston, Francis Donnell. Papers.
Winston, Patrick Henry. Papers.
Winston, Robert Watson. Papers.

ORAL INTERVIEWS (FOUND IN THE BART F. SMALLWOOD PAPERS)

Ballance, Alice
Bazemore, Aaron
Bond, Catherine
Bond, Roseatte
Cherry, Andrew Jackson
Cherry, Lord Cornwallis
Creecy, C. Melvin
Etheridge, Rosetta
Henry, Leo
Hill, Lucinda
Jarvis, Erich
Jonathan, Garfield
Jones, Althea
Joseph, Laura.
Lockler, Leon, Chief
Outlaw, Polly Holley
Pugh, Annie
Pugh, James S.
Smallwood, Lois Marie
Smallwood, Freddie
Watiford, Tanya

SOUTH CAROLINA HISTORICAL SOCIETY, CHARLESTON, SC, AND THE SOUTH CAROLINA STATE LIBRARY, COLUMBIA, SC

White, Wes. Papers.

SPECIAL COLLECTIONS, J.Y. JOYNER LIBRARY, EAST CAROLINA UNIVERSITY, GREENVILLE, NC

Askew. Papers.

Hatcher, William Carlyle. Collection.

King, Henry T. Collection .

King, Henry T. Collection. Newspaper Clippings.

Larkins, John Davis Jr. U.S. District Court Cases.

Rodman, William Blount. Papers.

SPECIAL COLLECTIONS, JAMES MONROE MUSEUM AND MEMORIAL LIBRARY, FREDERICKSBURG, VA

Monroe, James. Papers.

SPECIAL COLLECTIONS, PERKINS LIBRARY, DUKE UNIVERSITY, DURHAM, NC

Bagley, Warren. Diary.

Caswell, Richard. Papers.

Coolidge, Oliver S. Papers.

De Charlevoix, Pierre François Xavier. Papers.

Lahontan, Louis Armand de Lom d'Arce. Papers.

Documents on slaves and slavery in the United States.

Long, John. Papers.

New York (colony) Treaties etc.

Perrot, Nicolas. Papers.

Radisson, Pierre Esprit. Papers.

Slade, William. Papers.

Stuart, Jeremiah. Papers.

SPECIAL COLLECTIONS, SAMPSON-LIVERMORE LIBRARY, UNIVERSITY OF NORTH CAROLINA AT PEMBROKE, NC

Cheraw Indian. Folder.

Hacther, Eddie. Folder. Newspaper clippings.

Indians of Robeson County. Folder. Newspaper clippings.

Indian Identification. Folder .Newspaper clippings.

Indian Nation. Folder. Newspaper clippings.

Indian Population. Folder. Newspaper clippings.

Lowery, Henry Berry. Folder. Newspaper clippings.

Lumbee Indian. Folder. Newspaper clippings.

Lumbee Origins. Folder. Newspaper clippings.

Native Americans. Folder. Newspaper clippings.

Pierce, Julian T. Folder.

THE MASSACHUSETTS HISTORICAL SOCIETY, BOSTON, MA

Francis, Turbot, 1775. 2 folders. Speeches delivered at meetings of the Chiefs of the Six Nations and Indian Commissioners to secure the support of the Six Nations in the Revolutionary War against Britain.

UNITED STATES. BUREAU OF INDIAN AFFAIRS. 1875 1880 1 V.

Indian Agent Ledger includes records of Daniel Sherman on reservation life of the Tuscarora Indians of New York.

UNIVERSITY OF VIRGINIA, CHARLOTTESVILLE, VA

Virginia Electric and Power Company archived records including articles of incorporation, materials on early financing, mergers, and reports.

NEWSPAPERS

Bertie Ledger-Advance (Windsor, NC)
News-Herald (Ahoskie, NC)
Niagara Gazette
The News and Observer (Raleigh, NC)

SECONDARY SOURCES

MAGAZINES AND JOURNALS

American Anthropologist
American Historical Association, Annual Report
American Historical Association Papers
American Historical Review
American History Illustrated
Agricultural History
American Indian Culture and Research Journal
American Indian Quarterly
American Magazine and History Chronicle
American Quarterly
Anthropology and Humanism Quarterly
Caribbean Studies
Ceres
Chronicles of Oklahoma
Cultural Anthropology
Earth Island Journal
Ethnohistory
Florida Anthropologist
Harvard Journal on Legislation
History Today
Human Biology
Indian Historian
International Organization
Irish Sword
James Sprunt Historical Publications
Journal of American Culture
Journal of American History
Journal of Early Southern Decorative Arts
Journal of Family History
Journal of Negro History
Journal of Social History
Journal of Washington Academy of Sciences
Magazine of American History
Mid-America; An Historical Review
Military Collector and Historian
Mississippi Quarterly
Mississippi Valley Historical Review
Negro History Bulletin
New England Review
New York History
North Carolina Booklet
North Carolina Historical Review
Pennsylvania History
Pennsylvania Magazine of History and Biography

Political Science Quarterly
Popular Science Monthly
Recherches Amerindiennes au Quebec
Smithsonian
South Carolina Historical and Genealogical Magazine
Southern Exposure
The American Historical Review
The Association of American Geographers Annals
The Enterprise. Harvest Edition
The History Teacher
The Journal of the Council on Abandoned Military Posts
The Journal of Southern History
The Outlook
The Public Historian
The Southern Patriot
The State A Weekly Survey of North Carolina
The Western Historical Quarterly
Transactions of the Charles S. Pierce Society
Trinity College Historical Society, Papers
Virginia Magazine of History and Biography
We The People of North Carolina
William and Mary Quarterly

CENSUS RECORDS

United States census records from the colonial times to 2000.

THESES AND DISSERTATIONS CONSULTED

Anderson, Ralph V. Ph.D. Diss., University of North Carolina, Chapel Hill, 1974.
Benson, Donna Johanna. Ph.D. Diss., Duke University, 1984.
Blu, Karen I. Ph.D. Diss., University of Chicago, 1972.
Bogger, Tommy Lee. Ph.D. Diss., University of Virginia, 1976.
Boyce, Douglas Wesley. Ph.D. Diss., University of North Carolina, Chapel Hill, 1973.
Boyce, Douglas Wesley. M.A. Thesis, University of North Carolina at Chapel Hill, 1971.
Brooks, Evelyn. Ph.D. Diss., The University of Rochester, 1984.
Brown, Kathleen Mary. Ph.D. Diss., The University of Wisconsin at Madison, 1990.
Brown, William R. Ph.D. Diss., University of North Carolina at Chapel Hill, 1983.
Butler, Reginald Dewin. Ph.D. Diss., The Johns Hopkins University, 1989.
Bynum, Victoria E. Ph. D Diss., University of California, San Diego, 1987.
Carriker, Grady Isaiah. M.A. Thesis Wake Forest College, 1950
Champion, Walter Thomas. Thesis M.S. Western Illinois University, Macomb, Ill 1975.
Chujo, Ken. Ph.D. Diss., Duke University, 1988.
Clegg, Brenda Faye. Ph. D Diss., The University of Michigan, 1983.
Cromartie, John. M.A. University of North Carolina at Chapel Hill, 1983.
Counihan, Harold J. Ph.D. Diss., Chapel Hill: University of North Carolina, 1971.
Daniell, Mark Drew. Thesis M.E. Wayne State University, 1972.
Darling, Marsha Jean. Ph.D. Diss., Duke University, 1982.
Elmore, Ashby Dunn, M. A. Thesis, East Carolina University, 1971.
Eng, Eugenia. Ph.D. Diss., The University of North Carolina at Chapel Hill, 1983.
Farrar, Hayward. Ph.D. Diss., The University of Chicago, 1983.
Fitzpatrick, Leigh Jerome. Thesis M.A. Wake Forest University, 1993.
Gay, Dorothy Ann. Ph.D. Diss., Chapel Hill: University of North Carolina, 1975.
Good, Reg. Ph.D. Diss., University of Saskatchewan, 1994.
Gordon, Beverly. Ph.D. Diss., University of Wisconsin Madison, 1984.

Gregg, Robert Standish. Ph.D. Diss., University of Pennsylvania, 1989.
Haley, John Hamilton, III. Ph.D. Diss., University of North Carolina, Chapel Hill, 1981.
Hamlin, Walter Richard. Ph.D. Diss., The University of Rochester, 1980.
Jones, Maxine Deloris. Ph.D. Diss., The Florida State University, 1982.
Korchynski, Christina Denise. Thesis (M.U.P.) SUNY Buffalo, 1995.
Lewis, Earl. Ph.D. Diss., University of Minnesota, 1984.
Limeburner, Wayne T. Thesis M.A. Central Connecticut State University, 1985.
Lockhart, Walter Samuel. Thesis M.A. University of North Carolina at Chapel Hill, 1972.
McClain, Bahati M. Qualifying Paper, Harvard Graduate School of Education, 1980.
McClain, Kimberly Ann. A.B. Honors Thesis, Harvard University, 1989.
O'Donnell, William J. Honors Essay, University of North Carolina, Chapel Hill, 1993.
Paschel, Herbert Richard. Thesis M.A. University of North Carolina at Chapel Hill, 1953.
Peacock, Gregory Tyler. Paper Presented at the Historic Hope Foundation, 2001.
Powell, William S. M.A. Thesis University of North Carolina at Chapel Hill, 1947.
Price, Edward T. Ph.D. Diss., University of California Berkeley, 1950.
Randall-David, Elizabeth Wilson. Ph.D. Diss., University of Florida, 1985.
Reilly, Stephen Edward. Ph.D. Diss., Duke University, 1983.
Rudes, Blair A. Dissertation Ph.D. State University of New York, Buffalo, 1976.
Sauve, Stephanie L. D.Min. Diss., Colgate Rochester Divinity School, Crozer Theological Seminary, 1995.
Scarborough, William K. Ph.D. Diss., University of North Carolina, Chapel Hill, 1961.
Schlotterbeck, John T. Ph.D. Diss., The Johns Hopkins University, 1980.
Shinoda, Yasuko. Ph.D. dissertation, Chapel Hill: University of North Carolina, 1971.
Smallwood, Arwin D. M. A. Thesis, Durham: North Carolina Central University, 1990.
Smallwood, Arwin D. Ph.D. Diss., Columbus: The Ohio State University, 1997.
Speller Benjamin F. Jr. "Guide to African American Churches in Bertie County"
Speller, Benjamin F. Jr. "African American Soldiers & Sailors from The Civil War"
Styrna, Christine Ann. Ph.D. Diss., College of William and Mary, 1990.
Thompson, Robert Farris. Paper presented, Bertie County Historical Association, 1967.
Urquhart, Helen Holt. Thesis M.A. East Carolina University, 1988.
White, Marylin Mildred. Ph.D. Diss., The University of Texas Austin, 1983.
Williams, Marianne Mithun. Ph.D. Diss., Yale University, 1974.
Winch, Julie Patricia. Ph.D. Diss., Bryn Mawr College, 1982.

BOOKS

See preface for locations of archived bibliography with a complete list of the books on Native American, African-American, American, European, and Southern history that were consulted in this work.

INDEX

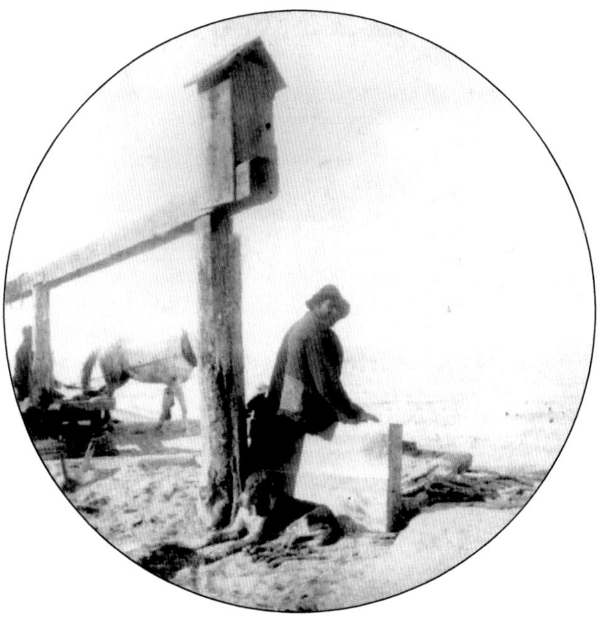

A black fisherman rests after a haul in the 1890s. (Courtesy of NCSAH.)